ARMS & ARMOUR OF THE
Medieval Knight

ARMS & ARMOUR OF THE
Medieval
Knight

David Edge & John Miles Paddock

BISON GROUP

Published by
Bison Books Ltd
Kimbolton House
117A Fulham Road
London, SW3 6RL
England

ISBN 0 86124 414 1

Printed in China
Reprinted 1991
Reprinted 1994
Reprinted 1995

Library of Congress Cataloging-in-
Publication Data
Edge, David & Paddock, John M
  Arms & armor of the medieval knight by
David Edge & John M Paddock
    p.   cm.
    ISBN 0-517-64468-1 $12.98
    1. Arms and armor—History.   2. Knights
and knighthood.
I. Title.   II. Title: Arms and armor of the
medieval knight.
U810.T87 1988
623.4'41—dc19   87-33101 CIP

Acknowledgements

This book does not claim to be based upon new research, but is
intended rather as a fresh presentation of current knowledge
about the armor and weapons of the Mediaeval Knight. We
hope that it will serve as an introduction to this vast and
fascinating field of study to which we, the authors, are relative
newcomers. We owe much to the scholarship, dedication and
research of others; in particular, we are especially indebted to
the published works of Claude Blair (former Keeper of
Metalwork at the Victoria and Albert Museum) and Vesey
Norman (Master of the Armouries). A note of personal thanks is
due to all those who helped directly with the production of this
work, and to the staff of the Royal Armouries, the Wallace
Collection and the Museum of the Order of St John for their
assistance and encouragement. Finally we owe a tremendous
debt of gratitude to Christine Frances Crickmore, who gallantly
saw this enterprise through all its stages of production and who
contributed much information and the fruits of her own
research on costume. This book is accordingly dedicated to her.

*David Edge is Senior
Conservation Officer and Curator
of the Armoury Department at
the Wallace Collection. His
interests include collecting and
restoring antique arms and
armour. (Chapters 1, 2, 6
and 7)*

*John Miles Paddock is a graduate
of the Institute of Archaeology,
University of London. He is
currently researching a Ph.D.
thesis on Roman Republican
Arms and Armour. He is
Assistant Curator at the Museum
of the Order of St John.
(Chapters 3, 4 and 5)*

Page 1: The Triumph of
Maximilian c *1516-18, shows
knights wearing armour for the
Scharfrennen (Rennen).*

*Pages 2-3: Frankish infantry and
cavalry of the Carolingian
Empire, from the* Golden
Psalter.

*Below: The effigy of John of
Eltham, Earl of Cornwall
c 1334.*

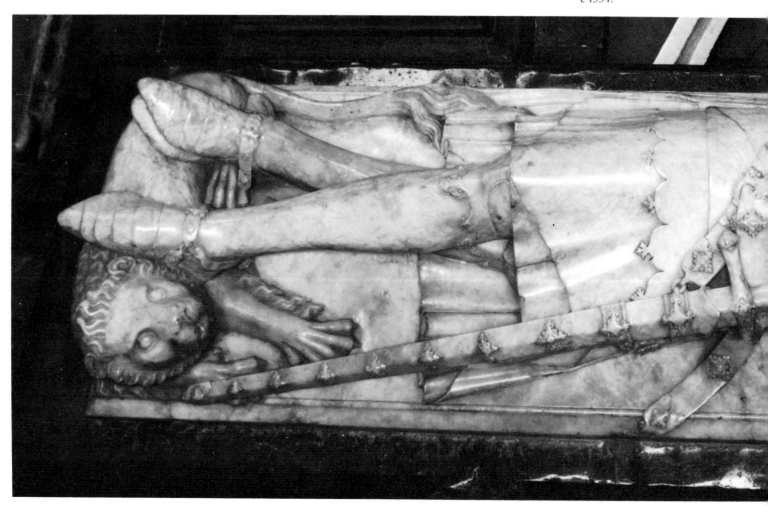

Contents

INTRODUCTION
The Origins of the Knight

Right: The helmet from the Sutton Hoo Ship Burial, seventh century. This is clearly derived from the late Roman Spangenhelm form and is of iron inlaid with silver and with gilded and tinned ornaments.

The medieval knight is generally perceived as a mounted warrior, armed *cap-à-pied*, bound by the codes of chivalry. The close association of the knight and his horse is clearly shown by the titles by which he was known throughout Europe; in France he was a *chevalier*, in Italy a *cavaliere*, in Spain a *caballero*, and in Germany a *ritter*, from the word meaning to ride. Even the name for the code by which the knight was later to be bound, chivalry, derives from the French *cheval*. It is only in England that the word 'knight' has no direct association with the horse. It comes from the Anglo-Saxon word *cniht*, meaning household retainer or servant, and it is not until the twelfth century that knighthood and chivalry become inextricably associated with gentle birth.

From the earliest civilized times the mounted warrior, whether in a chariot or upon horseback, had a pre-eminent social position. The effect of the mounted man was so great upon societies which knew nothing of the horse, that he gave rise to legendary creatures, such as the centaur of ancient Greece. The very cost of keeping, breeding and training war horses meant that for the most part mounted warriors were drawn from the highest strata of society. In the classical civilizations of both Greece and Rome the *hippeus* and *equites* formed a distinct social class which was between highest aristocracy and the citizen body in general, although the military systems of the great Mediterranean civilizations, especially those of Greece and Rome, were based primarily upon the infantryman.

The history of the development of the Roman army is one of adaptation and innovation, adopting aspects of nearly every military system with which it came into contact. According to Polybius, the second century BC Greek historian, the Romans adopted the equipment and tactical deployment of armoured cavalry from the Hellenistic Greeks, substituting long spears instead of javelins. By the fourth century AD the Roman army had developed heavily armoured cavalry, riding armoured horses, known as *cataphractarii*. These costly and élite units did not survive the break-up of the Western Empire in the fifth and sixth centuries, but by this time they had made a distinct impression upon their opponents. As a rule the Germanic invaders of the Western Empire fought on foot without armour; traditionally each ruler was surrounded by a body of picked warriors, usually around 300 in number, bound by ties of kinship, honour and reward. Men gave their loyalty to death and beyond – if their Chieftain was killed in battle, their duty was to avenge him or die in the attempt. This philosophy is illustrated in the epic *Beowulf*, among others. The knight was to evolve from the welding of these two traditions.

In the seventh century AD the only people in Western Europe to use the horse extensively in battle were the Lombards. These people swept into Eastern Europe and thence into Italy where they established the Kingdom of Lombardy. They proved an extremely dangerous enemy, as is amply attested by contemporary Byzantine historians. The Frankish army of Charles Martel which defeated the Saracens so convincingly at Poitiers in 733 was composed almost entirely of infantry based around an élite body of mail-clad troops. However, shortly after Poitiers the Franks began to raise large numbers of cavalry and laws were enacted both to recruit and equip them. Land was even confiscated from the Church to pay for their equipment and upkeep. Charlemagne conquered Lombardy in 774 and recruited large numbers of Lombards into his army

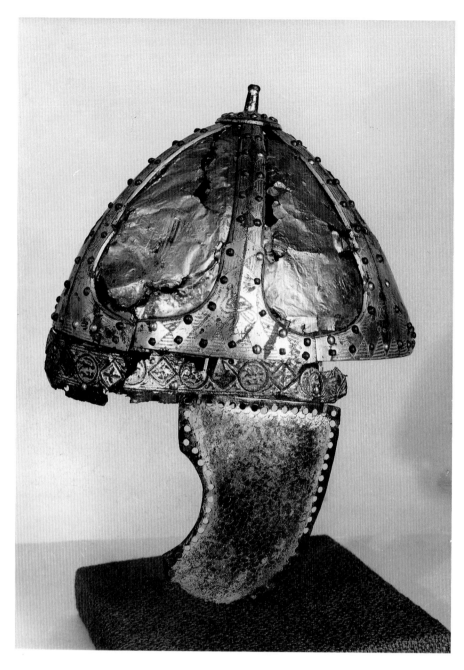

Above: An Ostrogothic Spangenhelm from Ravenna, Italy, seventh century.

authority of the emperor waned, and the defence of the outposts of the empire fell more and more into the hands of the Imperial Counts, their fortresses and their mounted retainers. These retainers were granted land in return for supporting their lord in his quarrels and in war, and it is from this that the feudal system evolved. The first chivalric poems and tales are woven around the lives of these retainers; the *Song of Roland* and the tales about King Arthur and the Knights of the Round Table have a similar origin. By the thirteenth century the chivalric tradition had become almost as much a part of the knight as his horse. The shedding of blood in battle and the concept of honour and loyalty to one's lord and, latterly, the the Church, were its cornerstones. However, the concepts were part of Germanic tribal life as early as the first century AD, and among the Celtic and other European tribal traditions a warrior élite was supported by an agrarian society in return for its protection. In other words, the traditions of the knight, as well as the form of his equipment and armour, are influenced by, if not descended from, those of Late Antiquity, and these were themselves strongly influenced by the Celts.

The first knights, the Paladins, were equipped in what is basically a debased form of late Roman armour. For the most part they wore round or conical helmets constructed of a number of pieces, to which the modern term *Spangenhelm* has been applied. These are direct descendants of the late Roman helmets produced at the Imperial Arms Factories during the fourth and fifth centuries. As most of these factories and their workers fell into the hands of the migrating German tribes, this is hardly surprising.

The *Spangenhelm* was at first constructed of three pieces, consisting of two half skulls riveted to a central comb, but later examples consisted of an iron framework of ribs extending from a brow band converging at the apex of the helmet. In between these were triangular plates of iron, which were sometimes plated with bronze or silver and decorated with semi-precious stones (as is the fourth century helmet from Duerne, Holland, and the examples from Interçissa and Berkasovo in Yugoslavia). Late Roman examples such as the fifth century helmet excavated at Dêr el Medîneh, Egypt, were equipped with cheek pieces, a separate neck guard and quite often a nasal, which was

and by the eighth century an armoured cavalry elite had evolved in both the social and military sense. In order to support these new troops Charlemagne instituted laws whereby all subjects were obliged to render military service in one form or another, but instead of a general levy each group of four men were to contribute to equip a fifth. This was supported by a War Tax which was levied on all free men. After his election as Holy Roman Emperor, this became law throughout his realm.

The earliest contenders for the title of knight are the Paladins of Charlemagne's Court, who held the Latin title *eques*. These were mailed horsemen who served the Emperor in his Frankish realm. Under Charlemagne's successors the central formed in one with stylized eyebrows and was riveted to the front of the helmet. Helmets of this type were found throughout Europe in the sixth and seventh centuries; for instance the Mörken helmet is from a princely Frankish grave, the Sutton Hoo helmet, found in England, is clearly derived from a late Roman type, and the Wendel helmet from Scandinavia is of a very similar form. The cheek pieces and neck guard were abandoned in about the late seventh or early eighth century, and this type of helmet remained apparently unchanged from then until well into the second half of the thirteenth century.

On their bodies the Paladins wore either mail birnies or hauberks, scale shirts or, more unusually, coats of lamellar armour. Examples of the latter have been found in the graves of the Wendel people of Scandinavia and are depicted in the *Golden Psalter*. The shirt of mail, formed of interlinked metal rings, first appears in Celtic graves, and the Roman author Varro assigned its invention to the Celts. It was first used in the Classical World in the third century BC and became widely disseminated. The Carolingian mail shirt was normally knee-length or a little shorter, and was pulled on over the head. It had a plain round neck opening with a centre-front slit, and invariably had short sleeves, which only occasionally reached as far as the elbow. At the centre back and front it was split from hem to groin level to enable the wearer to ride. Early mail shirts were worn over an ordinary woollen tunic, with apparently no special garment beneath. An Edict of Charlemagne dated 805 required all those individuals who owned more than 300 acres of land to supply themselves with a mail birnie. The early knights were armed with swords designed to cut and thrust, broad-bladed spears and round, convex shields.

This panoply was predominant throughout Europe and, although there were small modifications to individual items, remained virtually unchanged until the end of the eleventh century. The eighth century saga *Beowulf* describes the Geats thus:

Each tough hand-linked coat of mail sparkled, and the shimmering ringlets of iron clinked in their corselets. When they arrived in armour at the hall, the sea-beaten men unslung their broad double-proofed shields and ranged them against the palace wall. Then they seated themselves on

the bench; their corselets rang. The seafarers' weapons, iron-headed ash spears, were neatly piled. They were a well equipped company.

Above: Two plain iron Spangenhelms said to date from the fifth century.

Beowulf, their leader, was helmeted, he carried an ancestral patterned sword of the finest metal, and wore a corselet of mail which he claimed was the best in the world as it was made for his grandfather Hrethel by Wayland Smith himself. This mail was later seen to be of such quality that the monstrous mother of Grendel could not force her tallons between its closely woven links.

Charlemagne's accession in 742 AD marked a radical change in warfare in Europe. He enforced strict discipline on his levy and concentrated his expenditure on increasing his striking force of cavalry, to

ET SYRIAM SOBAL · ET CONYERTIT
IOAB · ET PERCYSSIT EDOM INVAL
LE SALINARVM · XII MILIA ·

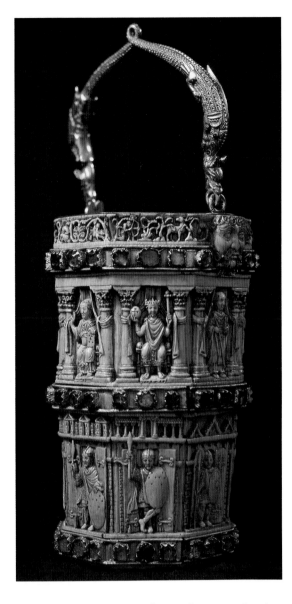

spear was developed at the same time which had lugs at its base to prevent it penetrating too far. It is often depicted being used with two hands, and the lugs may have been necessary because stirrups were introduced which, in conjunction with a new type of saddle with a more prominent cantle and pommel, enabled the weight and speed of the horse to be harnessed to a lance thrust. Certainly stirrups allow a rider to make a stronger downward cut with a sword and give him more stability on rough ground and in a melee. Stirrups appear to have been invented in China sometime in the fifth century and are first recorded as having been used by the Arabs in the seventh century. They arrived in the West in the early years of the eighth century, apparently brought by the Avars and Lombardic invaders.

The knight's equipment of the tenth century was also influenced by the Vikings. They wore mail shirts or lamellar armour, and helmets and carried flat, circular shields. Their principal weapons were the sword, axe and spear. Njal's saga tells how Skarphedin's axe severed Hallgrim's thigh, and Gunnar's was capable of severing the neck of Thorkell. The Vikings ascribed properties and names to their weapons, and the almost religious veneration with which the sword came to be regarded at this time may be the result of Viking influence. It is possibly the time, labour and money needed to produce a pattern-welded sword that gave it this position.

Far left: A page from the ninth century Frankish work known as the 'Golden Psalter of St Gall'. It shows typical Carolingian cavalry and infantry, equipped with Spangenhelms, mail shirts, winged spears and round shields.

Left: A holy water stoop from the Cathedral Treasury at Aachen, dating to the ninth century. Made of ivory and silver, the lower half depicts Carolingian warriors wearing Spangenhelms and mail shirts. They carry spears and shields.

counter the raids made on his Empire by Avar, Lombard and Saracen horsemen. He introduced a series of laws whereby land owners were to supply a cavalryman equipped with shield, lance, sword and dagger. Sixty years after Charlemagne's death in around 875, the Monk of St Gall described him as follows: 'Then appeared the Iron King, crowned with his iron helm, with sleeves of iron and his breast protected by a mail shirt . . . His thighs were mail covered, though other men preferred to leave them unprotected . . . His legs and those of most of his army were protected by iron greaves.' He is also said to have carried a plain iron shield. Allowing for a degree of poetic licence, this gives a fair indication of what the better equipped cavalryman wore.

Throughout the eighth and ninth centuries the long swords produced in the Carolingian Rhineland were especially valued by the Byzantines and Saracens. A heavy thrusting

Left: A ninth century Viking helmet, found in Coppergate, York. It is of Spangenhelm construction with cheek-pieces and a nasal guard incorporating stylized eyebrows.

The rank and file of both the Scandinavian and Frankish armies were, for the most part, equipped only with shield and spear; however, both used the bow and the Franks had a primitive form of crossbow and a sling as projectile weapons. The importance of the bow in battle is attested by Wiglaf's funeral oration over the pyre of Beowulf in which he paints an eloquent picture of the shield wall behind which Saxon warriors fought:

Now let the black flames shoot up and fire swallow this prince of fighting-men, who so often faced a rain of steel, when sped by bowstrings, a gale of arrows hurtled over sheltering shields, and the feather-flighted shaft did its work, driving home the barb.

The Viking raids and wars of conquest spread their weapons and aggressive styles of warfare throughout northwest Europe and this, allied with the native tradition of the Frankish Empire, was to produce not only the armies which subdued Normandy, England and Sicily but also the famed Varangian Guard. The latter was the personal bodyguard of the Emperors of Byzantium in which no less a person than Harald Hardrada, King of Norway, himself served.

By the tenth century the main characteristics of the medieval knight had evolved. He was a mounted warrior with rank and authority and his position and relationship to others was clearly defined. The duties and service he owed to those of a higher social rank were minutely laid down by the feudal system, as were the duties and service owed to him by his inferiors; and by the strength of his arm and his courage he might rise into the ranks of the aristocracy. His social prestige was further enhanced by the fact that all noblemen, no matter what their rank, were knights, and knightly warfare became the monopoly of an aristocratic caste.

The necessary curbs on the behaviour of one knight to another were formalized early into the code of chivalry. This governed the conduct of those of knightly rank to their peers but, apart from religious injunctions about mercy to the weak and charity to the poor, it did not extend to other classes.

At first knighthood could be granted by another knight but, slowly, this became the

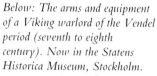

Below: The arms and equipment of a Viking warlord of the Vendel period (seventh to eighth century). Now in the Statens Historica Museum, Stockholm.

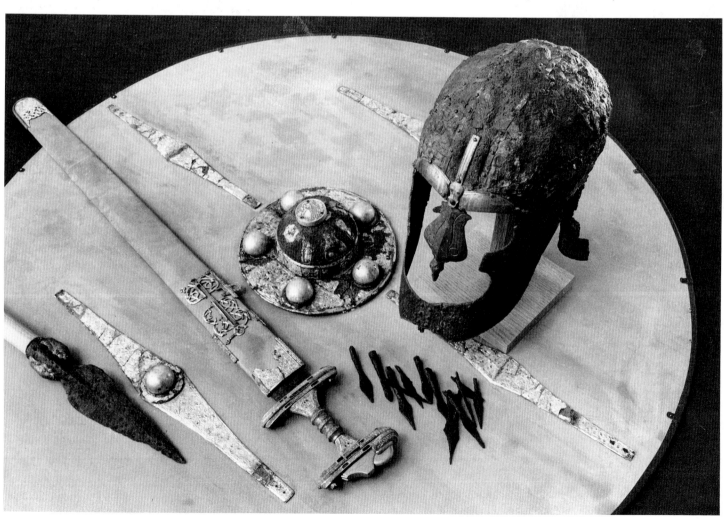

HIC WILLELM:DVX

prerogative of the monarch alone and became increasingly enshrined in religious ceremony. Without his knights a ruler was unable to enforce his will. The knight's rank, status and wealth depended on the size of his fiefdom. As land became gradually scarcer within the kingdoms of western Europe, the

only way a knight could win greater wealth and position was by marriage or by hiring himself out as a mercenary or as part of a free–lance – it was by the promise of fiefdoms to his own vassals as well as to mercenaries that William of Normandy raised the army which conquered England.

Above: William I of Normandy (left), depicted on the Bayeux Tapestry carrying a mace, already a symbol of rank and an effective weapon against mail. He is ready for the battle which will decide the outcome of his bid for the throne of England.

13

CHAPTER ONE
The Eleventh Century Adventurers to Aristocrats

Few early medieval rulers in Europe could afford a standing army large enough to protect their lands, especially with the mounting cost of equipping, feeding and maintaining such armies. The feudal system, which existed throughout Europe in one form or another for five centuries, was a way in which this cost could be spread across the whole spectrum of society. In essence, feudalism was a rural-based system dependent upon mutual co-operation; the giving of military or agricultural service to a lord (ultimately the king or prince of a realm) in return for which the vassal was entitled to his lord's protection, and to make his living from the feudal benefice (land known as a 'fee' or 'fief') granted to him. In some cases, of course, kings themselves could be vassals; thus William I of England was a vassal of the King of France by reason of his dukedom of Normandy. The 'great' vassals were more usually noblemen or churchmen, 'tenants-in-chief' of the king to whom all land ultimately belonged, and from whom their estates and power were derived. These lands could be divided and 'sub-let' to lesser vassals who would then owe service to the tenant-in-chief and through him to the king.

Due to the impracticality of fielding an army composed of many small elements with different, and usually conflicting, immediate loyalties, it was not long before debts of service were being commuted to 'scutage,' cash payments which could be used to hire professional troops loyal only to their paymaster. Such payments were already common in England by the middle of the eleventh century (some towns were allowed to pay in lieu of service – Oxford, for example, could pay £20 to the king instead of providing 20 men). Fines for failure to comply with one's feudal obligations were also common.

England prior to the Norman Conquest possessed one of the most sophisticated and formidable feudal defence systems in medieval Europe, despite the fact that as a nation the kingdom was far from united. King Canute 'the Great', England's Danish conqueror and king from 1017, had divided his kingdom into four great 'earldoms' – Wessex, Mercia, East Anglia and Northumbria. The 'earls' who ruled these were the king's vassals and answerable to him for their actions. The earl also had his own household troops, as many as 300 professional soldiers known as 'housecarls', whom the king could call upon at need. The king's own housecarls numbered approximately 3000 and these experienced, well-trained warriors formed the nucleus of any army that he might field. Canute first instituted the royal corps of housecarls in around 1018, financed by the Danegeld (a land tax originally levied to buy off the Danish raiders) and the Heregeld (a tax to pay for Danish mercenaries). At the time these taxes were almost unique in Europe, and were the main reason that English kings were able to raise and maintain such a large loyal standing army. In peacetime these troops were garrisoned all over the kingdom, but they were almost invariably mounted and could therefore be concentrated relatively swiftly if need be.

Below the forces of the king and the earls lay another level of military organization; that of the common feudal levies. These existed elsewhere in Europe too; in France they were known as the *arrière ban*, and the *Heerban* was a similar force in the German states. In England, the earldoms were divided into shires administered by a shire reeve or sheriff who was responsible for raising and commanding the shire levies or 'great fyrd'. This was the rank and file of the Anglo-Saxon army, consisting of every free

IAT:HAROLDVM

 SE

DEEXER

CITV

ELLMI

IS

man in a threatened area; they were often therefore highly motivated, but also ill-equipped, unmounted and lacking in training, so were rarely used outside their own shire. The 'select' fyrd were usually mounted and therefore capable of swift deployment, although (in common with the housecarls) they usually dismounted to fight on foot in Anglo-Saxon and Norse tradition. Not as numerous (probably 15,000 to 20,000 men nationwide) they were better trained and equipped, and of far more practical use as an independent military force. Military service in the select fyrd was dependent upon landholding; a similar system operated in Europe under laws first enacted by Charlemagne in the eighth century.

The select fyrd were a military elite with a strong bond of honour and loyalty; when incorporated into a much larger force under the command of an earl or even the king himself, they still retained their unit identity. Technically, service in the select fyrd was a feudal obligation, but by the middle of the eleventh century it had become an honour; and many could be considered lesser knights. The whole system reinforced the ancient Anglo-Saxon right of every free man to bear arms and tradition that it was honourable to die with one's lord upon the battlefield, and dishonourable to leave it alive if he were slain.

This was the military ethos and organization that the Normans inherited in 1066; after the conquest the more directly feudal system of Norman rule was imposed upon it from above, but the basic hierarchy with all its feudal ties remained. Landholders who had not fought against William or opposed his rule retained their estates; other estates became knight's fiefs to be granted to those who had assisted the duke in his invasion. Existing Saxon landholders therefore owed the same knight-service to William that his own Norman knights did. By the end of the Conqueror's reign in 1087 there were some 5000 knights' fees owing service to the king, of which perhaps 170 could be counted as tenants-in-chief. Although 'knight' in English is derived from the Anglo-Saxon for 'household retainer', by the second half of the eleventh century they had become a landed class valuing military prowess, honour and glory above all, with hereditary titles and estates. The latter provided them with revenues of their own rather than wages for their service to an overlord.

The increasing requirement for offensive military operations in this and subsequent centuries, however, was something that the feudal system was simply not designed to fulfil; rulers therefore increasingly sought to maintain units of professional troops themselves, and also supplemented their forces by employing mercenaries. Due to their high cost mercenaries did not replace the levies of the feudal army but merely reinforced them; neither could they replace the knights themselves, established as they were at the top of the feudal pyramid.

Like England, Normandy at the beginning of the eleventh century was a rich and well-administered state, already truly feudal in that the duchy was subdivided into fiefs, each owing knight-service to the duke in direct proportion to its size and value. There was no obligation to serve beyond the borders of Normandy itself, however, and still less overseas; when the army did finally embark for England, nearly one half of it was composed of mercenaries, lesser knights and those seeking to advance their fortune or social status through booty or new estates. Many of those who did accompany the duke did so more from feelings of personal loyalty and trust in him as a leader than because the feudal system compelled them to. William's knights, however, were the essential nucleus of his army; it was this full-time military professionalism that led to the social elevation of the knightly class throughout Europe. Before the 'bestowal of arms' that constituted the ceremony of knighthood, the knight had to undergo a long period of apprenticeship as an 'armiger' (squire), during which he became skilled in the craft of war. Such was the expense of his weapons, armour, horse and other equipment, however, together with the necessity for free time in which to devote himself to constant training and practice, that inevitably it was largely only the noble class who could aspire to such rank, eventually regarding it as their own especial right. There were many landless or 'lesser' knights in the service of their more powerful and well-established fellows, of course, but the 'enfeoffed' knight was always regarded as a social superior. The landed knights under William and his tenants-in-chief were called 'barones'; landed free-men who had not yet attained the rank of knight were known as 'vavasseurs', and those possessing less than a full knight's fee were known as 'sergeants', and were similarly armed and armoured mounted troops who fought alongside the knight in battle, but without possessing his rank or status.

The duchy of Normandy was not large, and with the sons of knights themselves holding the rank of knight, often the only way to found a new household was to seek estates elsewhere; thus by 1066 the Normans had expanded from northern France and established a firm foothold in Italy. The first settlement, at Aversa, was founded by Rannulf in 1030; in 1059 Robert Guiscard was declared Duke of Apulia and Calabria, and in 1071 the Normans captured Palermo from the Saracens. William, meanwhile, had taken England and proceeded to make his conquest secure. The Normans completed the conquest of Sicily in 1091, consolidating their hold over most of Italy, and in the closing years of the century played a major part in the First Crusade, taking Antioch from the Saracen Turks in 1098 to found a new state ruled by a Norman, Bohemond. Jerusalem fell in 1099, the only time it was ever to fall to a Crusader army.

The significance of the Normans therefore extended far beyond their conquest of England, and it is for this reason that the embroidery known as the Bayeux 'Tapestry' is the single most important source of information for the armour and weapons of mid-eleventh century Europe. This embroidery was probably commissioned by Bishop Odo for his new cathedral at Bayeux, dedicated in 1077. Equally as significant as the portrayal of the battle of Hastings, however, is the emphasis put upon the importance of feudal obligations as well as rightful succession to kingship. Prior to the death of Edward the Confessor and Harold's assumption of the crown of England, he is shown receiving gifts of arms from William; as much as the subsequent oath of allegiance supporting William's claim to the throne, this marked Harold as having become the duke's man, with all that that entailed. In many ways, however, our reliance upon the Bayeux embroidery is unfortunate, for there is a limit to what stitches alone can portray; many of the representations are conventionalized and need comparative material to make them fully understandable. Other sources (the early thirteenth century Norwegian Tapestry from Baldishol, for example) are subject to the same limitations. Very little

Left: A coin of Roger I, the Norman conqueror of Sicily, who died in 1101. It portrays a Norman knight just like the Bayeux Tapestry illustrations.

survives of the artefacts themselves; the pagan practice of burying a king or warlord with his arms, armour, and treasure ceased upon the widespread conversion of the European peoples to Christianity, so even archaeological evidence is scarce.

The helmets depicted in the Bayeux Tapestry are similar to the late Roman or Migration Period *spangenhelms* known from archaeological sites throughout central Europe. These were built around a framework of bronze or iron strips, the infills being made from beaten panels of iron (often plated

Below: Seventh century Frankish Spangenhelm, constructed of five iron segments within a bronze frame. It is likely that many eleventh century Norman helmets were made in this fashion.

Above: This Norwegian tapestry fragment from Baldishol Church is believed to be early thirteenth century, but depicts an eleventh or twelfth century knight similar to those of the Bayeux Tapestry. The figure on the left is probably wearing a split hauberk of lamellar or scale armour.

Far right, above: Tenth or eleventh century conical helmet, possibly Polish in origin.

Far right: The helmet of St Wenceslaus, who died in 935, now in the Treasury of Prague Cathedral.

or overlaid with other metals) riveted onto the main frame; occasionally thin sheets of bronze or even organic materials such as horn or hardened leather might have been used, but these rarely survive in an archaeological context. A tenth or eleventh century helmet of *spangenhelm* type now in the Royal Armouries at H M Tower of London is made of iron plates overlaid on the outside with sheets of gilt copper secured by silver-capped nails; such methods of construction and decoration clearly remained unchanged for centuries. The nasal guard characteristic of Norman helmets was generally riveted onto a reinforcing band around the bottom rim. At one point in the Tapestry, William reveals his face by raising his helmet, to dispel rumours of his death; this implies that the nasal guard could be quite large. Cheek-pieces seem to have been discarded by the eleventh century. In some cases, segmented helmets seem to have been made without a framework, the panels simply being riveted together along the vertical edges, converging at the top, with a nasal guard riveted onto the bottom edge at the front; such a helmet as this is in the Metropolitan Museum, New York, although it has lost its nasal and is very corroded. Helmets forged entirely in one piece were probably stronger, though requiring

more skill to manufacture; one is preserved in the Cathedral Treasury in Prague, and is said to have belonged to Saint Wenceslaus of Bohemia, who died in 935 AD. The iron skull is forged in one piece, with an iron nasal and bottom reinforcing rim riveted in place and decorated with silver overlay in the form of interlaced strapwork; the nasal is decorated in the same manner with a conventionalized crucifix motif. Another helmet of this type is in the Vienna Waffensammlung; it is forged entirely in one piece including the nasal guard, a series of holes around the bottom rim indicating that there was probably once a reinforcing band. Others are in Polish museum collections at Glucka Purzcza, Ostrów Wednicki and the State Archaeological Museum, Warsaw. The Bayeux Tapestry shows some helmets with extensions at the rear; other (manuscript) sources show two broad ribbons (presumably of coloured cloth) hanging down from the back of the helmet. Conical helmets of 'Norman' type seem to have proved an effective defence against sword, axe and mace, since they remained popular in various parts of Europe, especially the east, until well into the thirteenth century.

Most of the warriors in the Tapestry are shown wearing close-fitting mail hoods or 'coifs' underneath their helmets. These seem to have been made in one with the mail hauberk, although this is not evident on the hauberks being carried to the Norman ships prior to the invasion, nor in later scenes of the dead being stripped. Those without helmets sometimes wear only a coif. Civilian clothes probably also incorporated such hoods, made in fabric; where the stitch patterns indicating mail or scale armour are missing, coifs of cloth may have been intended. It is rare to find coifs separate from the hauberk. The only other headpiece (popularly worn by common infantry and archers) was a form of 'Phrygian' cap, possibly of leather. This was probably a cheap alternative for those of the lower orders who could not afford a helmet. Needless to say, none has survived to the present for examination.

The main body armour of the period was the knee-length mail shirt, the birnie or hauberk. The earliest surviving dates from the twelfth century and is preserved in Prague Cathedral as supposedly being that of Saint Wenceslaus, but it is in too poor a condition to tell us much. The early hauberks were invariably of riveted mail, probably weighing about 31 pounds (14kg). Mail found in the seventh century royal ship burial at Sutton Hoo appeared to have butted links, but X-radiography and scanning electron microscopy have established that this too is riveted. Hauberks were put on over the head, and were split at the front and back to enable the wearer to ride (although the Wenceslaus hauberk is split only down the back). The sleeves extended to mid-way down the forearm, the wrist being covered with another material, presumably cloth or leather; this could be an integral lining or the sleeve end of a garment worn under the mail. Occasionally, the stitch patterns indicate mail covering this part of the forearm also. The scenes of the dead being stripped show the bodies naked under their hauberks; common sense and practical experiment are at odds with this conclusion, however, and by the twelfth century other sources reveal knee-length garments of cloth under the mail. Many eleventh century hauberks have a rectangle covering the upper chest, outlined with broad (usually coloured) bands like those at the cuffs and hem, suggesting that the vulnerable neck opening was protected by a lined reinforce of mail. Very rarely, the hilt of the knight's sword protrudes from a

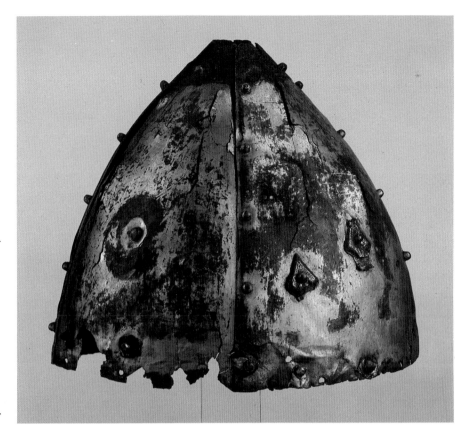

small slit over the left hip. Wearing the sword under the mail as opposed to the more usual practice of wearing it hung from a waist-belt

Left: An early eleventh century Byzantine carved ivory plaque of St Demetrius. His body is protected by a hauberk of overlapping metal scales, with sleeves and skirt probably of lamellar armour. The pattern formed by lamellar armour is reproduced almost exactly in the hauberk of the standing figure in the Norwegian Baldishol tapestry illustrated on page 18.

on the outside would obviously protect the sword and scabbard from being damaged or cut loose during a battle. Some late Anglo-Saxon manuscripts depict this feature, and it is clearly shown once in the Tapestry, where duke William honours Harold with a gift of arms for his part in the expedition against Count Conan. Harold's sword hilt is visible on his left hip, appearing from the slit in his hauberk; the foot of the scabbard protrudes below the hem of the mail. Early Anglo-Saxon manuscript sources imply that the mail shirt was rare and highly prized – only leaders or important warriors possessed one, but like the sword they later became an integral part of the early knight's equipment and an indication of his profession, status and rank. Like swords also, some hauberks were even christened with their own name; King Harald Hardrada, we are told in the Harald Saga, had a mail shirt called 'Emma'.

We know from other contemporary sources that hauberks were also constructed from overlapping metal scales sewn, laced or, more probably, riveted to a base garment (presumably of leather or stout cloth). Manuscripts describe different types of mail, such as 'double' and 'triple' mail; differing stitch patterns in the Tapestry may conceivably indicate these, but simple artistic licence

is just as likely. Hauberks made of two or three layers of mail would have been exceptionally heavy to wear; 'double' and 'triple' may therefore refer to the closeness of the mesh. 'Banded' mail in contemporary illustrations, especially from the twelfth and thirteenth centuries, may represent alternate rows of riveted rings and rings made by punching complete closed circles of metal from a thin sheet of iron. This would both confer strength (there being no 'weak' link in unriveted rings) and also reduce the labour of assembly by halving the quantity of rings needing to be riveted. In Europe from the fourteenth century onwards, however, it is extremely rare to find any exception to wholly riveted mail. Forms of 'soft armour' were certainly in general use by the mid-twelfth century; defences of thickly padded, quilted cloth were a cheap, practical and

Above: An eleventh century conical helmet from Moravia. Made of iron, it is forged in one piece.

Left: The symbolic arming of Harold by William of Normandy, in the Bayeux Tapestry. Note Harold's sword, worn under his hauberk with only the hilt protruding.

21

Above: The lower border of the Bayeux Tapestry showing the stripping of the dead at the Battle of Hastings. Their hauberks are being pulled off over their heads.

Below: The provisioning of William's invasion fleet, as shown in the Bayeux Tapestry. Note the hauberks being transported on poles, and the helmets being carried by their nasals.

comfortable alternative to those made of metal. The early evidence for their use is inconclusive, however; the Tapestry depiction of Bishop Odo at the battle of Hastings shows him wearing a hauberk composed of large, differently-coloured triangles, possibly scale armour or, equally feasible, a quilted 'gambeson'. William himself wears one of these puzzling garments in his military expedition against Count Conan of Brittany, and a third is worn by Count Guy of Ponthieu; but the latter is more likely to be scale armour, since its surface is covered with rows of wavy horizontal lines having the effect of overlapped semi-circular plates of metal. Contemporary manuscript sources such as the late eleventh century *Song of Roland* also contain references to 'jazerant', or garments made 'of jaz'rain'. Little evidence exists as to what this actually was; the word may derive from the Arab 'kazaghand',

which the twelfth century Saracen Usàmah describes as being one or more shirts of mail sandwiched between two thicknesses of padded cloth.

The legs do not appear to have been protected at all in the eleventh century, although a few figures in the Tapestry wear mail leggings ('chausses'), either as stockings or, more likely at this date, mail covering only the front of the leg, laced across the calf at the back. There is no evidence for plate leg defences, despite the ninth century precedent for greaves of iron. Only important figures, such as William himself and some of the other leaders, wear chausses; most of the other soldiers are wearing ordinary cloth hose, sometimes cross-gartered or spirally bound, with shoes of civilian form.

The traditional form of the warrior's shield throughout the latter Dark Ages was circular (or occasionally oval), usually not larger than

about 3 feet (1m) in diameter, and constructed of wooden planks laid next to each other or cross-grained like plywood. The surface was frequently covered with leather and/or painted; contemporary texts often describe Viking shields as brightly coloured and decorated with pictures of dragons or other beasts. Specific types and shapes of round shield varied, of course, depending on their place of origin, but the principles of construction were largely the same. A hole was cut in the centre, across which an iron hand-grip was riveted; a metal boss ('umbo') covered this on the outside, protecting the hand. The shield's rim could also be reinforced with metal. From rivets found on archaeological sites it is estimated that the thickness of such shields varied from .6-1.2 inches (15-30mm); even so, the sagas often tell of them being hacked to pieces early in the battle. Shields were used both defensively and as a weapon; to parry blows, thrust into the face and, wielded edge-wise, to strike at an opponent or knock aside his weapon. Warriors either fought hand-to-hand in individual combats (individual prowess in battle counting for everything) or side-by-side with others in the formation known as the shield wall, each man protected by the shield of his neighbour on his vulnerable left side. The larger round shields had a strap for the forearm, anticipating the way in which the large kite-shaped shields of the Normans were carried and used.

Most of the shields depicted in the Bayeux Tapestry are of the familiar Norman elongated 'kite' form, which probably originated in southern Europe. Some English soldiers have oblong shields, while others carry what appear to be, in profile, round wooden shields of traditional Viking and Anglo-Saxon form. Round shields persisted in use

Below: A scene from the Bayeux Tapestry interpretation of the Battle of Hastings. On the extreme left is Bishop Odo, wearing what may be a hauberk of scale armour and carrying a mace of cudgel form.
On the extreme right, William of Normandy raises his helmet by its nasal to dispel rumours of his death.

Right: The great seal of Henry II (1154-1189) shows how the shield was carried.

Far right: A twelfth century stone carving of Roland, on the portico of Verona Cathedral. He carries a kite-shaped shield with an umbo.

Below: One of the figures on a gilt bronze chandelier (c 1140), formerly in the Abbey Church of Gross-Comburg. Note the curvature of the shield.

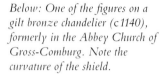

sometimes (for instance they are depicted in eleventh century Spanish manuscripts) but were regarded as old-fashioned by the second half of the century. They were not ideal for cavalry and had drawbacks even in infantry use – Magnus Barefoot, king of Norway 1093-1103, no doubt called his sword 'Leg Biter' for that very reason – whereas the round-topped kite-shaped shields of the eleventh century, carried by foot soldier or horseman, provided protection for the whole body including the legs. None of these shields has survived; the earliest one still in existence is a knight's shield from Seedorf in Switzerland, dating to the very early years of the thirteenth century. On horseback they were hung on the left side of the rider by a loose strap called a 'guige' around the neck, with a pair of shorter vertical straps ('enarmes') held firmly in the left hand. On foot, the shield was carried in much the same way, the guige enabling it to be slung on the back when not required. Their construction is largely conjectural; presumably wooden (borne out by the Tapestry's depiction of arrows sticking in them), probably covered with leather and painted, with a rim of metal or possibly wood. They were not flat, but slightly curved in the vertical plane so as to afford a measure of protection to the sides as well as to the front of the body. Relatively few of the shields are decorated with anything other than plain colours, groups of dots or simple four-armed 'swirling cross' designs; a few bear dragon motifs, but their apportionment seems largely arbitrary, and heraldic display on armour is not seen until the early years of the twelfth century.

In some manuscript illustrations and in such representations of Norman-style knights as the twelfth century 'pyx' figures in the Burrell Collection and the Wallace Collection, the kite-shaped shields appear to have umbos. References to shield bosses of 'gleaming brass' occur in contemporary literature, and in the *Song of Roland*, Roland's companion Oliver carries a shield with a 'golden boss'. It seems unlikely from what we know of these shields that such bosses were intended to be functional, however, especially for use on horseback.

In the eleventh century the European knight revered the sword above all other weapons. It was regarded not simply as a weapon of war but also as a symbol of his status and power, was used in the ceremony

of his knighthood and also served as an emblem of authority and the adjunct of ceremony on other significant occasions such as the coronation of kings. Furthermore, largely due to the influence of the Crusades which took place between 1096 and 1291 the simple cross-hilted sword of the knight became both a symbol of his Christian religion and the very instrument of God's will on earth. The veneration with which the Vikings had regarded their swords was thus perpetuated and as the literary traditions of the early sagas evolved into the medieval chivalric Romances, the image of both knight and sword was enhanced still further. The ancient custom of naming one's sword continued: Roland's sword is called 'Durendal' (Enduring), while that of the Emperor Charlemagne is 'Joyeuse' (Joyous). Other knightly protagonists carry swords with names such as 'Hauteclaire' (High-bright) and 'Murgleys' (Death brand). Their Saracen enemy, the Emir Baligant, names his own sword 'Précieuse' (Precious), so that it will not appear inferior to Charlemagne's. It was still widely believed that the personal courage, strength and renown of a warrior could somehow be absorbed by his sword, and that subsequent possession of this weapon would bestow the same distinction upon the new owner. Swords therefore continued to be highly valued and handed down from generation to generation.

The eleventh century sword owed much to Viking traditions. The warriors of the Scandinavian kingdoms (chiefly Norway and Denmark) had raided the coasts of Europe for centuries, and their reputation for military prowess was much admired and widely emulated. The sword was their principal and most prized fighting weapon, and from the end of the ninth century, if not before, Scandinavia had become a manufacturing and trading centre for swords, in particular fine blades rivalling those made for export in the Rhineland. These were of the highest quality, made of steel that was flexible, shock-resistant and capable of taking a keen edge.

The finest early blades were made by 'pattern-welding', a process probably first developed by Celtic smiths during the early Dark Ages. Obtaining a completely homogenous length of tempered steel sufficiently free from forging flaws and similar weaknesses so as not to break in use was a serious

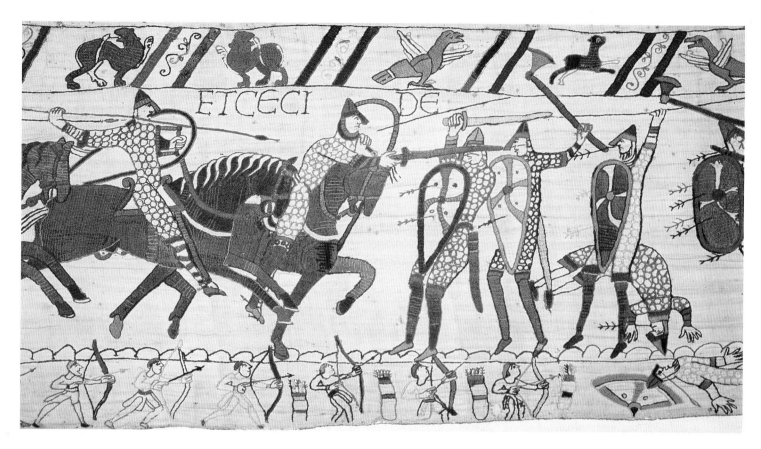

Above: A scene from the Bayeux Tapestry in which mounted Norman knights, armed with swords and light spears held over-arm for throwing, attack Harold's infantry at the Battle of Hastings. The English are similarly armed and equipped, but are also shown wielding battle-axes. A variety of shield shapes are depicted, the kite form being the most common on both sides.

technological problem; pattern-welding enabled the smith not only to overcome such limitations but also to utilize both inferior and good-quality iron (a necessary expedient when 'good' iron was a scarce and valuable commodity). A pattern-welded blade of the highest quality could take a month to make, and involved so much time and skill in the forging that its value in the mid-tenth century 'heriot' (the war-trappings due to a lord upon the death of a vassal) was said to be equivalent to 120 oxen or 15 slaves. Such blades were made of many separate parts; a centre bar of complex structure forged into one, and two edges made from a long billet of relatively homogenous steel bent back on itself into a tight 'V', which was then hammer-welded into place along each side of the centre bar to give the blade a hard cutting edge and point. To make the centre, several thin rods of malleable wrought iron were first case-hardened in a charcoal fire. Through this process the iron on the surface was carburized (that is, it absorbed carbon) to form a skin of hard steel. The rods were then heated red-hot and tightly twisted together, and finally were hammer-welded at white heat to forge all the constituent parts together. Depending on the way in which the twisting and forging was done, different repeating patterns could be formed within

the structure of the metal. Once these main bars had been forged together and the blade given its approximate shape, the fuller was put in. This was a broad, shallow hollow forged along the centre on each side, designed both to lighten and strengthen the blade on the same principle as the modern H-bar girder. Then, after it had been ground and filed to its final shape, the blade was heated and quenched to give the steel edge its hardness. The relatively soft iron in the centre core gave it resilience and prevented it from being liable to fracture. The pattern along the central fuller (referred to in *Beowulf* as being 'wave patterned' or 'variegated like a snake') could be enhanced with acid after the final polishing, the carburized parts showing a lighter colour than the softer iron. The description of Beowulf's borrowed sword 'Destroyer' hints at this process: 'an ancient heirloom, trusty and tried; its blade was of iron, with etched design.'

The swords which have survived do not retain this original finish; however, a contemporary description occurs in a letter written in AD 520 by Cassiodorus, secretary of Theodoric the Ostrogoth, Emperor of Rome, acknowledging a gift of swords from Thrasamund, King of the Varni:

You have sent us swords capable even of cutting

through armour. They are more precious for the iron of which they are made than for the gold that enriches them; with their strikingly perfect polish, they shine so that they reflect the face of whoever looks at them . . . The admirably hollowed middle part of their blades seem to be veined and patterned. There is the play of so many different shadows that one would think the metal is interlaced with elements of different colours.

These swords invariably had a broad double-edged blade usually not more than about 2 ft 6 ins (76cm) long, with a slightly rounded point, clearly intended for cutting and slashing rather than for thrusting only. They were used in one hand, although the sagas tell of Harald Hardrada disdaining to use his shield, and wielding his sword with both hands to deliver especially powerful blows. Most blades were mass-produced in a relatively few centres in Europe, and were occasionally struck, incised or inlaid with the name of the bladesmith (for instance INGELRI, spelt in a variety of ways) or an inscription (sometimes apparently meaningless). Good-quality blades could be inlaid with latten, copper or bronze; silver and gold were now more rarely employed.

Pattern-welded blades continued to be produced in Europe until about 1050. From the late eighth century, however, Viking smiths developed the technology to make blades of homogenous steel that equalled or even surpassed the performance of the pattern-welded ones. The name Ulfberht, a smith or family of smiths possibly originating from the Rhineland (near Sölingen), is often found on later blades of this type, frequently inlaid in iron; such inlay is never found in conjunction with pattern-welding. Lighter, tougher, and more sharply-tapered blades better able to pierce mail then evolved, and swords became less blade-heavy, enabling them to be used with more speed and dexterity than before.

Hilts were dependent upon national types and then upon the personal taste, wealth and purpose of the owner. The same general form was employed throughout Europe with only relatively minor national variations; the far-ranging nature of warfare as pursued by the Scandinavian warriors together with the flourishing trade in such weapons ensured the wide dissemination of both hilt types and styles of decoration.

Sweden, in particular, was noted for the manufacture and export of sword hilts richly decorated with gold, silver and niello; these have been found in archaeological deposits across Europe, from Ireland to Byzantium. The decoration on swords was usually applied by 'counterfeit damascening'; the iron was covered with a network of very finely chiselled cuts to roughen the surface, then softer non-ferrous or precious metal in the form of thin wire or foil was hammered onto this ground, which due to its roughened surface was able to retain the overlay. By the late tenth and eleventh centuries, relatively simple designs worked in latten or similar alloys were widely popular, usually letters or simple patterns incorporated into a background of fine vertical lines. Rarely, the names of hilt makers are found: LEOFRIC ME FEC ('Leofric made me') on a detached cross-guard from a late Viking sword in the British Museum, or HLITER (either a name, or possibly the word in old Norse for 'protection') on a sword in the Wallace Collection.

The form of the hilt was the same throughout most of Europe; a short, stubby iron cross-guard, a hand-grip covering the tang of the blade, and a flat iron pommel approximately semi-circular in shape (like a 'tea cosy'), sometimes divided into three, five or even seven 'lobes', set on a straight or slightly curved base. The hand-grip was usually of wood, bone or horn wrapped with cloth or leather and occasionally bound with cord or thonging; gold or silver wire also occurs but is much more rare. The weight of the hilt counterbalanced the blade and gave the weapon good handling characteristics, though invariably it was blade-heavy. National variants do occur; for example, on some Viking and Anglo-Saxon swords the ends of the cross-guard were not straight but inclined downwards. The pommel resembled a 'cocked hat' in shape – its base inclined upwards at each end away from the blade, in the opposite direction to the bend of the quillons. On Danish swords of the tenth and eleventh centuries the centre top of the pommel was divided into three lobes; these swords have also appeared on archaeological sites in London, presumably brought there by Canute and the Danish invaders.

Trilobate pommels were popular even as far south as Spain, occuring in the tenth to eleventh century 'Commentaries to the Apocalypse' of the St Beatus of Liébana, and

A Viking sword, c1000, found in the River Thames, London. Its blade is inlaid in iron with the maker's name, INGELRI.

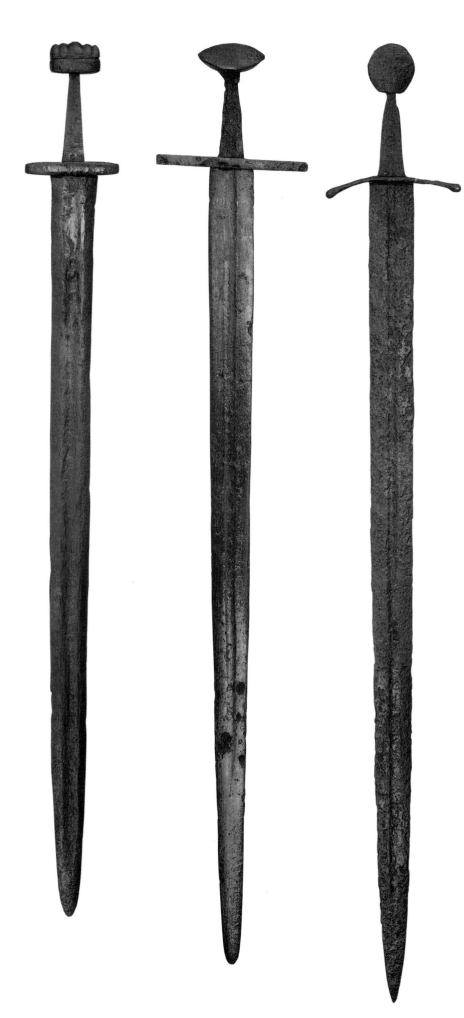

similar manuscript sources. By the early eleventh century, however, in northern and central Europe this form of pommel was evolving towards the 'brazil nut' shape so popular in the twelfth and thirteenth centuries. This was accompanied by a lengthening of the cross-guard, which also became more rounded in cross-section. The brazil nut pommel first appeared at the end of the tenth century, simultaneously with the first flat disc-shaped pommels, which were probably of southern European origin. These 'wheel' pommels became common in Europe following their widespread introduction and popularity during the first two Crusades (1096-99 and 1147-49).

Throughout this entire period the sword was usually carried in, and used from, a scabbard hung on the left hip from a waist belt secured by means of straps, thongs or buckles, as shown in the Bayeux Tapestry. The scabbard consisted of two thin laths of wood along either side of the blade, moulded to its shape and probably glued together along the edges with animal glue, then covered with leather which could be elaborately tooled and embossed. The inside was lined with fleece, the lanolin in the wool probably helping to curtail rust; the 'lay' of the wool was upwards to enable the sword to be drawn smoothly and easily, while its springiness helped to keep the blade firmly sheathed (important if the sword were being carried on horseback). In later centuries the knight's sword was carried in a tighter-fitting wooden scabbard made without this fleece lining. Very occasionally such swords and scabbards were carried not secured to a waist belt but to a simple baldric (usually a single leather strap) slung over the right shoulder. Belts, baldrics and straps generally had metal buckles and strap-ends, usually made of iron or various copper alloys; these could be gilded, enamelled or inlaid with semi-precious stones. In Scandinavia and Germany a sword-belt that tied closed was preferred. The metal fittings on the scabbard (a locket to protect the mouth and a chape for the bottom tip) were often similarly decorated. Gold or, more commonly, silver mounts and fittings are not unknown. As a general rule, however, sword and scabbard furniture became plainer, rather than more ornate, in the so-called Age of Chivalry.

The spear is the staff-weapon of a foot soldier; the lance that of a horseman. By the end of the Middle Ages these two were as far apart in appearance as they were ever to become, but at the beginning of this period, from the fourth to the tenth century, there was very little to distinguish between them. Spears were the most cost-effective and therefore the commonest weapons of the Dark Ages, and the use of a combination of spear and shield was the most popular form of combat. In eleventh century England a large proportion even of the select fyrd were armed with the spear as their primary weapon. Under the laws of Canute laid down between 1020 and 1023, the heriot stipulated twice as many spears as swords, making it quite clear that the spear was a class-less weapon used by all. An earl's heriot was '8 horses, 4 saddled and 4 unsaddled, and 4 helmets and 4 coats of mail and 8 spears and as many shields and 4 swords and 200 mancuses of gold.' The estate of a lesser thegn owed 'a horse and its trappings, and his

weapons . . . [but] if he has a more intimate relation with the king: 2 horses, 1 saddled and 1 unsaddled and a sword and 2 spears and 2 shields and 50 mancuses of gold.'

There was little established tradition for separating or categorizing the various types and functions of the spear, although obviously there were differences in weight, length and the form of head to suit different purposes. The Carolingians used a 'winged' spear-head with twin projecting lugs at the base of the blade to prevent over-deep penetration. The Bayeux Tapestry and other sources depict spears with single or double (and in some cases even triple) cross-pieces at the base of the blade-head, probably derived from this Carolingian form; although occasionally used by fighting horsemen, they seem to be primarily an infantry weapon. The archaeological evidence from late Dark Age burial sites indicates considerable variation in the lengths of spears, as well as a

Far left: Three swords in the Wallace Collection, London. The sword on the left is Scandinavian, c850-950. The hilt is overlaid with latten decoration incorporating the letters HLITER. The centre sword is German, eleventh century (in use until 1150). The hilt has a 'brazil nut' pommel. The right-hand sword is southern European (possibly Italian), twelfth century. The pommel consists of a thin, flat iron disc (forerunner of the true 'wheel' pommel).

Left: The Battle of Macchabees as depicted in the Bible of Rhodes (late tenth or eleventh century). This is another early illustration of horsemen carrying their lances couched under the right arm.

spear-heads with two such splits have been found. The heads were then riveted tightly to the shaft, sometimes additionally secured with leather thonging. Steel was quite difficult for the early smiths to make, and often imported as a raw material from steel-producing countries such as Sweden, Russia or Spain. The early spear-heads were often pattern-welded, and sometimes decorated like sword hilts, Scandinavian styles and workmanship predominating. This decoration was always situated so as not to interfere with the function of the blade or impede the sharpening or honing of its edge.

The Bayeux Tapestry shows spears used both as couched lances held under the right arm, and also as weapons carried over and under-hand to stab and probe at an enemy's defences, mainly in hand-to-hand combats. Spears are also shown hurled through the air as javelins, sometimes apparently from horseback; these are frequently shown with barbed heads in the shape of a 'V' and many of them also have cross-pieces below the blade. The spears carried to the boats prior to the invasion are all of this type. Some of the Norman knights carry couched lances with thick shafts bearing pennons flying from their tips, the forerunners of the traditional knight's lance of later centuries; a stout, long thrusting weapon, with a steel head either of long, thin triangular form or with a double-edged leaf blade, used in an all-out cavalry charge of tremendous weight and momentum such as frequently occurs in the early Romances. In the Tapestry scene where William rides at the head of his knights at Hastings the group is led by three knights galloping with such lances couched under their arms, followed by a much larger crowd of mounted knights who seem to be armed with the lighter types of spear, many of them having barbed heads.

The *Song of Roland* makes absolutely clear the power of the horseman's lance: 'He splits the shield, and cleaves the closely-woven hauberk, clean through his breast drives lance and pennon both', or again, 'Into the torso lance-point and pennon plough, from breast to back the shaft runs through and out.' It is also clear that such injuries are the result of a definite 'charge' on horseback, relying upon the speed and weight of the destrier as much as the strength of the warrior's right arm to inflict a death-dealing blow; the final shock of collision is such that the body

Above: Medieval spear and lanceheads excavated in London. Unlike the two Viking period types on the top right, the four on the top left were clearly designed to penetrate early plate armour (fourteenth century), as was the rarer tanged example (bottom left). Next to this is a 'winged' form, based on Carolingian prototypes, but dating to the fifteenth century. At the bottom right is a hunting spearhead of similar date.

diversity of spear-head types. The average length is about 6 feet 6 inches (2m) which is fairly short for cavalry use if couched under the arm, but these early spears clearly were not. As the spear evolved into the horseman's lance it tended to increase in length. By the thirteenth century such lances were rarely less than about 10 feet (3m) long. The wood was usually ash; this is recorded in Beowulf and also in the *Song of Roland*, where the knights have 'lances of ash and apple-beam'. The heads were of iron or steel; in some cases, points or edges of steel were hammer-welded into the iron, a technique developed in the last years of the Roman Empire. Most were socketed, the tang section having been hammered flat and forged around to form a socket with a single longitudinal split at the side, although in England many socketed

of the hapless victim is usually flung 'a full spear's length dead from the saddle' upon the ground.

Frequent mention is made of the lances bearing pennons; in the Bayeux Tapestry a number of the spears and lances carry small rectangular flags with tails or 'flies' (usually three in number) attached to them. Similar banners occur in the illuminated manuscript of the Winchester Bible (*c* 1150). These were called 'gonfanons' or 'gonfalons'. They seem to be closely associated with the mounted knights, as it is mainly horsemen who are depicted carrying them, and also they clearly constitute a mark of rank or authority. In the ceremonial arming of Harold by duke William, the latter bestows a lance bearing a gonfalon upon the English earl. The Saxons, fighting on foot, also have them; one warrior in each of the two groups representing the Saxon shield wall carries one of these banners on his spear, obviously as a symbol of authority and a rallying marker. The 'sacred cross' banner given to the Normans by the Pope to sanctify and legalize their enterprise is similarly of gonfalon shape, though longer and having its flies individually twisted into decorative knots. The only other form of battle flag depicted in the Tapestry is the traditional 'dragon' standard of the period; the cut-out shape of a wyvern attached by its head to the top of a staff. Two of these are

carried by Harold's standard bearers in the little group of warriors denoting the English 'command centre' during the battle.

Throughout eleventh century Europe the use of sword and spear was universal; other weapons varied in popularity, however. The battle-axe was a favourite weapon of the Scandinavian kingdoms, introduced into Anglo-Saxon England by Canute's Danish warriors at the beginning of the century. Paradoxically, the archaeological evidence for their use in England is fairly thin; they are a rare find on purely Anglo-Saxon sites, and those that do turn up are often the smaller, single-handed type known as the 'skeggox', which could be used in hand-to-hand fighting or could be hurled as a missile. It was similar to the 'bearded' axe-head of the Vikings, of which many have been found in the River Thames, London. They were probably initially developed from simple all-purpose tools. By the eleventh century, however, the most popular type was the Scandinavian 'broad-axe', which could be 4-5 feet (120-150cm) long overall, with an angular neck and a head (often decorated) measuring up to 10 inches (25cm) between the upper and lower points of its broad cutting edge. This edge was often of steel, quite capable of severing limbs and heads, as the tales of the sagas and the illustrations of dismembered corpses along the bottom border of the

Above: This Bayeux Tapestry scene of the Norman knights riding to battle shows the leaders with couched lances bearing 'gonfalon' pennants, while those behind carry lighter spears or javelins.

Above: Viking age spearheads and broad axe heads found in the River Thames, near London Bridge. Battle-axes such as these were capable of severing a man's head from his shoulders.

Bayeux Tapestry attest. They do not yet seem to have been furnished with iron langets or 'cheeks' to prevent the head being hacked off in battle; in fact, there is a scene in the Tapestry where this is clearly happening. It is also interesting to note the completely different shape of the head on the felling axes, and the 'T' shaped heads and shorter shafts of the small axes being used by the shipwrights building William's invasion fleet. These tools were clearly different from the axe heads made for war. One of the reasons suggested for the surprising scarcity of battle axe heads on archaeological sites is that they were too valuable to discard – they could be reused as tools or reforged into other objects and implements relatively early.

The Bayeux Tapestry shows both sides wielding battle-axes, but it is likely that fewer Normans than English were armed in this way, due to the preponderance of cavalry on the Norman side. The axe was largely an infantry weapon, without the social status or implications of the sword, but nonetheless tremendously effective in battle; this is why it was used by dismounted knights and noblemen as well as by common soldiery. Against mail armour it was particularly effective, having both a percussive and a cutting effect. During combat an axe was usually wielded with both hands, without a shield; the warrior either relied upon his own agility and skill to defend himself or, occasionally, fought alongside a companion armed with a sword or spear, and a shield. Mounted knights tended to rely upon the sword as a

subsidiary weapon after their spear or lance had been broken or lost, due to the practical difficulties of swinging a large axe from horseback; this is possibly also why the Normans generally seem to have favoured a shorter shaft and a smaller axe-head than the traditional two-handed Viking broad-axe, the type most illustrated in the Tapestry. Elsewhere on the continent, the axe does not appear to have become popular until the twelfth and thirteenth centuries.

The only other weapons of note that seem to have attained relatively widespread military use in the eleventh century are the mace and the bow. Both of these, however, were still in the formative years of their development, and unfortunately in both cases virtually no examples have survived to the present day for assessment. Both types of mace are shown quite frequently in the Bayeux Tapestry. In its early form it is a simple club or cudgel, probably made from wood, hence, perhaps, its sometimes rather knobbly appearance. Also seen is a slim, straight-shafted weapon with a trilobate head, presumably made of metal, clearly a forerunner of the all-metal maces of later centuries. There is evidence that the mace was used as an emblem of authority; William, for example, is shown bearing what is probably a wooden mace at the head of his army as he advances towards Hastings, and his half-brother Bishop Odo is depicted during the battle, mace in hand, 'rallying the young men' (possibly those who had not yet become knights), according to the Latin caption embroidered above his head. Both these cudgels and the metal-headed maces are depicted being used in this way, and they are generally only seen in the hands of leaders or warriors of some consequence. The only exception seems to be a group of fleeing English, most of whom are carrying trilobate-headed maces. They were definitely used as weapons – in the battle one is shown flying through the air towards the Normans, presumably having been hurled from behind the Saxon shield wall. There is no reason why both axes and maces should not have been so thrown, especially in the heat of battle. Such weapons of percussion were especially effective against mail armour; repeated blows could shatter bones and kill the victim without even breaking a single riveted link of his hauberk. In this situation the flexibility of mail, an advantage in other respects, was a positive disadvantage. The only defensive measure was to wear increasingly thick, heavy padded garments under the mail or, eventually, to supplement it with plate. This was not to happen for another century or more, however.

The bow had been in use for centuries as a weapon of war and its effectiveness on the battlefield was already well-known in Europe by the beginning of the medieval period. The Vikings (and Scandinavian peoples in general) had always had a particularly strong tradition of archery, and archers were present on both sides at Hastings. The vast majority of these were infantry, although in the aftermath of the battle a single mounted archer is depicted in the Tapestry as part of the cavalry force pursuing the fleeing Saxons.

There is little evidence that the Saxons made any great use of the bow in war, however; for the noble classes, spear and sword were the true weapons of the warrior. Whether this was due to the relative low power of the early medieval bows, compared to that of the fourteenth and fifteenth century longbow, it is impossible to say. In contrast, other northern European lands continued to maintain a strong tradition of archery, and in men of all classes, skill with the bow was recognized and applauded. This is evident in the sagas of the Norsemen. Snorri Sturluson tells of Harald Hardrada's legendary skill as an archer; he used his bow to lethal effect at the Battle of Nissa in 1062, and his prowess was widely recognized. It is also recorded that earls made and strung their own bows.

The Vikings had settled Normandy in about 800 AD; Charlemagne had promoted the use of archers in his armies, but after his death the Franks did not generally continue this policy; William, though, was quick to recognize the effectiveness of the bow in war, and encouraged it both in his own feudal levies and also by employing large numbers of mercenary archers to supplement his forces. Most of the archers depicted in the Bayeux Tapestry seem to be relatively poor, humble men, clad for the most part in civilian dress; only one bowman wears a hauberk and helmet, for instance, and none possesses swords or any other kind of weapon. As to the bows themselves, of course, none has survived to the present day. No archaeological discovery yet has done for eleventh century bows what the wreck of the *Mary*

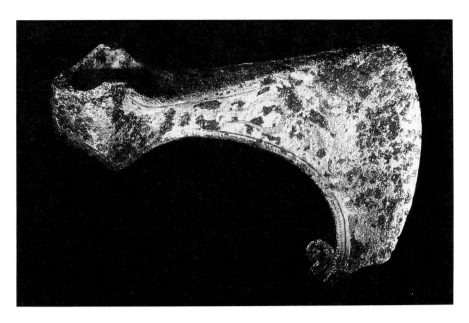

Eleventh or twelfth century axe head from central Europe. Such weapons as these, despite their fine form and decoration, were not used solely for hand-to-hand fighting but could also be thrown, often with deadly accuracy.

Rose did for the sixteenth century longbow. However, such evidence as we do have indicates that the early bows were similar in shape and form to their later descendants, often of 'D' section wood (yew, ash and elm being most frequently used), with horn nocks to carry the string. They seem to have been shorter in length than the medieval longbow or 'English' bow at the height of its fame. Instead of being pulled back to the ear, the bow string was only pulled to the chest, implying perhaps a less flexible or a weaker bow-stave. The arrows were carried in cylindrical quivers slung on a strap over the right shoulder or on the right hip; one Tapestry illustration shows an archer holding four arrows and his bow all in the left hand, while drawing a fifth to shoot. The bow-staves seem to be shorter than the height of a man, giving perhaps an estimated effective killing range of about 100 yards (90m). Reference to mail 'of proof' is sometimes found, indicating that such armour could not be penetrated by arrows; on the other hand, the mere fact that it was necessary to make this distinction implies that mail was indeed frequently pierced. Arrows rarely occur on archaelogical sites and the larger iron arrow-heads are easily confused with the heads of light throwing spears or javelins. Both were frequently barbed (the sagas often mention barbed arrow-heads), or otherwise had smaller leaf-shaped heads which could be either socketed or tanged. An arrow-head with a tang was probably easier (and therefore cheaper) to make in quantity than the socketed type. Tanged spear-heads, on the other hand, seem to have been much more

rare. The shafts were commonly of ash about 20 inches (50cm) in length, often with four feathered flights rather than the three more usually encountered later. These were both glued and secured in place with bindings of tarred or waxed twine, which would also have prevented the shaft from splitting during use. Self-nocks (a notch cut in the end of the shaft, to take the bowstring) were common, and there is also some evidence for inserts of horn being used for this purpose, as in later medieval arrows; of all the organic materials used during this period, however, horn is the one least likely to survive in an archaeological context, and so the evidence for widespread use of horn nocks is inconclusive. Virtually no complete early medieval arrows have survived, and certainly none has both head and flights.

It is known from other sources that the Normans took crossbows with them to England, but no such bows now exist and none occur in the Bayeux Tapestry. A hand-bow with a wooden stock or 'tiller' to which a short bow-stave was set at right angles, enabling it to be held, aimed and discharged from or on the shoulder, was known to the

Romans; Vegetius mentions it in a military treatise circa 385 AD. References to such weapons in Europe are comparatively rare until the tenth and eleventh centuries, when they start occurring quite frequently; the tenth century *Historia* by Richer relates how King Lewis and his army attacking the city of Senlis in 947 were repulsed not only by the strength of its towers but also by the vigorous activity of its crossbowmen, and the Domesday Book (1086) mentions one 'Odo the crossbowman'. Its popularity probably stemmed in part from its being a weapon useful both for war and for sport; William II's accidental (or perhaps not so accidental) death in 1100 while hunting in the New Forest was reputedly due to an arrow shot from a crossbow. As early as the late eleventh century, the force and speed of such an arrow (termed a 'quarrel' or 'bolt') was already sufficiently notable for it to be used as a simile in literature; the dying Roland for example, speeds toward Spain 'as a quarrel flies from a drawn crossbow.' By the twelfth century, the Byzantine chronicler Anna Comnena (writing between 1118 and 1148) was able to remark 'not only can a crossbow bolt penetrate a buckler, but a man and his armour, right through.'

The earliest crossbows almost certainly had a wooden stave, but this would not have been able to deliver a bolt with tremendous power. In particular, it would have been liable to warping or snapping, and after some use would probably have taken a 'set' and lost its springiness. By the end of the eleventh century it is likely that many crossbow staves were of 'composite' construction, like those of the Saracens, who had long been famous for their archery. These bow staves were made using horn, a tough 'springy' material unlikely to break, and sinew, which pulled the stave back into shape after shooting. Quite often at this date such materials would still have been used in conjunction with a springy wood such as yew. Contemporary references to 'horn' bows almost certainly refer to composite bow-staves; the Crusades brought knowledge of these bows and the methods of their construction to most of Europe, and by the end of the next century certain areas of southern Europe (Genoa, for example) had become famous for the manufacture of composite bows, and for the 'export' of mercenary crossbowmen. The earliest recorded crossbow maker in England seems to have been one 'Peter the Saracen', who was working for King John in 1205; the name is perhaps a further indication of where these bows originally stemmed from.

Little is known of other weapons such as the sling, but it is likely that their military use was limited. Simple hand-slings, probably using stones for ammunition, are depicted in the Bayeux Tapestry, but never in a military context despite the precedents for such use in classical and Biblical history. They are shown being used for hunting small game such as birds. Their chief merit probably lay in their suitability as secondary weapons for common foot-soldiers of peasant stock. Although effective against bare flesh they were of limited value against mail armour, and no use at all against plate; despite a number of contemporary references to 'slingers' taking part in battles of the late Dark Ages and the early medieval period, their use does not seem to have been widespread.

The use of daggers or knives in battle does not seem to have become necessary or popular until the thirteenth century, when the dagger begins to appear as part of the personal equipment of a knight, worn on the right hip to counterbalance his sword on the left. However personal knives, used as tools, for cutting and preparing food, or, if pressed, as a weapon both for defence and attack, had always been carried by their owners. The most common knife at this date was the Anglo-Saxon 'scramasax', with a single-edged blade having an angled back-edge extending from the point to the thickened 'back' of the blade for perhaps one third of its total length. The tang was usually set into a simple grip of bone or wood, with little or no guard and no pommel. The shape and size of these knives varied enormously; excavated examples range from 3 inches (7.5cm) to 2 feet 6 inches (76cm) in length, the latter almost certainly being a weapon. The average is perhaps 6 inches (15cm) or less; this is the 'handseax', a general-purpose knife used by all classes. The Norse spearmen, however, favoured the long-bladed 'langseax' as an alternative weapon to the sword; occasionally the grips of such blades seem to have been very long as well, possibly so as to wield them using both hands.

In a sense, the horse should also feature in this discussion since, after all, this was the most effective and significant weapon the knight had; the basis of his pre-eminent position in society and on the battlefield. The relative value in terms of cost, and in the effort of training, of the destrier as opposed to the ordinary riding horse or 'rounsey' has been stressed. The Tapestry shows unequivocally that the war-horses used by the Norman knights are all stallions. Also clearly portrayed is the type of saddle used. This was secured by an single breast-band and girth, and had an upright bow in front with an equally high cantle behind, both curling gracefully outwards. Most important of all, it was furnished with long stirrup leathers in order to give a deep straight-legged seat, so that the knight was virtually standing in the saddle. This enabled him to use it as a fight-

Below: Eleventh century Anglo-Saxon 'scramasax' knives from the River Thames, London. All three are pattern-welded blades; the longest measures 12 inches (301mm) overall.

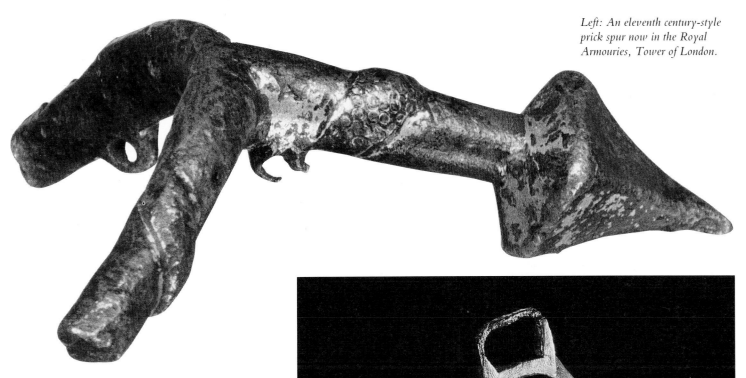

Left: An eleventh century-style prick spur now in the Royal Armouries, Tower of London.

ing platform, both to take his weight and also to hold him securely in place while delivering or receiving blows. The Romances stress this; the *Song of Roland* describes Oliver and Roland as receiving blows or injuries that, but for their saddles, would have dashed them to the ground.

The Greeks and Romans never used the stirrup, but they certainly used the spur, and those of the early medieval period were for the most part direct descendants of classical prototypes. In the eleventh century all mounted men wore 'prick' spurs. A semi-circular arch of metal half-enclosed the heel and was secured to the foot with straps and buckles; to the outer curve was fixed a ball or pyramid-shaped base bearing a short stubby circular-section point. They were mostly of iron, but were frequently decorated or even gilded overall; these latter were probably the 'golden' spurs of the knight so often mentioned in the Romances. Wheel or rowel spurs were not introduced until the thirteen century. The Bayeux Tapestry shows all mounted military men wearing spurs, and even in the scenes of hawking those presumably of knightly rank but depicted on foot in civilian dress wear them.

In the final battle Harold and the bulk of his men are not shown wearing spurs, however; they took the high ground at Hastings, and fought on foot. As long as they maintained this defensive position, they were able to withstand the onslaught of the Norman cavalry; as soon as they foolishly left it to

counterattack, they were first cut off, and then cut down. Ironically, similar tactics were to be employed in the next century by the Saracen light cavalry against the armoured heavy cavalry of the European knights, the spiritual (and in some cases actual) descendants of the Normans.

Above: Tenth or eleventh century iron stirrup overlaid with bronze, with incised and pointillé decoration.

CHAPTER TWO
The Twelfth Century
The Era of the Crusades

Far right: A page from the Winchester Bible (English, c1170). It purports to show scenes from the life of David, but the military dress and equipment is entirely contemporary. Note the more rounded profile of the helmets compared to earlier examples. Many of the soldiers are wearing mail 'mufflers' made (like the coif) all in one with the hauberk. As on the Hunterian Psalter figure, the skirts of a garment worn under the mail have now descended below the hauberk's hemline.

In general form and principle, the armour worn throughout Europe in the eleventh century continued relatively unchanged during most of the twelfth. After the Norman era, under the rule of the Angevin kings, the role of the knight was strongly reinforced both socially and militarily; with this confirmation of status came increased power and, inevitably, wealth. This was to show itself in increased expenditure on the knight's personal weapons, armour and all the ceremonial appertaining to knighthood, together with a more lavish sense of display in the form and decoration of his equipment and the full panoply of his rank.

Above all, however, the twelfth century was dominated by the ideals and grim realities of the Crusades. By the end of the century, largely due to the harsh lessons learned in three successive military expeditions to the Holy Land, it was apparent that large bodies of cavalry were becoming used to the idea of manoeuvring and charging as one, in a relatively ordered, disciplined way. Although reliant upon the massed force of the group to achieve maximum impact in the initial charge, however, the knight in battle was still very much an individual, seeking to fight a series of individual combats with equals, rather than acting as a single subordinate element within a unit. This, it could be argued, did not actually occur until well after the medieval period, as cavalry warfare gradually ceased to be the prerogative of an aristocracy anxious to win personal honour and glory often at the expense of unity and military strategy.

From the end of the eleventh to the beginning of the thirteenth century there were four Crusades; 1096-9, 1147-9, 1189 and 1202-04. The first was perhaps the most successful, resulting in the fall of Jerusalem in 1099 and the establishment of four wholly feudal Christian states (one centred upon the holy city itself and the others around Antioch, Tripoli and Edessa). The number of knights involved was usually relatively small; in the First Crusade about 3000 set out from Constantinople, of whom probably less than half were present at the start of Jerusalem's siege

Right: Twelfth century warrior from the Hunterian Psalter, showing how little the arms and armour of the knight changed in the century and a half after the Norman Conquest.

Above: This initial letter in an illuminated manuscript of William of Tyre (written c 1250-60) depicts Saladin's army ravaging the Holy Land. Their panoply is that current in Europe throughout the twelfth and early thirteenth centuries.

nearly overwhelmed by Saracen invasions, constituting a threat to both the religion and political integrity of Western European society. Consequently, the ideals of 'holy war', including the forcible conversion of heathens, were openly advocated by both religious and political leaders.

By this time, of course, the Church of Rome had become wealthy and powerful in its own right, gathering revenue from property and estates throughout Europe; it was therefore in its interest to harness the ideals of the warrior code for its own defence. In the 'Policraticus' (c 1150) John of Salisbury set out the aims of the knight as being to 'defend the Church, assail the Infidel, venerate the priesthood, protect the poor and pacify the province'. As can be seen, the Church figured high in the list of priorities for knightly behaviour. The rulers of Europe would also benefit, of course; they were increasingly able to wage what were in fact political wars under the guise of religious conviction. Political expediency was not alien to the Papacy; Pope Leo IX in the mid-eleventh century had attempted to halt the advance of the Normans into southern Italy by condemning them as a threat to Christianity. On the other hand, one of his sucessors, Alexander II, gave Papal sanction to the Norman invasion of 'heretic' England in 1066, absolving all those who took part and granting the invaders a sacred banner to lead and inspire them on the battlefield. The gains to the Church from the success of such 'crusades' were not inconsiderable; in particular, vast wealth and lands accrued to the Church during the two centuries of crusading to the Holy Land.

The era of the Crusades also saw the founding of various religious and military Orders of Knighthood, devoted to furthering the aims and ambitions of the Church Militant. Some of these were to last into the sixteenth century and beyond, reinforcing the role of the knight as a soldier of Christ, defender of the faith, and chivalrous protector of the poor and weak. The Knights Templar are reputed to have owed their origin to a little band of nine knights calling themselves the 'Poor Knights of Christ', who from 1115 escorted pilgrims through the Holy Land. The Templars were the first true warrior-monks, vowing themselves to poverty and religion, and committed to making war upon the Infidel regardless of the odds, refusing

(together with around 12,000 infantry). Once campaigning was over, following the city's fall, many knights returned home to Europe; there were then only about 500 available for the defence of Jerusalem, and the pilgrim routes leading to it. Nonetheless, the initial impact of the heavily armoured European knights upon their Eastern opponents cannot be overstated. Such was their effectiveness that in 1177 a force of less than 400 knights charged and routed Saladin's entire army, and it was not unknown for less than this number to attack Saracen formations comprising thousands of men.

The social and military effects of the Crusades on Europe for the next two centuries were almost as dramatic and, some would say, altogether out of proportion to the actual number of combatants involved. In particular, the strong associations between knight and church were confirmed, the often gratuitous violence and pillage of the Crusades being made respectable by the concept of 'holy war'. This concept was not new, though it was far removed from the ideals of the primitive Christian Church at the beginning of the millenium.

By the sixth century, the principle of 'conversion by force' had already started to become acceptable, especially in the West. In the eighth century Spain and France were ransom and fighting to the death if necessary. By the middle of the twelfth century their power and influence was felt not just in the Holy Land but throughout Europe where, thanks to donations, the Order eventually owned over 9000 feudal manors and lordships. By the second half of the century they had become the biggest landowners in Syria and Palestine, and had also developed a sophisticated banking system which extended across Western Europe to the East.

Equally significant as the Templars were the Knights of St John of Jerusalem. The Order was based upon the founding of a hospital for pilgrims in 1099, in Jerusalem; this provided for the sick and wounded, and eventually many such hospitals were established throughout the Holy Land. By about 1140 the Knights of St John were also fielding a military force, although it was not until the end of the century that this became sufficiently large to rival the Templars.

The Crusaders were drawn from all parts of Western Europe, with France perhaps providing the largest number. England at the beginning of the century saw little involvement; Henry I had succeeded his brother William Rufus in 1100, and the Battle of Tinchebray won him Normandy from his other brother, Robert. For most of the second quarter of the century, however, England was torn by civil war between Henry's daughter Matilda and Stephen of Blois, which led to feudal anarchy until 1153. Henry II, Matilda's son, became king after Stephen in 1154 and under this monarch order was restored; large bands of mercenaries were dismissed or disbanded, unlicensed castles were razed to the ground and Northumberland and Cumberland were regained from the Scots. Henry spent less than half his reign in England, due to the extent of his Angevin empire in Europe; nonetheless, under his auspices a feudal revolt in 1173–4 was successfully put down (the only time that large numbers of mercenary troops were employed) and in 1181 the 'Assize of Arms' ensured the complete reorganization of England's feudal levies. Scutage, which Henry I had levied on the clergy, was now extended by Henry II to knight's fees, because of his need for costly non-feudal troops across the Channel. The year 1188 saw the introduction of a 'Saladin tax' in response to the Saracens' capture of Jerusalem. In 1189, soon after his accession to the throne,

Richard I Coeur de Lion embarked on the third Crusade, competing for glory, honour and the fruits of conquest with his personal and political rival, Philip II of France. Richard was captured on his return by Duke Leopold of Austria, and held for ransom by the Emperor Henry VI. Upon buying his freedom in 1194, he spent the rest of his reign in a military struggle on the continent with Philip II, building Chateau Gaillard on the Seine, the first castle built in accordance with lessons learned in the East, as an outpost

Below: An early thirteenth century figure carved in stone, from Rheims Cathedral. The warrior, probably modelled on a contemporary Byzantine warrior, is wearing scale armour.

against Philip. Richard was still engaged in this conflict on his death in 1199; his brother John then became king.

In France the early Capetian kings spent the first part of the twelfth century consolidating their frontiers, subduing feudal resistance and opposing the threat of Anglo-Norman ambitions in Europe. Under the relative peace and order of feudalism, Western Europe saw economic recovery, urban development and the growth of the bourgeoisie; this century also saw the establishment of a royal administration that significantly strengthened the French monarchy. Louis VII (1137-80) inspired the disastrous Second Crusade; following this defeat, the annullment of his marriage with Eleanor of Aquitaine cost him the territories of Poitou, Guienne and Gascony held by her, for she immediately married Henry, Duke of Normandy. Henry had already succeeded his father as Count of Anjou, Maine and Touraine, and when finally in 1154 he succeeded as Henry II to the English throne also, the so-called Angevin Empire stretched from England to the Pyrenees. Louis VII's successor, Philip II, was an able ruler who soon consolidated his position on the throne against baronial opposition, but was unsuccessful towards the end of the century in his quarrels with Richard Coeur de Lion, following the Third Crusade. It was not until the reign of King John at the beginning of the thirteenth century that Philip was able to regain control of the Angevin lands north of the Loire, leaving those in the south to be reconquered by his successors.

In central and southern Europe at the beginning of the century Emperor Henry V was successful in confirming his Imperial power in the German and northern Italian states, and in securing its ratification by the Papacy. The Concordat of Worms in 1122 ended the controversy of the Imperial investiture, but not the rivalry between Emperor and Pope. Henry left no heir, and the election of Lothair II as Emperor in 1125 was the signal for civil war in the German states, lasting until 1135. The imperial pretensions of Lothair's opponents, the Hohenstaufens, were fulfilled in 1138 with the Emperor's death and the election of Conrad III of Hohenstaufen; this dynasty was to continue until 1268. Conrad took part in the Second Crusade, but in his absence the lack of centralized control took its toll, and there was widespread unrest and revolt. The rest of his reign was spent in trying to repair this damage. The consequent devotion of the Emperors to a policy of centralization and the aggrandisement of Imperial lay power brought them into conflict once more with the political aspirations of the Papacy, especially in Italy. Elsewhere, the Empire expanded its sphere of influence and territorial conquests in the direction of Scandinavia and the lands under domination by the Slavs.

The Emperor Frederick 'Barbarossa' I (Barbarossa meaning 'red beard') was elected in 1152; the embodiment of the 'ideal' German medieval king, he saw himself as inheriting the traditions of Constantine, Justinian and Charlemagne, and consequently termed himself 'Holy Roman Emperor'. This title was to remain for the rest of the medieval period and beyond. Frederick was able to consolidate the power of the Emperors, stemming the anarchy and factional rivalries which were rife throughout Conrad's reign, but due to his own rivalry with the Papacy he became enmeshed in constant military expeditions to Italy, culminating in the disastrous Battle of Legnano in 1176. Frederick was defeated by the combined forces of the Lombard League; significantly, this was the first major defeat of feudal heavy cavalry by largely bourgeois infantry. From this point on, the Italian and German states, even where they owed allegiance to the same Imperial overlord, tended to pursue different lines of development. Peace between the Pope, Frederick and the Lombard towns was ratified in 1183. The following year, at the Great Diet of Mainz, Frederick's two sons were knighted with great pageantry and a huge tournament was held, in the presence of (reputedly) 70 princes and 70,000 knights. Even allowing for the probable exaggeration of these numbers, the occasion was undoubtedly one of the greatest that medieval Europe had ever seen. Frederick 'took the Cross' in 1186, in common with so many other European knights; until his death in 1190 he then led the Third Crusade in the traditional role of Knight-Emperor and champion of Christendom. His successor, Henry VI, was already 'Caesar' and regent, and on being crowned Emperor in 1191 managed to consolidate most of Frederick's gains against powerful German and Papal opposition. His death in 1197, however, was followed by civil war in Germany

The martyrdom of St Thomas à Becket, in a late twelfth century Latin Psalter. This illumination clearly shows the helmet types in current use; a flat-topped cylindrical helm, the earlier rounded form, and a mail coif with ventail covering the mouth and chin. St Thomas himself seems to have been wearing a 'Phrygian' cap (now lying at his feet).

and a bitter anti-imperial reaction in the Italian states. Order was only restored upon the accession of Frederick II in 1212, but the Empire was never again to achieve the unity and territorial expansion of the reigns of Frederick Barbarossa and Henry VI.

The Iberian peninsula in the twelfth century was divided into many small kingdoms (Granada under the Moors, Castile, Barcelona, Catalonia, Navarre, Aragon and Portugal). These generally played little part in the political rivalries of the rest of Europe, however, being primarily engaged from the eleventh century onwards in the *reconquista* –

the freedom of Spain from Moorish influence. This took the form of incessant wars against the occupying Muslim forces in the southern half of Spain, during which the great Spanish military Orders were founded. In addition, the states indulged in constant dynastic and territorial rivalries with each other, frequently supported by military intervention. Gradually, through a slow process of intermarriage, alliance and annexation, the smaller and weaker of these states were amalgamated. By the beginning of the thirteenth century the largest and most politically significant kingdoms were Castile, Aragon and Portugal (the French retaining a strong influence in Navarre).

The conical helmet shape of the Normans continued in use throughout most of Europe, with few variations, until the middle of the century; the skull then became rounded rather than pointed, and in many cases the nasal bar ceased to be fitted. An illustration in the English 'Psalter of St Louis' (*c* 1200) shows just such a helmet worn over the coif, which is still clearly part of the hauberk. In this particular instance, however, the nasal has been retained. Towards the end of the century, a flatter-topped helmet shape seems to have become popular, the sides either vertical or tapering slightly towards the base. The top is usually very slightly domed or flat; after the glancing surfaces presented by the previous forms of helmet, one would have

thought this shape to have been somewhat impractical, and indeed contemporary manuscript sources often contain illustrations of similar helmets being cut in half by a powerful downward blow from sword or axe. One can only presume that the construction of the helmet was made heavier to withstand such punishment.

At the very end of the century, iron face-guards pierced with sights, and occasionally ventilation holes, made an appearance; these too are occasionally depicted, appearing in the Maciejowski Bible (*c* 1250) and elsewhere. The coif during this period remained largely unchanged, although in the last quarter of the century the 'ventail' (an additional flap of mail fastening across the mouth and lower face) became popular, although it was not to become widespread until the thirteenth century. The *Song of Roland*, written at the end of the eleventh century, contains a particularly early reference to it:

The hauberk's ventaille he has shattered with the stroke,
And split his throat wide open at the collar-bone

This leaves us in no doubt as to the precise nature both of the armour and of the part of the body it was designed to protect. Similarly, the broad-brimmed, open-faced helmet widely known as a 'kettle-hat', although more normally associated with the thirteenth century, made its first appearance in Europe

Right: Three of the carved walrus-ivory chess pieces found at Uig on the Isle of Lewis, probably Norse, dating to the end of the twelfth century. They combine both up-to-date and rather 'old-fashioned' features; the ear-pieces on the conical helmet of the mounted knight on the left are rarely seen in other contemporary illustrations, yet the horseman in the centre wears the new style of rounded helm.

Left: Stone relief, c1128, from Angoulême Cathedral depicting a pair of knights wearing hauberks of scale armour, jousting with couched lances. Their fluted helmets are extended at the rear to protect the back of the neck.

during the twelfth; an example of such a helmet is clearly depicted on one of the Isle of Lewis chessmen (a group of carved ivory figures believed to be twelfth century Norse). One of the mounted figures has ear flaps on his conical helmet, but this does not seem to have been a common feature elsewhere in Europe at this date.

The body armour of the eleventh century also continued relatively unchanged into the twelfth, still consisting primarily of the mail, or, occasionally, scale, hauberk with an integral coif. Two figures carved on the late twelfth century Porta Romana in Milan, Italy, depict hauberks of mail and scale respectively, and there is sufficient detail present to be sure that the contrast was intended. Otherwise, their helmets, shields and spears all conform to the 'Norman' pattern, and are virtually identical to each other.

By the middle of the twelfth century mail chausses on the legs were far more common than they had been a century previously, and there are many more extant contemporary illustrations of them in use. For the most part, the type which laced up at the back of the calf was still more popular than the full mail stocking gartered at the knee. The latter are found on some church effigies and sculptural monuments dating from the early part of the next century. The foot was now more commonly protected with mail than previously, and the arms also; in the last few decades of the twelfth century the sleeves of the hauberk became longer, ending in mitten-shaped mail gloves called 'mufflers', which were slit at the wrist to permit the hands to be withdrawn at will. The palms were not covered with mail, however, since this would have impeded one's grip of a weapon; instead, they were usually made of cloth or leather. Early forms of muffler sometimes left the fingers and thumbs completely exposed: this can be seen very clearly on the figures of knights incorporated in the illuminated initial letter of the Book of Joshua in the Winchester Bible (*c* 1165-1170).

The same illumination also shows the knights wearing 'surcoats'; long, usually sleeveless, full-skirted cloth gowns which the knight wore over the armour. These first appear in the second half of the twelfth century, but did not become widely popular until the thirteenth century. It is possible that they developed through the influence of the Crusades. Armour worn under the blistering sun of the Middle East would not have been at all comfortable to wear; the best compromise, therefore, was perhaps a white surcoat to deflect the worst of the sun's rays. This does not, of course, explain why they should have become so universally popular throughout Europe during the next century. One very early illustration of a knight wearing a surcoat which occurs on the charter seal of the Earl of Worcester shows a surcoat complete with sleeves; this seems to be an isolated example of a feature more normally found a century later.

Evidence that a lining or undergarment was worn beneath the hauberk is still inconclusive, although it does seem that in the first half of the century such a garment does appear, peeping below the hem of the mail shirt. It can be seen on the twelfth century gilt bronze 'Temple Pyx' figures in both the Bur-

Above: An initial from the Winchester Bible c1170, showing loose-flowing surcoats worn over the mail, and mail sleeves ending in integral fingerless mittens.

rell and Wallace Collections. This 'dropped hem-line' is in many cases virtually the only way in which illustrations of eleventh century mail armour can be distinguished from those of the early twelfth.

'Soft' armour continued to be worn throughout the century, but the confusion regarding terminology persists at least until the thirteenth century, and is not fully resolved even then. As stated before, it is likely that the terms 'gambeson', 'aketon', and 'pourpoint' tended to be used rather arbitrarily; by the thirteenth and fourteenth centuries, at least, there is sufficent documentary evidence to enable the scholar to draw at least some conclusions as to the precise nature of these garments.

The form of the shield carried by knights during the twelfth century remained for the most part similar to that of the eleventh, until towards the end of the century the rounded

profile to the upper edge became gradually straighter, and the whole shield tended to become shorter; this was largely because of the practical considerations of fighting in large groups on horseback, relying upon the charge with lance and sword to obtain the initial advantage over an enemy. In this situation, a large shield tended to be an encumbrance, especially since the increasing use of mail armour for the limbs rendered it unnecessary. Shields were still decorated; by the end of the century sometimes with the coat of arms of their owners, or devices symbolic of their calling, such as the Cross of the Crusaders.

The sword and lance remained the primary weapons of the knight. The form of the lance remained much the same as in the previous century. Its length was rarely less than 10–12 feet (3–3.7m), and there are indications that the head became gradually smaller as its profile became more sharply pointed and consequently more penetrative. The shaft was still basically that of a spear, however; it was long and relatively thin with parallel sides for most of its length, and made in one piece from solid wood (usually ash) as before.

The development of the sword was more marked, following trends established in the last quarter of the eleventh century. Pattern-welded blades had largely ceased to be made in Europe by then except sometimes for knife blades (many of which, according to archaeological evidence, seem to have been made in this way well into the twelfth century). A considerable number of early sword blades were still being used, however, and several examples of contemporary rehilting have survived to the present day. The type of simple cross-hilt with elongated quillons and a brazil-nut or wheel pommel had found most favour in the south but its popularity was slowly moving north and west, stimulated perhaps by the influence of returning Crusader knights who had adopted this form of hilt during their passage to and from the Holy Land. Their pommels were usually made of iron but could alternatively be of bronze or, more rarely, other rich and exotic materials like rock crystal or semiprecious stone. Reflecting the importance increasingly accorded to religion, a few of them even contained holy relics (such relics could alternatively be incorporated into the grip of the sword). The medieval Romances often mention weapons of this nature.

The blades of twelfth century swords were now frequently inlaid or incised with religious inscriptions as well as the names of bladesmiths. This again probably had much to do with the religious ideals of the Crusaders, the so-called 'Men of God'; one of the most common inscriptions was HOMO DEI (Man of God) or IN NOMINE DOMINI (In the name of the Lord), and other variants can be found. Letters and words on sword blades could also signify blessings, religious quotations or abbreviations of the same, which would obviously have meaning for their owners. Mysterious repetitive sequences of letters or symbols often occur, and seem to have been used as a form of ornamentation; it may be that they were never intended to have a meaning. The sword was still generally used in one hand as a cut-and-thrust weapon; the blade length was variable but rarely more than 25–30 inches (63.5-76cm), rather shorter than many swords of the next century. The broad slashing blades of the previous century remained popular until the 1200s.

Above: Twelfth century manuscript illustration from the 'Life of St Guthlac'. Note the shields, by now starting to become shorter and more flat-topped in shape.

inventories between ordinary general-purpose knives and those regarded as weapons. By the next century daggers seem to have become relatively common; the Maciejowski Bible contains some battle scenes where they almost appear to outnumber swords. In the twelfth century, knights are rarely shown wearing daggers. Early daggers generally had blades which were approximately 8-10 inches (20-25cm) long, usually double-edged, with a very short arched guard, the quillon-ends curving in the direction of the blade. The pommel was shorter and was similarly arched, resembling a pair of horns or an upturned crescent; the ends curved in the opposite direction to that of the guard. This shape of hilt (basically an 'H' lying on its side) became increasingly popular all over Europe, evolving into the type of dagger or short sword later known as the 'baselard'. Otherwise, daggers often resembled nothing less than miniature swords, usually with much reduced quillons.

Daggers in the twelfth century had not yet become an integral part of the knight's panoply, but nonetheless were slowly developing from their early origins as the Anglo-Saxon or Scandinavian 'seax' into the basic form that they were to retain for the next five centuries or more. The contemporary European names for this weapon were 'coustel' or 'cultellus'. They were used initially by common foot soldiers, and sometimes acquired a rather unsavoury reputation as a result; in fact, by the middle of the twelfth century the term 'coustillers' was being applied to roving bands of brigands. The term 'dagger' was just beginning to be used in this century; a statute of William the Lion, King of Scotland (1165-1214), mentions the 'cultellus which is called a dagger' and gradually the term came to supersede all others for general use. Relatively early in the medieval period it came to be used especially in relation to those knives intended primarily for fighting; these were usually held in the hand with the blade pointing downwards, and used with a stabbing motion. Specific types of dagger, of course, continued to be referred to by specific names, and, increasingly, distinctions were drawn in lists and

Right: A knight armoured with a hauberk of scale, and carrying a wheel-pommel sword; part of the decoration on the Gross-Comburg chandelier, c 1140.

The mace and axe retained their appeal for those of noble class, the battle-axe in particular finding great favour with warriors of high rank. The chronicler Roger de Hoveden recorded that King Stephen of England at the Battle of Lincoln in 1141 was 'equal to a thunderbolt, slaying some with his immense battle-axe and striking down many others.' When, through the sheer number of blows, this axe eventually broke, the king then drew his sword, clearly indicating that the sword tended to be worn as a matter of course by those of knightly rank, regardless of the nature of the 'primary' weapon being used at the time. The form of both mace and axe remained largely unchanged from the previous century, however, except that in some cases a lighter axe-head was preferred; even so, the actual width of the cutting edge tended to remain as broad as before.

The most popular form of bow in twelfth century Europe remained the crossbow; in the hands of common infantry, this was increasingly threatening the superiority of the mounted knight on the battlefield. The rulers of Europe had mixed feelings about this situation; on one hand, there were obvious advantages to be gained by employing skilled crossbowmen, but on the other hand they were hated by many, and especially by those of noble rank. In 1139 Pope Innocent II issued through the Lateran Council his famous 'anathema' against 'the deadly art, hated by God, of crossbowmen and archers', with the proviso that it was perfectly acceptable to practise the art against non-Christians. Such was the effectiveness of the crossbow in war, however, that the edict was widely ignored.

It is likely that the Crusades did much to establish the popularity of the crossbow, or 'French' bow as Anna Comnena called it, perhaps because their stout wooden or composite horn and sinew bowstaves were more resistant to desert conditions than those of the weaker hand or 'self' bows. In twelfth century Wales the foundations of a new generation of more powerful self bows were already being laid. Gerald de Barri (known as 'Gerald the Welshman'), writing shortly after 1188, recorded the power of the Welsh bow at the siege of Abergavenny Castle in 1182; there, this forerunner of the English longbow was seen to shoot arrows into a solid oak door to a depth of 'nearly a hand'. On another occasion an arrow was said to

have penetrated the mail chausse of a mounted soldier, pinning him through his leg to the saddle, and inflicting a mortal wound upon his horse. The broad-bladed hunting and war arrowheads of previous centuries were increasingly supplemented by arrowheads designed specifically for war; case-hardened needle-pointed 'bodkin' heads that could pierce mail and, later, plate armour.

These bows were not yet the smoothly contoured yew longbows of Agincourt or Crécy, but were apparently made of rough and 'knobbly' wild elm. Nonetheless, in the hands of trained and skilled men they were already a fearsome weapon. They were potentially more deadly even than the crossbow, owing to their extremely rapid rate of fire and their great power and range. As yet, however, their use remained largely confined within the borders of their native land.

Above: Twelfth century silver plaque in the Abbaye de St Maurice, Valais, Switzerland. It depicts a mounted knight in the panoply that was universal throughout most of Europe at this date. His shield bears a cross, symbol of Christianity, instead of the previously arbitrary patterns of decoration.

CHAPTER THREE
Paladins and Paynims
The Thirteenth Century

At the beginning of the thirteenth century warfare, both in Europe and the Holy Land, was still dominated by the feudal, heavily armed, mounted knight. The knight was used primarily in cavalry charges of great violence and weight, and these had, for the past two centuries, proved difficult to withstand. In the eleventh century the Byzantine armies in southern Italy had been unable to deal with the small forces of Norman knights set against them, and at first the Saracens had been quickly overturned by the shock of these charges, which smashed into the ranks of their lightly armed cavalry. However, the Saracens, aided by their swift mounts, soon learnt to evade these charges and to draw the Crusaders on, pelting them at a distance with arrows until they were exhausted by heat and exertion. Then, and only then, did they close in for the kill.

The deadly lessons taught in the Holy Land slowly altered Western military thinking, and contact with Byzantine tactics and military thinkers led the kings of Europe and the Crusaders of Outremer to supplement their forces with light cavalry or *turcopoles*

Right: 'Christ leading the Crusaders', from a thirteenth century manuscript.

Above: A knight from a relief in the Church of St Justina, Padua. It shows a typical knight of around 1210 with a developed form of helmet with a rudimentary face mask, and a large shield carried on a guige.

spearmen fought for the kings of France and England and the cities of Italy, alongside the crossbowmen of northern Italy.

Europe in the thirteenth century was dominated by power struggles between over-powerful nobles and their feudal over-lords, and saw a drastic restructuring of the European kingdoms. In 1204 the Duchy of Normandy was wrested from the hands of King John of England and the powerful Angevin Empire, which had been created by Henry II of England, crumbled. The disastrous foreign policy of John and the Papal Interdict under which he was placed in 1208 led to the enforced signing of Magna Carta in 1215 and the subsequent Barons War of his son, Henry III. The effect was to keep England on the fringe of European affairs for the rest of the century. However, the accession of Edward I and his reforms of the English military system during his Welsh and Scottish campaigns were to leave England prepared to take the stage in her wars on the Continent in the fourteenth century. The occasion for this re-entry was provided by the struggle between Philip IV of France and Edward I for the control of Aquitaine. Edward had made an alliance with Flanders to threaten France on two fronts. The resultant war, along with a series of campaigns which the French waged in Flanders, became the main burden of the French Exchequer.

The decline of English power in France during Henry III's reign allowed the French kings to regain control of their domains and create the most powerful military state in Europe, and it was during the three Crusades of the reign of Louis IX (Saint Louis) that the pre-eminent position of the French knight was attained. Most French territorial gains in this century were at the expense of the English kings, but in 1285 Philip III invaded Aragon and intervened in the disputed succession in Navarre and Castile which involved France in a Navarrese war and an abortive invasion of Castile.

For the first half of the 13th century, the Holy Roman Empire was torn by incipient civil war. Although Frederick II acceded to the title of Emperor of the Romans in 1212, it was not until 1215 that he could be crowned King of Germany. For the rest of his reign, until his death in 1250, Frederick tried to reorganize the Holy Roman Empire and place it once and for all in the hands of the

and disciplined, well-equipped infantry. In Europe, however, since the knight was not faced by lightly equipped horse archers, older forms of tactics remained in use and it was not until the fourteenth century that these innovations were taken to their logical conclusion. The feudal armies of Europe were increasingly supplemented by mercenaries; from the twelfth century Brabançon

Emperor. This aroused constant opposition, not the least of which came from his son Henry, King of the Romans. Frederick's power base was the Kingdom of Sicily and while he established control over Italy, and to a certain extent the Pope, he failed to establish a firm position in his German territories. The communes or city states of Italy were also drawn into the struggle between Emperor and Pope for control, giving rise to the long-lived and bitter rivalry of the Guelph and Ghibelline factions. Following Frederick's death there was a power struggle for control of southern Italy. The final victor was Charles of Anjou, brother of Louis IX and candidate of Pope Innocent IV, who defeated Frederick's illegitimate son Manfred at the Battle of Benevento in 1266. This established French control over Italy and the papacy and eliminated the Emperor as a force to be reckoned with in Italian affairs.

Frederick II had spent little time north of the Alps and on the death of his legitimate heir 'Conradin' at the hands of Charles of Anjou, the power of the Hohenstaufens waned. The year 1257 saw the election of no less than two contenders to the title of Holy Roman Emperor, Richard Duke of Cornwall and Alfonso of Castile, neither of whom was able to consolidate his position. As a consequence, there was effectively no Emperor for the next two decades, until the election of Rudolph of Hapsburg in 1273.

Much of Spain remained isolated in its struggles against the Moorish occupation, but the claims of the House of Aragon to the Kingdom of Sicily through the marriage of Pedro the Great of Aragon and Constance, daughter of Emperor Frederick, led to Aragon's emergence as a great sea power in the Mediterranean.

During the thirteenth century the equipment of the knight varied little throughout Europe. It consisted basically of a mail hauberk with an integral coif and mufflers, mail chausses for the legs, a helmet of some form and a sword, lance and shield.

From the beginning of the thirteenth century the flat-topped helmet current at the end of the twelfth century was fitted with a face guard which contained two slits for the eyes, called sights, and was pierced by holes for ventilation, called breaths. These are clearly shown on the Shrine of Charlemagne in Aachen Cathedral, made between 1200 and 1207, as are the padded arming caps which were worn beneath them. By the 1220s, this helm had evolved a narrow, fixed neck-guard which, during that decade, extended round to join the face guard to form a flat-topped but cylindrical helmet known as the 'great helm' or 'heaume'. This was equipped with breaths and was sometimes reinforced at the front by a cruciform metal bracing pierced with horizontal sights. Slowly, over the next 20 years, the front of the helm was extended downwards to protect the wearer's neck. There are very few surviving examples of this type of helmet but perhaps the best was excavated in the Schlossberg bei Dargen in Pomerania, now in the Museum für Deutsche Geschichte, Berlin. This form of helm remained unchanged until the 1260s, after which its crown was given a taper, presumably as a result of the inability of the flat-topped helm to deflect a sword cut. Depictions of these flat-topped helmets being split by swords of war occur throughout the century, especially in the Maciejowski Bible. In the last quarter of the century the crown was given an even more pronounced taper, as is clearly shown on the brass of Sir Roger de Trumpington in Trumpington Church, Cambridgeshire.

From as early as the late twelfth century the great helm was fitted with a crest. This perhaps served two functions: firstly it allowed the knight to indulge in an ostentatious display of martial magnificence; and secondly, because the knight's face was completely enclosed by the great helm, it served to identify him in battle. The fact that contemporary open-faced helmets are not equipped with crests reinforces this theory.

Left: A thirteenth century prick spur, now in the Royal Armouries, HM Tower of London.

Right: Part of the Silver Shrine of Charlemagne in Aachen Cathedral, c1207. It shows knights wearing the flat-topped helmets and carrying the large shields typical of the early part of the thirteenth century.

The earliest known representation of a crest comes from the second Great Seal of King Richard I of England and dates to 1194. It shows a fan-shaped crest emblazoned with the leopard of England. At the beginning of the thirteenth century crests invariably took this form but very quickly new types started to appear; pennons, and free-standing devices in the form of stylized animals and birds. These crests were probably made of a variety of different materials, for the most part parchment, feathers, *cuir bouilli* and gesso. They were often brightly painted and sometimes gilded. When a crest was not worn, the great helm was often adorned by a coronet appropriate to the rank of the

Right: This panel of the Silver Shrine shows Charlemagne besieging a city. The knights on the right have flat-topped helmets with nasal guards; not all of them wear surcoats.

Left: Another panel from the Silver Shrine of Charlemagne. The right-hand figures are wearing helmets with rudimentary face and neck guards; those on the left wear coifs; the left-hand figure in the tent is wearing an arming cap.

wearer. To accompany the crest a roll of cloth was sometimes worn around the helm, especially in Germany.

The great helm was worn with a padded arming cap, worn either over or under a mail coif. Two forms are known. The more usual one is simply a heavily quilted version of the civilian coif; rather less common is the variety depicted on the front of Wells Cathedral, *c* 1230, which is an arming cap with an additional roll of padding set about the brow of the wearer. This roll would ease the weight of the helmet off the top of the head and help to spread it rather more evenly on the skull.

The conical helmet, with or without a nasal, continued to be used by the knight until the 1250s but was increasingly replaced by a domed version, the most popular form of which is known as the *cervelière* or basinet. This was a small hemispherical skull cap which was often worn beneath the mail coif, as can be seen from the outline of contemporary monuments. This was increasingly worn under the great helm or simply on its own over the coif.

The end of the twelfth century saw the introduction of a completely new type of helmet known as the *chapel de fer* or kettle hat. It is known as a kettle hat because of its close resemblance to a medieval cauldron or kettle; indeed, scenes from the Maciejowski Bible

show them slung from the sides of carts in a similar way to cauldrons. There were two forms of this helmet, one was shaped and made like an upturned bucket of hoop-and-stave construction, but this type did not outlast the century. The other consisted of a round bowl with a wide brim, sometimes of one piece, but often assembled from a number of plates riveted together, as was the earlier *spangenhelm*. The skull was formed by a cross of steel, and the intervening spaces were filled by plates. This was extensively used by the knightly class and was often worn with a basinet and mail coif underneath. However, worn alone or with a coif, it was to remain the common soldier's favourite up until the mid-fifteenth century. Part of the reason for the popularity of this helmet, especially among infantrymen, was that it offered protection from a downward cut, but gave all-round vision. It was particularly useful in siegework, because the brim helped to deflect missiles from the face.

The main body defence remained the mail hauberk. This reached to mid-thigh and had an integral coif which had a ventail or flap of mail which could be drawn across the mouth and closed with a strap. This is clearly shown on the wooden effigy attributed to Robert of Normandy in Gloucester Cathedral, England. The coif was also equipped with a thong which passed round the wearer's brow

*Right: A knight on the west front
of Wells Cathedral. English
c1230-40. It shows an almost
fully developed great helm.*

and was interwoven through the mail; this
presumably served the function of stopping
drag on the neck. Below this a broad fillet or
brow band is sometimes depicted, which
occasionally seems to have been jewelled and
is a mark of rank. Towards the end of the
century the separate mail coif once more
made an appearance; this is possibly connected with the wearing of additional body
defences. The coif quite often was attached to
this defence.

The hauberk had long sleeves which, from
the end of the twelfth century, ended in mufflers or mitten-like extensions with an opening which could be closed with a lace just
below the wrist, so that the hand could be
removed. By the mid-century these often
had separate fingers. In order to provide
extra protection for the neck, a reinforce of
small plates or thickened rings was placed
inside the coif. Although mail hauberks were
by far the most common form of defence, the
coats of scale worn in the twelfth century
were still to be seen at the very beginning of
the thirteenth.

Mail alone was found to be an inadequate
defence for the body and from the end of the
twelfth century there are references to a rigid
defence known as a *cuirie* or cuirasse. Its exact
form cannot be ascertained since it was between the hauberk and the all-enveloping

*Far right: The brass of Sir Roger
de Trumpington, from
Trumpington Church,
Cambridgeshire. It shows the
developed form of the heaume
with a tapered crown.*

surcoat. However, at first it was obviously made of leather, probably *cuir bouilli*, as its name is derived from the French *cuir* (leather). It is shown on two English monuments, one from the Temple Church in London and the other from Pershore Abbey, Worcestershire, which date to the 1260s. It takes the form of a rigid defence consisting of a front and back plate strapped together at the shoulder and under the arm. As a supplementary defence, the front of the surcoat was occasionally reinforced by rectangular steel plates riveted to the inside of the material in vertical rows three plates deep. These can be seen clearly on the sleeping guard from part of a sculpture of the resurrection of Christ from Wienhausen, now in the Provinzial Museum, Hanover. A further type of body defence appearing mid-century which spread throughout Europe is depicted on the statue of St Maurice in Magdeburg Cathedral. This garment was shaped like an inverted cross with one long arm. Near the junction of this arm was a central neck opening which had a mail coif permanently attached to it. The wearer would put his head through this, with the rest of the arm hanging down his back. The three other arms formed the front and sides of the garment, and were lined with oblong plates retained by rivets at top and bottom. The side flaps, which reached from the wearer's arm pit to his hip, wrapped around his body and buckled at the rear over the back of the garment. Plates from what appears to be this type of defence were excavated at the Castle of Montfort in the Holy Land, and must date to before 1271, when the castle fell to the Saracens.

Mail is not a rigid defence and, although it will stop a cut, the force of a blow is transferred directly through it, causing injuries of a type known as blunt trauma, that is broken bones and haemorrhaging. Furthermore, it gives inadequate protection against a thrust with a sharply pointed weapon or from arrows or crossbow bolts, all of which can burst the links apart. These problems were dealt with in two ways: partially by wearing the rigid defences mentioned above over the mail, and partly by the adoption of quilted and padded undergarments. The latter were separate defences which could be worn by the knight either as an accompaniment to his mail hauberk or, on occasions, in its stead. These are referred to in contemporary sources as 'aketons', 'gambesons' or 'pour-

points'. These terms seem to have been interchangeable but the weight of evidence suggests that 'aketon' refers to garments worn under the mail while gambesons were worn over or instead of it. Pourpoints (meaning 'for points') probably refers to any garment for the upper body to which the hose were attached. All these garments seem to have been vertically quilted. They were usually made of two or more layers of linen stuffed with tow, rags or other material. When worn under armour the aketon had long sleeves and reached to the knee. Gambesons are often referred to as being covered in silk, embroidered or emblazoned, bearing out the assumption that they were intended to be seen. The gambeson is often referred to in contemporary accounts as being worn by the common soldiery and, indeed, is part of the equipment required by the Assize of Arms of 1185 of Edward I of England.

Over his armour the knight wore the surcoat. This seems to have been generally adopted around the year 1210. Numerous reasons have been put forward for the adoption of the surcoat. It may have been worn simply to keep the armour clean, as is suggested by the following lines from the contemporary poem, *The Avowing of King Arthur*.

Gay gowns of grene
to hold thayr armur clene
And were hitte fro the wete.

Below: A Spanish gilt bronze ornament in the form of a mounted knight, c1290. Noteworthy are the aillettes and the helmet crest in the form of antlers.

Right: A late thirteenth century tournament scene showing a great helm in the process of being split by a sword of war.

Others suggest they were a garment modelled on the flowing robes of the Saracens, designed to keep the armour cool in the heat of the Holy Land. Finally, perhaps they were simply adopted to display the wearer's coat of arms. The last suggestion is the least likely because although heraldry was in its infancy at this time, the earliest surcoats were invariably plain, without any heraldic adornment. The second hypothesis, that

they were derived from Saracen garments is possible, although the knights of Sicily, Southern France, Italy and Greece must also have needed to keep their armour cool, and may independently have had the idea. Also the form of the garment is extremely basic, contains no exotic element, and is very similar to civilian garments worn at the time.

A number of different forms of surcoat are represented in contemporary sources – sleeved and unsleeved, longer and shorter – but by the early thirteenth century the most common form of surcoat was a sleeveless, loose-fitting garment reaching to mid-calf with a slit in the skirts to allow for riding. However, the façade of Wells Cathedral has sculptures dated to *c* 1240 which show two types of surcoat: the first is like that described above, but the second is smooth in the body and stands proud from both neck and shoulder, and may already incorporate some form of additional defence.

At first the knight had no additional defences for his arms other than the sleeves of his hauberk. However, the elbows are a particulary vulnerable part of the body, and as early as 1260 small disc-shaped plates known as couters were laced or strapped to the hauberk to protect them. However, couters are extremely rare before the end of the century. About 1290 numerous references to gauntlets constructed of whalebone first appear. These are presumably the long and deeply flared cuffed items which are depicted

Right: An illustration from the Lives of the Two Offas *by Matthew Paris, English, c1250. It shows a battle between the forces of two Mercian Kings.*

in contemporary illustrations; they were probably leather, faced with plaques of whalebone. Steel-plated gauntlets, presumably constructed in the same way, are first mentioned in 1296 but the vast majority of knights continued to make do with mufflers of mail. Separate gauntlets were probably developed because the muffler failed to give adequate protection to the exposed fingers of the sword hand, as little or no padding could be worn beneath it. The cross bar of the sword hilt was also insufficient defence.

Additional shoulder defences, called espaulers, were first mentioned at the end of the century, but the form these took and of what material they were made is unclear. Finally, mention must be made of ailettes. These were flat, disc-, square- or diamond-shaped plates which were strapped to the point of the shoulder. They were made of parchment or leather and bore the coat of arms of the wearer. It has been suggested that these served as an additional defence to protect the neck from a sideways cut, but they were too flimsy for this. They seem simply to have been designed to allow the wearer to be recognized from the side.

Above: An illustration from the Maciejowski Bible, French, c1250. The battle scene shows a variety of helmets and arms and armour and illustrates the effectiveness of the sword of war.

Left: A sleeping guard from a reliquary from Wienhausen Monastery, Germany, c1270. It shows a reinforced surcoat.

The defences for the leg developed in advance of those for the arm because when the knight was mounted the legs were particularly vulnerable to infantrymen. Two types of mail chausse had been common throughout Europe from about 1150. The first was a complete hose of mail, closely fitted and gartered below the knee, presumably to stop the legs from dragging. Most of these had two individual legs, which presumably tied on to a waist belt or were laced to the aketon or pourpoint. The other variety was simply shaped to the front of the leg and foot only and was laced up the back of the leg. However, at the Battle of Bouvines in 1214

Reginald de Boulogne was saved from a thrust which passed beneath his hauberk, presumably by joined leg chausses. By about 1220 a new type of defence for the thigh had appeared: these were called gamboised cuisses and consisted of quilted and padded tubes of cloth, often covered with rich materials such as silk or velvet, and occasionally embroidered. They were funnel-shaped and seem to have been simply pulled on over the leg, as is shown in the Maciejowski Bible. It is likely, however, that they too were laced to the aketon in order to keep them up.

By the middle of the century this defence was supplemented by a cup-shaped plate of

Right: 'Stripping the Dead', a scene from the Maciejowski Bible. Most of the combatants wear chausses of mail and carry a variety of staff weapons.

steel known as a poleyn, designed to protect the knee-cap. These were simply laced or strapped onto the chausses. It was not until the end of the century, and even then only very rarely, that any defence for the lower leg other than the mail chausse was worn. In the last quarter of the century gutter-shaped shin guards of steel known as schynbalds appeared. These were quite short and protected only the front of the leg and were simply strapped on over the chausses. These items appear in a list of armour supplied to Edward I's sons, Edward Prince of Wales (later Edward II) and John Duke of Lancaster, for the campaigns in Scotland in 1299.

Throughout the twelfth century the knight had used the kite-shaped shield to the virtual exclusion of all other types. However, at the beginning of the thirteenth century it was shortened and the top of the shield lost its very prominent curve. In conjunction with this the profile of the shield became less convex and took on a triangular shape. These changes were possibly because of the improvements in helmet design and the introduction of the great helm, which meant that the shield was no longer needed to defend the face. However, until the 1250s the

shield was still moderately large. Within the next 20 years the shield became smaller and its sides convex – thus assuming the shape it was to take for the next century. This was probably due to the additional body and leg defences developed in this period which meant that a large shield was no longer necessary. The shield was still equipped with a guige or strap from which it could be slung round the neck, and two enarmes for the forearm. Throughout the century, the shield was used to display the bearer's coat of arms.

English Statues of Arms of the thirteenth century speak of 'covered horses'. Whether or not this refers to mail or quilted caparisons is not made clear, but by the 1250s the knight's horse was sometimes equipped with a complete mail trapper composed of two parts, the front covering the horse from head to knee and the rear enclosing the rump to the hocks. However, the cost and weight of such items must have severely limited their use and there can be no doubt that most knights simply used quilted cloth or leather caparisons. From the middle of the century protection for the horse's head, known as a 'shaffron', was used. This seems at first to have been made of leather, but towards the

Above: A battle scene from the Maciejowsky Bible showing infantry wearing gambesons and kettle hats and using crossbows and staff weapons.

Right: A relief from the tomb of Gugliemo Beradi, c1289, in the Church of Santa Annunziata, Florence. Note the elaborately decorated leg defences, probably of cuir boulli, *strapped over the mail chausses.*

end of the century was probably made of iron or steel. The shaffron was often decorated with a crest similar to that worn on the rider's great helm.

The weapons of the thirteenth century knight were characterized by modification to increase their effectiveness against an armoured opponent, especially by the use of heavy cleaving weapons. The lance and sword remained the paramount weapons of the knight in the thirteenth century, but the introduction of solid body armour and the great helm had a reciprocal effect on the design of the knightly sword. The need for a greater cutting power led to an increase in both the weight and length of the sword, to produce what were then known as 'swords of war'. These were equipped with wider cross-guards, either of spatulate form and straight, or tapering and inclined towards the blade. They had heavy wheel-, ball- or trefoil-shaped pommels to balance the new, weightier blades, and slightly longer grips to allow for the use of both hands. The blades were lengthened to about 40-42 inches (101-106cm)

and were given a central channel or fuller to lighten them. At the very end of the century a new type of sword appeared, which was to be exceedingly popular in the next century. This was designed specifically for thrusting and had a stiff, sharply pointed blade of diamond section. These two types of sword were increasingly supplemented by a single-edged sword kown as a falchion, which was shaped rather like a modern machete. The widening of its blade towards the point gave it great cleaving power and it thus gained much popularity with all classes.

From the middle of the century the knight started to wear a dagger to accompany his sword. This was a two-edged stabbing weapon, shaped like a small version of the sword and known as a quillon dagger. It was worn on the right hip to balance the sword on the left.

The lance and spear of the thirteenth century remained virtually unchanged from their twelfth century counterparts. The knight also used a number of supplementary weapons, most notably either the two-handed or a short, single-handed axe, and the mace. In general the axe was given a larger and heavier head and mounted onto a 4 or 5 foot (1.20 or 1.50m) shaft to give it greater leverage. The mace, a weapon known from the earliest times, started to gain great popularity with the knightly classes since it was capable of crushing the supplementary defences. It usually took the form of a bronze or iron head mounted on a short, wooden shaft, in general not more than 3 feet (1m) in length. However, larger, two-handed versions were also used. The head of the mace was either flanged vertically or was covered with a number of projecting, pyramidal lugs.

Partly as a result of the internecine power struggles throughout Europe in the later twelfth and thirteenth centuries, and partly

because of the Crusaders' experiences in the Holy Land, the common foot soldier was becoming better organized and equipped, a process encouraged in England by the Statutes of Arms promulgated in the twelfth century. Thus the knight was increasingly faced by more effective opposition, not only from his own class, but from that of his social inferiors. Even Richard I, the foremost knight in Europe, was fatally wounded at the siege of Le Mans in 1199 by a crossbow bolt shot by a commoner. The levy troops in most countries continued to use the spear as their primary weapon, but the Crusades had encouraged the use of a number of agriculturally based weapons which were to give rise to a whole family of new and increasingly effective staff weapons. The spear,

Below right: The sword of Fernando de la Cerda, a son of Alphonso X of Castille, c1270, in the Monastery de las Huezeas, Burgos. The grip of the sword is bound with red and yellow silk, the pommel is bronze and the cross is iron. The belt fittings on the scabbard are of buckskin.

Below: The sword and scabbard of St Maurice, c1200-50. It has a 'brazil nut' pommel, a large spatulate cross and the blade has a large central fuller.

therefore, was supplemented by a bewildering array of arms based on the hedging bill, scythe, flail and pitchfork.

The crossbow and the sling remained the most popular missile weapons. The crossbow had shown its true worth at the battle of Assouf in 1191, where Richard I had deployed it to such effect among his knights and infantry that he soundly defeated the Saracens. This force consisted of about 2000 infantry, of which a quarter were crossbowmen, and 50 mounted knights. He deployed his infantry so that each crossbowman was supported by at least one spearman, behind whose shield he could shelter. Therefore the crossbowman could fire while protected from the Saracen cavalry. This practice seems to have been quite common in the thirteenth century, as in 1259 the infantry of Florence were divided into separate companies of spearmen and crossbowmen. From then on, all armies had sizeable proportions of crossbowmen and groups of professional crossbowmen started to take service as mercenaries all over Europe.

The bow of the crossbow was increasingly powerful. It was usually made of laminated layers of wood, horn and sinew, covered with leather or parchment. The crossbow was fitted with a stirrup at the front of the tiller into which the crossbowman placed his foot. He knelt down and fixed the hook he

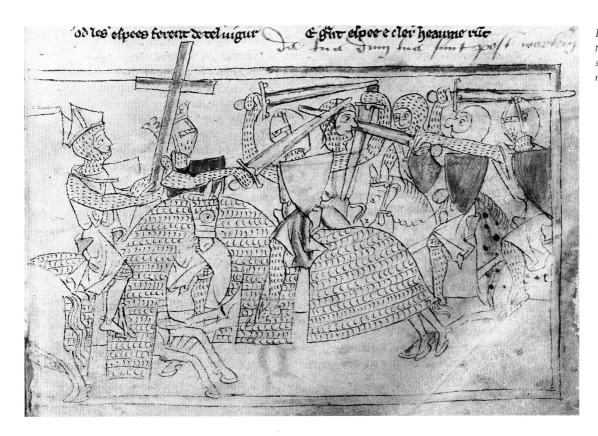

'od les espees ferent de cel uigur' & gur espee e clof heaume uic

Left: A battle scene from a thirteenth century manuscript showing 'covered horses' with mail bards.

wore attached to his waistbelt over the string and then stood up, keeping the crossbow in position with his foot, thus spanning the bow.

The sling was originally a peasant weapon, being cheap and easily constructed. It was usually made of leather or some textile, and consisted of a small pouch with a thong on either side. The projectile, either a rounded pebble or, in later times, a lead shot, was placed within the pouch, the sling was whirled round in one hand, and when it had gathered sufficient momentum one string was released, expelling the shot. These missiles could penetrate far into the bare flesh of horse and man, and would certainly produce severe bruising and perhaps broken bones. A larger version of this weapon, the fustibal, was attached to a stave and was used to throw larger projectiles, sometimes 'stinkpots' (clay vessels filled with burning sulphur or quicklime).

In his Welsh campaigns of 1282, Edward I used large bodies of English and Gascon crossbowmen but their use declined until in 1292 he had only 70 in his army. This is because at the end of the century a new weapon started to be widely adopted in England – the Welsh longbow. In the fourteenth century the longbow was to make England the paramount military nation in Europe.

In England Assizes of Arms, especially the Assize of 1242, laid down the minimum equipment required from each class and from this and contemporary illustrations an accurate picture of the common man's equipment can be made. The better off wore a full hauberk reaching to the knee with a mail coif or a short-sleeved harbergeon. A *chapel de fer* or *cervellière* was usually worn with both. Infantry used no form of leg defences as this would inhibit their marching and mobility on the battlefield. Since they were not as heavily armoured as the knights, and not mounted, agility was an important factor to make up for their lack of defensive equipment. Infantry, as laid down in the Assize of Arms of 1182, often wore one of two types of gambeson. One type was a sleeveless garment with a stiff collar and stiffened arm openings; the other was a plain quilted garment reaching to the knee, with full-length sleeves. The Maciejowski Bible shows these two being worn either individually or together. It was quite common throughout the thirteenth century for infantrymen, especially the poorer ones and the peasant levy, to go into battle completely unprotected; in fact this state of affairs was common for the English longbowman up to and including the Battle of Agincourt in 1415. Their only defence was a small round shield of approximately 1 foot (30cm) in diameter.

Opposite page, right: A shield bearing the arms of Von Nordech from Rabenau. The shield is constructed of three vertical planks, and covered in gesso and leather and painted.

Opposite page, left: The brass of Sir John D'Aubernoun in Stoke d'Abernon Church, Surrey. His scabbard was attached to the sword belt by thongs in a similar way to that of Fernando de la Cerda on page 63.

CHAPTER FOUR
The Fourteenth Century
The Parfait Gentil Knight

The feudal system was not an efficient method of raising armies and by the fourteenth century, this had become obvious. France and Germany clung tenaciously to this system of raising armies but they encountered more and more problems as generations passed, since the continual partition of fiefs among heirs produced such a complexity of tenure and consequent service that it was difficult to know which knight owed duty to which lord. Knights quite often held fiefs from more than one lord, and service was then given only to the principal or liege lord. The situation was further complicated where the estate or fief had descended to a minor or heiress. Then service was, from the end of the eleventh century, commuted to scutage or 'shield money'. Eventually, scutage was paid by all those who did not personally wish to take part in a campaign. In many ways this was advantageous, because the king could hire mercenaries, who were not only better trained but who would also serve indefinitely while paid.

The feudal system was designed primarily to supply the king with knights, and made no provision for the supply or recruitment of the increasingly necessary professional soldiers such as crossbowmen, spearmen and cannoneers. These could not be provided by the feudal levy of the *Heerban* of Germany or the *arrière-ban* of France. Furthermore, the length of service required of a feudal tenant was strictly stipulated as a maximum of 40 days, a fact which greatly limited an army's military efficiency as well as curtailing the scope of its operations. One of the main problems of the feudal military system was that it was designed primarily for the defence of the

Right: The gilt bronze effigy from Canterbury Cathedral of Edward, The Black Prince, who died in 1376. He commanded a wing of the English army at Crécy and defeated the French at Poitiers.

kingdom, not for offensive operations outside the realm, and therefore the kings of Europe had to expend vast amounts of money hiring professional soldiers of all classes to augment their forces. This was an extremely costly business and could swallow up as much as half the annual revenue of the kingdom in a protracted war. Owing to this the kings of England from the reign of Edward I began the practice of granting contracts or indentures to individual nobles, and later professional soldiers, to provide mercenaries to serve the king for an indefinite period. The indenture was written out twice on a single sheet; the sheet was then cut in two with a jagged or undulating line, and the authenticity of one half could be proved by matching its jagged edge against that of the other. Edward III took the indenture system to its logical conclusion; the contractor undertook to serve the King for an agreed wage, with an agreed number of followers, and for a set period of time. These forces consisted of large numbers of all types of professional soldiers who served almost indefinitely during a campaign. This promoted an *ésprit de corps*, thus paving the way for the success of the English campaigns on the Continent and enabling the king to garrison captured castles. This system slowly spread throughout most of Europe, becoming commonplace by the end of the fourteenth century and remaining in use in the armies of the Hundred Years War.

One of the undesirable side-effects of this system and the *chevauchée* (mounted raid) style of warfare in the Hundred Years War between England and France was the formation of the so-called 'free companies'. Usually formed of unemployed soldiers, at the end of a campaign these companies either set about looking for a new paymaster or lapsed into brigandage, usually establishing themselves in an area and holding it to ransom. After the French defeat at Poitiers in 1356, these companies overran much of France. Large numbers subsequently fought in the Italian wars, the most famous of which was the White Company under the command of Sir John Hawkwood. So powerful could these become that one, known as The Great Company, even forced the Pope in Avignon to buy them off for the huge sum of 30,000 florins.

As early as 1310 the *signori* of Italy such as the Visconti of Milan, the della Scala of Verona and the d'Este of Ferrara had begun to employ *compagnie de ventura*, mostly foreign mercenaries. Like the free companies, these often lapsed into brigandage at the end of their *condotta* (contract). The *condottieri* (commanders) of these companies were either men of noble blood who fought simply to finance their states or to serve their families, or professional soldiers, such as Sir John Hawkwood, who fought first for Pisa against Florence, then for Milan against the Pope, and finally again for Florence.

The fourteenth century saw great political upheaval, characterized all over western Europe by protracted, costly and bloody wars: the Hundred Years War between England and France; strife between France and Flanders; the struggle for the throne of Castile; the jockeying of the Italian city states and the Great Schism which resulted in the existence of two, and at one stage three, Popes simultaneously and in the expulsion of the papacy from Rome and its installation at Avignon; and the attempts of the Holy Roman Emperors to stem the tide of rising Swiss nationalism. Consequently it was a time of very great change for the knight and his equipment. It was a period of experiment both in tactics and in the manufacture of armour and witnessed a revolution in the tactical use and military position of the knight – indeed, it witnessed the eclipse of his pre-eminence on the battlefield.

It is a century punctuated by major defeats for the feudal forces of chivalry: in 1302 at the Battle of Courtrai, Flemish infantry defeated the best knights of Europe, the *puissant* chivalry of France; at the Battle of Bannockburn in 1314 the might of England, 23,000 picked men led by Edward II, was vanquished by *schiltrons* of just 10,000 Scottish spearmen. The English victory over the Scots at Hallidon Hill in 1333 saw the first wholesale tactical deployment in Europe of the knight as an infantryman, in conjunction with longbowmen, and it was this combination that was to shatter the armies of France at Crécy and Poitiers. Finally the defeat in 1386 of the Austrian army at Sempach by the peasants of the Swiss Confederation armed almost exclusively with pikes and the deadly halberd, sounded the death-knell of the feudal army and heralded its replacement by the professional soldiers of the fifteenth and sixteenth centuries.

The armour of the fourteenth century is characterized by the increasing use of plate defences for the body of various materials including latten (a brass-like copper alloy), whalebone, *cuir bouilli* and iron and steel, and the emergence by the end of the century of an almost complete harness of steel. Similarly the weaponry is characterized by its penetrative and percussive nature. Two-handed

Right: The effigy of Sir Hugh Despenser, c1349, from Tewkesbury Abbey, Gloucestershire. Sir Hugh's globular basinet clearly shows the vervelles and cord for attaching his aventail.

axes, maces and swords were designed specifically for thrusting. However, perhaps the most deadly of all the weapons used in the fourteenth century was the English longbow which, for the next hundred years, until the battle of Chastillon, was to make the English army unrivalled throughout Europe. At short range the longbow could penetrate even plate, and its rate of fire was second to none.

Finally, throughout the fourteeth century there was an increasing professionalism, especially in the English army, and an increase in the use of professional soldiers not of the knightly class in the armies of Europe. As these soldiers could expect little mercy if defeated and, indeed, showed little to their social superiors, the knight was particularly interested in all advances in defence.

Throughout the fourteenth century the great helm continued to be worn by the knight over a *cervellière* or basinet, and varied very little in its general form. However, after about 1350 its use tended to be restricted to the tournament, although it is sometimes illustrated in manuscripts being worn in battle as late as the early fifteenth century. This is possibly because it restricted the movement of the knight's head and his breathing. Weight was also a consideration,

although these helms were by no means as cumbersome as they look, weighing only 5 or 6 pounds.

By the last quarter of the thirteenth century the skull of the helm had become so tapered that it formed a truncated cone, and the side and the front of the helm were extended downwards almost to rest on the shoulders and the chest of the wearer. This provided a glancing surface off which the blades of weapons would slide: the flat-topped helm of the previous century had proved both vulnerable to, and ineffective against, the increasing weight of weapons such as the sword or battle axe, as is attested by many contemporary manuscript illustrations. Between the years 1300 and 1340 helms with pivoted visors were commonly illustrated, as in the Luttrell Psalter, but no actual examples survive.

Helms of similar form were used throughout Europe for most of the century. Three surviving late-fourteenth century examples from England, those belonging to the Black Prince and Sir Richard Pembridge, and one in the Royal Armouries, Tower of London, are very similar to the earlier forms represented by a helm preserved in the Castel Sant Angelo, Rome, from Bolzano in Northern Italy.

Above left: A late fourteenth century great helm from above the tomb of Sir Nicholas Hauberk, who died in 1407. The iron loops riveted at the front and rear are to attach it to the breast and backplates.

Above: A visored basinet, German or North Italian, c1370. This is a typical fighting helmet of the period.

However, towards the turn of the century the helm did change and there are three examples of this new type from England: that of Henry V in Westminster Abbey and two from Cobham Church, Kent. These were designed for the joust and consist of a high, truncated conical skull below which the lower edge of the sight is drawn forward to project well beyond the upper edge. In addition, loops were riveted to the base at the front and the back to attach it to the wearer's breastplate and backplate.

From the beginning of the fourteenth century the helm was equipped with a guard chain which was directly attached to the body armour. This ended in a toggle which fitted into a cruciform aperture in the lower right-hand edge of the front of the helm and was designed to stop the helmet being lost if knocked from the head in the midst of battle. The guard chain also served the useful function of supporting the helm; when action was not imminent it could be removed from the head for comfort and slung over the shoulder.

As in the thirteenth century, the helm was worn with a variety of crests, for the most part made either from *cuir bouilli* or parchment and whalebone. These took the form of moulded and painted horns, examples of which are preserved in Vienna and at Churburg, or of heraldic beasts and symbols. For those of the rank of Baron or above, crests usually surmounted a cap of maintenance, as can be seen on the surviving crest on the helmet of the Black Prince. Crests were not necessarily derived from one of the charges of the knight's coat of arms, but were usually the same colour as the principal charge. They were very popular in Germany, England and the Low Countries, but were seldom worn in the Iberian Peninsula, Italy and France. In Eastern Europe they were commonly replaced altogether by *panaches* of feathers, a fashion which spread throughout Europe. Crests were commonly accompanied by cloth mantling, usually in the main tinctures of the coat of arms, which may have been intended to lessen the effect of the heat of the sun on the back of the helmet. It has also been suggested that mantlings and torses might have been drenched with water as a further cooling measure.

As mentioned, the *cervellière* continued to be worn, and originally the term 'basinet' was synonymous with it. The *cervellière* was

worn either over or under the mail coif, and latterly was laced permanently to it, but by the 1330s the *cervellière* had been totally displaced by a developed form, the true basinet, of which there were at first three basic types. These were either deep and conical with an arched face opening, extended down to the base of the neck and often had a visor; small and of globular form, only just reaching to below the wearer's ears; or, finally, of a tall conical form, only just reaching to the tops of the ears.

All these types appeared regularly until the 1350s but after this the basic form of basinet was of medium height with a conical skull which extended at the rear and sides to cover the cheeks and the nape of the neck. By the end of the century it was extended to the base of the neck and the cheekbones, and the apex of the skull was slowly moved backwards to give an almost vertical rear face. In Germany

Above: The Pembridge Helm. This great helm was formerly hung in Hereford Cathedral over the tomb of Sir Richard Pembridge, who died in 1375. It is constructed of three plates of steel. The skull is pointed at the top to provide a glancing surface and the sight is formed between the skull and side plates. At the lower edge on each side is a cruciform piercing for the attachment of a toggle-ended chain.

Far left: A north Italian basinet, c1390. This basinet originally had a centrally pivoted visor; the present example is a replacement, probably made during the helmet's working lifetime. The aventail is associated.

a basinet with an ogival-shaped skull was popular throughout the period 1350-1400.

The aventail was a fan-shaped curtain of mail extending from the base of the basinet to the point of the shoulder, protecting the neck and throat but leaving the face exposed. It was at first riveted directly to the basinet, but later was attached by means of staples called vervelles which passed through a leather band at the top edge of the mail; a cord was then threaded through the staples above the leather. This had the advantage that the aventail could be removed for repair and cleaning. The lower edge of the aventail was sometimes laced to the *jupon*, as can be seen on the figure of a martial saint on an altarpiece carved by Jacques de Baerze around the end of the century for the Chartreuse de Champmol, which is in the Musée des Beaux Arts, Dijon.

When not worn under the great helm, the basinet was at first provided with its own globular visor which pivoted at the sides. In Italy and Germany there was an alternative form of face protection in the form of an embossed triangular plate, shaped to fit over the wearer's mouth and nose, which was attached to the aventail and hooked onto the basinet. Although this was heavily padded, the amount of protection it provided cannot have been very great. A further variant in use in Germany was a centrally pivoted visor known as the *Klappvisier*, a surviving example of which is preserved in the Museum of Sitten, Switzerland. This was a small, rounded visor which covered only the area left exposed by the aventail. It had flanged eye-slits or sights and was pierced by numerous small holes, known as 'breaths', which enabled the wearer to breath. Throughout Europe in about 1380 the visor began to develop a pronounced projecting

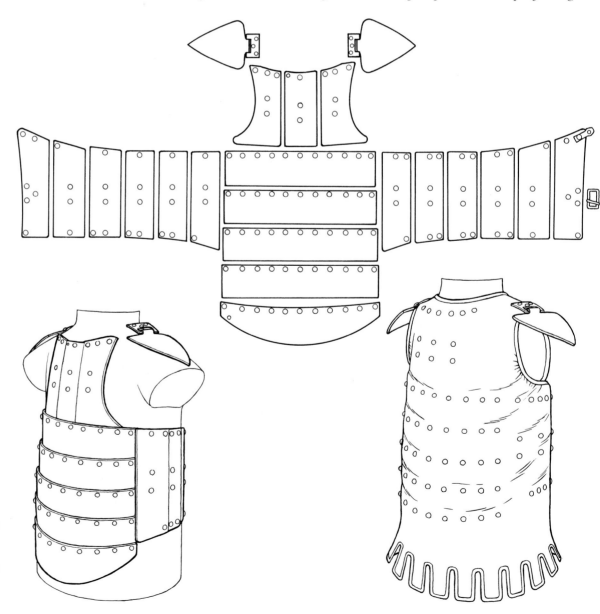

Right: A reconstruction drawing of a coat of plates based on finds from the battle graves at Wisby, c1361. It shows the layout of the plates beneath the cloth covering with the garment spread out (top), and the coat of plates with its covering, as it was worn (below right).

conical snout with flanged sights and mouth slit, pierced with numerous small breaths; these were essential as the visor now totally enclosed the knight's face. This type of visor is often called a 'hounskull' or 'dog-head' basinet, and was accompanied by another innovation in design in the form of a new type of pivot which allowed the visor to be removed when not required. This worked by incorporating what were, in effect, hinges, into the arms of the visor in front of the pivots. The hinges were equipped with removable pins, often with their own small guard chains to prevent loss.

A number of splendid examples of this type of late fourteenth century basinet are preserved in major European collections, for example at the Von Trapp Armoury at Churburg, the Wallace Collection in London and the Royal Armouries (Tower of London).

At the very end of the century the basinet was developed further by the replacement of the mail aventail by a plate defence to produce what is known as the 'Great Basinet'. There is a particularly fine example of this type in the Doges' Palace, Venice – the whole helmet (with the exception of the visor) is raised from a single piece of steel.

Alongside the great helm and the basinet, the *chapel de fer* or kettle hat continued to be very popular, particularly with the poorer knights as it was relatively cheap and easy to produce and gave good all-round vision. From about 1320 it is depicted with a tall conical skull, like the contemporary basinet. The *spangenhelm* form of kettle hat, previously made of a large number of overlapping plates, was henceforth made of one or two, and very rarely three, pieces.

After his death at the Battle of Courtrai in 1302, the inventory of the goods of Raoul de Nesle, listed his arms as consisting of gambesons, mail hauberks, basinets, kettle hats, padded cuisses and both half and full greaves and pairs of plates.

The 'pair of plates', commonly known today as a coat of plates, was a development of the type of thirteenth century surcoat which was sometimes reinforced with oblong vertical plates riveted to the cloth. Throughout the fourteenth century the most common form of body armour, especially up to the 1360s, was a textile or leather garment lined with plates. By 1330 they were very commonly mentioned in wills and inventories, but they are rarely seen in illustrations as

they were worn over the hauberk but beneath the surcoat. Sometimes, instead of the plates being riveted to the inside of a textile or leather garment, they were riveted to the outside, as is seen in the *Romance of Alexander*, an illuminated manuscript preserved in the Bodleian Library.

The most important source of information about this type of armour comes from the mass graves at Wisby. The Battle of Wisby was fought in 1361 between the Gotlanders and the Danes, and after the battle the dead were interred in graves along with some of their equipment. The coats of plates found consist of iron plates riveted to a textile

Left: Detail from a fourteenth century illuminated Address from the town of Prato to Robert of Anjou. It shows a knight wearing a kettle hat, mail hauberk, plate leg defences and a coat of plates.

Above: Detail from the Romance of Alexander (1338-44), showing two knights wearing plates attached to a lining and without a cover.

covering; the rivet heads often take the form of florets or heraldic devices. Coats of plates conformed for the most part to the basic pattern of a T-shaped garment with a hole in the centre of the vertical arm through which the wearer put his head. The horizontal arm of the T, which formed the front and side of the garment, was lined with plates and these wrapped around the wearer, passed over the rear of the garment and met at the back, where they were fastened with buckles and laces. Other forms of pairs of plates were found at Wisby and elsewhere which were constructed so as to form separate breast and back plates which joined at the shoulder and laced or buckled down one side. The majority of the knights who were present at the battles of Crécy and Poitiers fought in coats of plates.

By the 1350s effigies start to show the evolution of a single large plate covering the upper chest, accompanied by smaller plates to cover the shoulders. To prevent their loss in battle, guard chains were often attached to the helm, sword and dagger and then riveted to the breastplate. By the 1360s or so this plate had increased in size and covered the chest as far as the diaphragm; the skirts of the armour were sculpted as vertical rows of rivets in a cloth cover, which represented horizontal hoops of iron or steel. By the 1370s these waist lames had disappeared, to be replaced by a breastplate which finished at the top of the hips and a skirt or fauld of horizontal lames.

Although there is literary evidence for an independent breastplate as early as the 1340s, the first known depiction dates only from the 1370s, and shows the breastplate being worn over the coat of plates. It is not until the last two decades of the century that it can be regarded as at all common. In Italy and Germany it was sometimes worn independently with a short fauld and without any form of backplate, being held on by cross-straps at the back, as shown in the silver altar piece from Pistoia Cathedral (*c* 1376). An Italian velvet-covered breastplate of this form is preserved in the Bayerisches Museum, Munich, but shoulder attachments and lace holes down both sides would suggest that it was intended for use with a backplate. The effigies of Albert and Konrad von Limburg in the church at Burg Komburg in Wurtemburg show breastplates shaped to the neck and arms and ending at the waist, as does the monument of Walter von Hohenklingen, who was killed at the Battle of Sempach and is buried in Felbach Church, Switzerland. This monument shows a globular one-piece breastplate with a lance rest attached to the upper right-hand side, worn over a quilted coat armour. A lance rest is a small bracket,

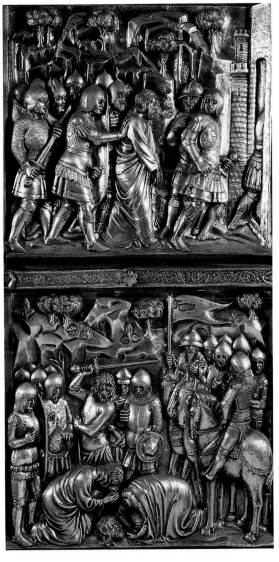

Left and below: Portions of a silver altar piece in Pistoia Cathedral, Italy, c1376, made by Leonardo di San Giovanni and Francesco di Niccolò. They show typical Italian armour of the late fourteenth century with deep, open-faced basinets and one-piece breastplates with faulds, at least one of which is held by straps at the rear.

Below left: The brass of Sir Miles and Lady Stapleton, from Ingham Church, Yorkshire. It shows body and leg defences constructed after the manner of a brigandine.

Prato in Italy, dated 1368. The earliest English reference to a brigandine is in the inventory of Thomas Duke of Gloucester, son of Edward III, dated 1397 – the year of his imprisonment and murder in Calais by Thomas Mowbray. The brigandine, to judge by surviving fifteenth century examples, was

Far left: A late fourteenth century breastplate with a fauld, covered in velvet. Probably north Italian.

Below: The tomb effigy of Walter von Hohenklingen, c1386, shows a one-piece breastplate worn over a gambeson.

designed to engage a small circular plate on the lance behind the grip, so that when the lance was couched the arm would not be driven back.

Two late fourteenth century independent breastplates survive at the Armoury at Churburg, one of which is clearly derived from a coat of plates. It consists of nine vertical plates, each edged with engaved brass strips and attached to a leather lining; the breast was defended by three plates with smaller plates disposed under each arm and held by cross-straps at the rear. It has a V-shaped bar riveted just below the neck to act as a stop-rib to prevent the point of a weapon from sliding into the wearer's neck. The breastplate is globular and is fitted with a folding lance rest. The second, which dates to about 1400, is made of a single piece of steel and is of globular form with a stop-rib.

During the later part of the fourteenth century a body defence known as a brigandine was developed. This was a piece of body armour which followed the principle of a coat of plates, and clearly descended from it, but using much smaller plates which worked over each other to give greater flexibility. These plates were riveted to a canvas garment which was usually covered in some finer material. One of the earliest mentions of this sort of defence comes from the letters of Francesco di Marco di Datini, a merchant of made of numerous overlapping small plates riveted to a cloth cover, with two larger and slightly globular L-shaped plates to protect the chest and lungs.

In addition to all these forms of body defence, a garment known as the coat armour was also worn. These were often used to display the wearer's coat of arms as an aid to identification on the field. At the very beginning of the century the knight still wore a surcoat or flowing gown over his armour, which probably proved a hindrance while fighting on foot, as it is often depicted tucked up into the belt. Later, the front of the gown was shortened to expose the bottom of the coat of plates. By the late 1340s it had risen to knee level both at the front and at the back. The coat armour, as it was known, was worn in different forms in different countries, but in Germany after 1360 it ceased to be worn at all. However, in general, especially in England, it was a tight-fitting padded garment which was sleeveless and reached to just below the hips. There are two surviving coat armours, both dating to the last quarter of the fourteenth century. The most complete is preserved in the Cathedral of Chartres and was probably deposited there around the year 1400 by Charles VI of France. The other, and perhaps more famous, is that of the Black Prince in Canterbury Cathedral. Both garments are quilted vertically.

The Chartres coat armour, or *jupon*, is in excellent condition and is made of quilted white linen stuffed with wool and covered with crimson silk damask woven with medallions containing heraldic birds and beasts, interspersed with foliage. It is mid-thigh length with a scalloped lower edge, closes at centre front with 25 wooden buttons covered with the same crimson damask and has long, loose sleeves which taper to the wrist. On the left side of the garment are two slits to accommodate the straps of the sword scabbard. Unfortunately, the Black Prince's coat armour is not in such good condition, but was made of red and blue velvet embroidered with the arms of France and England quarterly, and was lined with satin and padded with wool. It, too, fastens centre front, but with eyelets and lacing. Although the sleeves now reach only to the elbow, they may originally have been full length as only the upper quarters of the coat of arms survive.

There is another interesting piece in the Musée Historique des Tissus de Lyons, France. This is the so-called '*pourpoint* of the Blessed Charles de Blois', although it almost certainly postdates his death at the Battle of Auray in 1364. It has the fashionable cut of the last quarter of the fourteenth century, with sleeves being set *à grandes assiettes* and the characteristic pouter-pigeon chest and wasp-waist favoured by the dandies of the period. The front and sleeves fasten with cloth-covered wooden buttons, interestingly in the same disposition as those on the

Below: A composite armour of a Vogt of Match, in Schloss Churburg. North Italian, c1390. The breastplate is constructed of plates, the borders of which are edged with bands of decorative brasswork.

Left: The monumental brass of Sir John d'Abernon, c1340, in the Parish Church of St Mary, Stoke d'Abernon, Surrey. It shows an armour typical of the Crécy period, comprising a basinet and aventail, and a knee-length coat armour, with the surcoat shortened at the front.

Below: The effigy of Edward, the Black Prince (after Stothard), in Canterbury Cathedral. It shows an almost completely developed harness of plate.

Chartres coat armour: flat disc-shaped buttons below the waist, and domed buttons above. The garment is made of a silk damask similar to that used for the Chartres *jupon* with a pattern of heraldic lions and birds set in medallions, and is padded to give a smooth line. Although in the author's opinion this is probably a purely civilian garment, some historians believe that it is *jupon* of the type worn by the figure on the Champmol altarpiece mentioned above. The Champmol *jupon* is a sleeved garment reaching to groin level. Below the waist it fits closely to the hips and is fastened by lacing. Above the waist, the garment is, to judge from the carving, hardly, if at all, padded and both the body and sleeves are very loose. It fastens across the chest and up the sleeves with ball

buttons, and has an opening on the right to allow the lance rest to protrude.

For the duration of the fourteenth century the knight continued to wear his hauberk or habergeon under his armour but after about 1350, like the *jupon* it only reached to just below hip level and was often bordered by brass rings meshed like mail and shaped into a zig-zag fringe. Beneath this he wore his aketon which, by the mid-fourteenth century, had become shortened to the same length as the hauberk and was strongly waisted in form, like the contemporary civilian pourpoint.

The development of the plate arm harness was somewhat behind that of the defences of the leg and shows a certain amount of local variation. In different countries and at different times the parts of the arm defences were known by different names; in England the arm defence was called a 'bracer' and the individual components were the 'spaudler' for the point of the shoulder, the 'rerebrace' for the upper arm, the 'couter' for the elbow and the 'vambrace' for the lower arm. However, as the most eminent modern authorities use the term 'vambrace' to refer to the whole arm defence and 'upper and lower cannons' and 'couters' to refer to the upper and lower sections and the elbow defences

Above: The coat armour or jupon of Charles VI of France, deposited in Chartres Cathedral at the end of the fourteenth century. This is an almost unique survival and is in excellent condition.

Left: The effigy of Don Alvéro de Cabrera, who died in 1299. Don Alvéro has a reinforced surcoat and plate defences for the lower arms and legs.

respectively, it seems logical to follow this usage.

The earliest known full-plate arm harness appears on the monument of Don Alvéro de Cabrera in the Monastery of Santa Maria dei Belpuig de las Alvenas at Bellaguer, Spain. This consists of upper-arm defences constructed after the manner of a coat of plates and lower-arm defences of plate. From the 1320s monuments frequently show gutter-shaped plates strapped on to the upper and lower arm and a cup-like couter defending the elbow. These are accompanied by disk-like defences known as besagews, which are suspended so that they hang down to defend the armpit.

By 1325-30 the lower cannon of the arm defences started to be constructed of two plates to completely encircle the arm. On the Continent knights were quite often depicted wearing mail inside the upper defences but outside the lower. In Germany separate tubular or gutter-shaped defences for the upper and lower arm, worn with or without separate couters, were all attached individually by points or straps to the undergarments. About this time in England gutter-shaped upper and lower cannons made an appearance. These were joined to a couter with a small, disc-like wing by small laminations, with a separate laminated spaudler for the point of the shoulder. By 1340 these spaudlers were permanently attached to the upper cannon. This upper cannon was hinged down one side and strapped across the other. Up until about 1361 (the date of the Treaty of Brétigny, which ended the first phase of the Hundred Years War) these defences were used in conjunction with besagews which, after this date, disappear for some 40 years.

Italian arm harness, as represented by the armour preserved at Churburg, consisted of a short gutter-shaped upper cannon riveted to laminated couters and lower cannons of tulip form, that is, narrowing to the wrist and flaring at the cuff. Quite often these seem to have been worn without spaudlers or indeed any defence for the shoulder other than the mail sleeve of the hauberk.

The arm defences preserved with the *jupon* at Chartres are of a similar but slightly different construction. They have a short gutter-shaped upper cannon, a hinged lower cannon and a couter. The couter, however, was not joined to the upper and lower cannons by riveted lames, but would appear

to have been attached to internal leathers. From about 1275 until halfway through the fourteenth century, items known as ailettes were commonly worn throughout Europe, except in Germany. These were usually rectangular in form and laced to the point of the shoulder. However, these had little or no defensive value and their chief role was

Above: A French brass dating to 1333 shows a globular basinet and aventail, besagews laced to the sleeves of the haubergeon and schynbalds strapped over mail chausses.

Right: The brass of Sir Hugh Hastings, c1347. The plate arm defences now include gutter-shaped defences for the upper and lower arm, and besagews at the elbow and armpit. Gamboised cuisses and poleyns are worn over the chausses on the legs.

heraldic and thus recognitive.

To complete the arm defences the knight would don a pair of gauntlets. Towards the end of the thirteenth century plate defences for the hands started to evolve. The mail mufflers worn throughout this century all but disappeared by 1330. The new types of gauntlets were originally either deep-cuffed cloth gloves plated with whalebone (Froissart mentioned these as being part of the equipment of the men of Bruges at the battle of Roosebeke in 1382) or, alternatively, cloth or leather gloves lined with plates, constructed in a similar manner to the coat of plates, and a number of gauntlets of this type were excavated from Wisby. From the middle of the century the gauntlets most commonly associated with the fourteenth century appeared; these were of hour-glass form and consisted of a large plate shaped for the back and sides of the hand, constricted at the wrist and flared to form a short cuff. This plate was embossed for the shape of the knuckles and the base of the thumb, and the gauntlet was completed by small overlapping plates to protect the fingers and thumbs. This whole gauntlet was stitched to an internal glove either of leather or cloth. However, sometimes the plates themselves were covered in cloth, as is a gauntlet from Brick Hill Lane, London, now in the Royal Armouries (Tower of London). The finger defences were sometimes accompanied by gadlings or spikes attached to the knuckles, which could be used in the manner of knuckle-dusters. Those on the gauntlets of the Black Prince take the form of small lions.

Throughout the fourteenth century leg harness showed a gradual development with a great deal of variation. At the beginning of the century many knights wore simply mail *chausses* with little or no additional defence, those that were worn being simply gamboised cuisses and cup-like steel poleyns, and occasionally schynbalds or shin guards of plate. However, mail chausses continued to be shown commonly until 1350 and occasionally, in Spain and Germany, to the end of the century. However, after 1310 schynbalds are rare, being replaced by full and demi greaves. These were referred to in the Nesle inventory of 1302. By 1330 greaves constructed of two pieces hinged and strapped together were quite common, although splint-like defences were also in use, as can be seen on the monument of Guy Lord Bryan

(who fought at the Battle of Crécy) in Tewkesbury Abbey.

Up until 1340 gamboised cuisses were still common but from then until the middle of the century cuisses constructed after the fashion of a coat of plates were used, usually with globular poleyns, and it is in this period that the first plate cuisses appear. Plate sabatons of overlapping horizontal lames shaped to fit the pointed 'poulain' shoes of the period

Above: The vambrace and couter of a child's armour, c1390, from Chartres Cathedral. The vambrace is 'tulip' shaped and has an internal hinge. The poleyn has an oval side wing and was originally articulated on leathers.

Below: A bronze statuette of a mounted knight. He is equipped with ailettes and gamboised cuisses, and carries a lance with a vamplate.

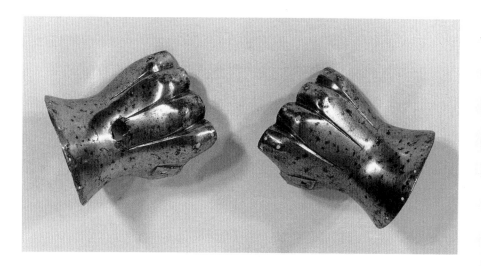

Right: A gauntlet, c 1375, excavated at Brick Hill Lane, London. This gauntlet is probably of English manufacture and was once covered in cloth attached by rivets.

Above: A pair of gauntlets from Chartres Cathedral, c 1390. These are of the typical hour-glass form common at the end of the century. The gauntlets have been stripped of their gilt-bronze ornament and have lost their finger plates. The holes on the knuckles are for mounting gadlings.

appeared at this time, superceding the earlier form constructed of small plates riveted to a cloth covering.

By the 1370s plate cuisses consisting of a single plate were common and had embossed lower edges to fit over the wearer's knees; these were articulated to the poleyns by rivets. The poleyns were skilfully shaped in

Right: A late fourteenth century misericord depicting a falling knight, from Lincoln Cathedral. It shows a back plate consisting of plates riveted to the cloth lining.

order to ride snugly over this bulge. Also at this time the poleyns developed a heart-shaped side wing to protect the tendons at the back of the knee. The leg harness preserved at Chartres Cathedral includes an almost complete right leg defence of this form but is unique in that it still retains its sabaton. The cuisse is embossed with a bulge over the knee and there is no articulating lame between it and the poleyn, which has a rounded side wing, and below this is an articulating plate to which are attached straps for securing it to the greaves. The greaves are made of two plates hinged on the inside and fastened by straps on the outside; closely modelled to the leg, its lower part is shaped for the ankle bones with an arch cut out over the instep and heel. The sabaton is composed of articulated horizontal lames with sharply pointed toes. All these plates overlap in a downward pointing direction. The lames of the sabaton articulate from a large plate shaped to the instep and terminate in a pointed metal 'toe cap', the edge of which is decorated with silver-gilt *fleurs-de-lys*.

By the last quarter of the century the upper leg defences consisted of a single plate protecting the front of the thigh with a hinged side plate for the outside of the leg. At the bottom of the main plate a small articulating lame was riveted to allow the poleyn to pivot. The poleyn had a lower lame which either strapped over or was attached to the greave. The greaves were of a similar style to those at Chartres described above.

As most people know, the shield of the medieval knight had two functions: first and foremost it was a defence, but it was also used for identification, displaying the personal heraldic arms of the bearer.

By the 1270s the shield had assumed the shape known today as the 'heater', because of its resemblance to the base of a clothes iron. It was in general of moderate size and very slightly curved to the body. It was made of

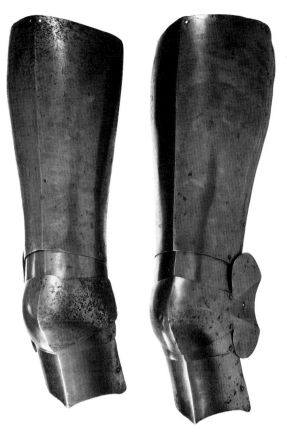

Left: Cuisses, probably north Italian, late fourteenth century, from the Armoury at Churburg.

thin wood, usually with an applied layer of canvas, over which was laid a layer of leather. The leather was either painted or decorated with applied moulded leather to represent the knight's coat of arms. Because of the very nature of their constituents very few fourteenth-century shields have survived; perhaps the most famous of these is the shield of Edward the Black Prince from above his tomb in Canterbury Cathedral. It measured some 28¾ inches (73cm) in height and 23¼ inches (59cm) in width. It is made of poplar wood joined centrally and covered with canvas and gesso, and then overlain by parchment and, finally, a layer of leather. This is decorated over all with cruciform punch marks and painted quarterly blue and red. The first and fourth quarters (observer's top left and bottom right) are powdered with moulded leather *fleurs-de-lys* and the second

Below left: The cuisse, poleyn and greave from a child's armour, c1390, at Chartres Cathedral. This is the most complete leg defence extant from the fourteenth century.

Below: The sabaton from the same armour at Chartres Cathedral. It still retains fragments of its silver-gilt decoration.

and third have three lions *passant guardant*. The inside of the shield is painted green and has no fixings for the arm straps; it therefore seems probable that the shield was only ever intended for funerary use. However, an example preserved in Sitten Museum in Switzerland which dates to the early years of the fourteenth century still has its original fixings; these consists of a pad for the arm and two enarmes and a guige. This particularly fine shield is blue and is decorated with a gold-painted raised eagle of leather and gesso.

Unfortunately no horse armour survives from the fourteenth century, with the possible exception of the Warwick shaffron which may be late fourteenth century or early fifteenth century, but there is ample pictorial and literary evidence from which to form a reasonable picture of its development. Mail trappers had been worn from the thirteenth century, but were rare in the fourteenth, perhaps because of either their great weight or the cost of producing them. However, early in the century defences constructed like coats of plates appeared. At first only the head and the chest of the horse were protected, by a *shaffron* and *peytral* respectively. Towards the end of the century this defence was generally replaced by large plates of either *cuir bouilli* or steel and these occasionally had flanchards, defences which hung down from the side of the saddle, and cruppers to defend the horse's rump.

The earliest form of *shaffron* can be seen on the statue of Cangrande della Scala in the Castel Vecchio in Verona. This consisted simply of a plate of leather or steel shaped to the horse's head to protect the forehead, and extending as far as the nose, but leaving the sides of the head bare. It had cut-outs to accommodate the ears and eyes but was embossed above the eye holes to form rudimentary eye-guards. By the mid-fourteenth century tubular defences for the ears were added to the shaffron and pierced, cup-like eye defences were also quite common. The final fourteenth century form is represented by the Warwick shaffron; this is now in the Royal Armouries but was until recently preserved in Warwick Castle where it had probably been since it was first made. Made entirely of steel, the main plate has a medial keel with a bulbous projection for the nose and hemispherical bosses for the eyes which are all pierced by numerous circular holes. It

Right: The brass of Sir Robert de Bures, c 1331, in the Church of All Saints, Acton, Suffolk. Sir Robert is equipped in a somewhat old-fashioned style. He has no plate arm defences and wears on his legs chausses, gamboised cuisses and poleyns.

has a riveted rear extension which gives the shaffron a voluminous appearance and encloses the rear of the horse's head. It would appear to have had riveted tubular ear guards originally.

Although in essence not part of the knight's armour, spurs were an intrinsic part of his panoply, which not only denoted his social rank and status but also served the useful function of driving his horse on. Even the most well-trained mount, when faced with the noise of battle and a hedge of spear points or an on-coming wall of opposing horses, might need some encouragement. Their importance is shown by the fact that spurs formed a part of the coronation insignia of a King of England; and that a knight was said to 'receive his spurs' on knighthood. When asked to send troops to aid his son the Black Prince during the battle of Crécy, Edward III is reported to have replied 'let the boy win his spurs.' Finally, the greatest hero of Richard II's reign was Sir Henry or Harry 'Hotspur' Percy.

Until the end of the thirteenth century a very basic form of spur known as the prick spur was used. This form is of very great antiquity and was used by both the Greeks and Romans. In the thirteenth century the prick spur consisted simply of a U-shaped bracket shaped to fit round the wearer's ankle bones with a moderately long stem projecting from the rear, which either had a pyramidal point or swelled to form a ball with a short spike projecting from its apex. These were so designed to stop the spur penetrating the horse's flesh too far. However, at the beginning of the fourteenth century a new and more elaborate form appeared known as a rowel spur. This was of the same general form as the prick spur, except that the end of the stem was divided and a spiked wheel inserted. This form remained in common use for more than 500 years, and is the type of 'jingling spur' commonly associated with the cowboy of the American West.

In the fourteenth century armour was decorated in a number of different ways, for example with cloth coverings, paint, or with applied and engraved adornments. From the beginning of the century the very construction of the coat of plates lent itself to a display of finery and conspicuous consumption. The richest knights could afford the finest materials with which to cover their armour. Materials such as silk, damask, and silk vel-

Above: The Warwick shaffron, probably English, second half of the fourteenth century, designed to enclose the whole of the horse's head.

Below: A rowel spur, possibly English, second half of the fourteenth century.

Right: The shield of Edward, the Black Prince, who died in 1376. Part of his funerary achievement, it is made of poplar wood covered in canvas, gesso and leather and painted.

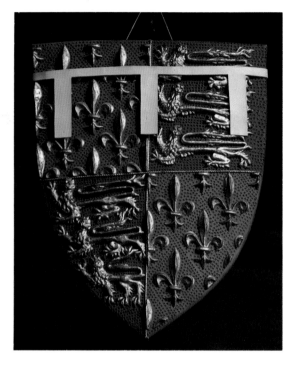

vet, both figured and unfigured, had become increasingly easily obtainable, although never cheap. It is a common misconception that the Middle Ages were drab and colourless. This may have been true for the poorer classes, but one has only to look at contemporary manuscripts and artifacts to see that, for the well off, nearly every surface was covered in decoration, usually in bright colours. The same is true of contemporary armour. The few surviving fragments of cloth-covered armour and the two coat armours that survive from the fourteenth century give but a tantalizingly small glimpse of the splendour of the richer man-at-arms. A breast plate that survives in the Bayerisches Museum, Munich, was originally covered in deep red silk velvet, and we read in numerous inventories of items covered in damask and other rich stuffs. The poorer had to make do with fustian (a cloth of wool and linen or latterly cotton, with a raised nap, giving the effect of velveteen) and linen. It was quite common throughout the Middle Ages to paint armour, often with heraldic patterns. However, due to the vulnerable nature of this decoration, very little survives.

Perhaps the most durable, and indeed the most impressive, embellishment of armour consisted of applied bands or motifs, usually of latten (a copper alloy) but sometimes of silver gilt. These varied from simple bands applied around the main edge of the armour to elaborately moulded and delicate decoration such as the silver-gilt *fleurs-de-lys* which

bordered the main edges of the boy's armour from Chartres. As can be seen on composite armour at Churburg, these bands were sometimes engraved, usually with quotations from the Bible or talismanic legends which were intended to protect the wearer. The breastplate of the Churburg armour bears the words: 'Jesus autem transiens per medium illorum ibat' (Luke 4:30; 'But he passing through the midst of them went his way'). From the same period, as with the Black Prince's gauntlets, more elaborate embellishment such as the zoomorphic gadlings are found.

From about 1300 the basinet was also decorated more or less elaborately, and contemporary accounts speak of gold, pearls and precious stones encrusting these. From this time we read of basinets being decorated by a roll of cloth or torse; this was often richly embellished and was commonly jewelled, as one can see on the monument of Thomas, eighth Lord Berkeley (d 1361) in Berkeley Church, Gloucestershire, and on the brass of Lord Willoughby d'Eresby (d *c* 1390) at Spilsby, Linconshire. Contemporary illustrations and accounts show basinets being worn with a coronet, although these were presumably, at least in theory, restricted to those entitled to them. The Duke of Alençon sheared one of the fleurons off the crown of Henry V at the Battle of Agincourt (1415) with his sword. Also common in the fourteenth century were mounts which were jewelled or enamelled, often with an heraldic motif; these were commonly attached to the

Right: One of a pair of hour-glass gauntlets, Milanese, c1380-1400. The gauntlet is decorated with applied brass decoration, the lower band of which is inscribed with the word 'AMOR'.

aventail and to coats of plates.

There is a unique survival, now preserved in the Cathedral of St Stanislaus at Krakow, of a fourteenth century basinet found underneath a tree at Sandomir. It had a jewelled crown made of four pieces in the shape of four *fleur-de-lys* which was decorated with 65 semi-precious stones and fitted to the outside of the basinet. In his Chronicles for 1385, Froissart described the crown on the basinet of the King of Castile as being a circlet of worked gold, set with precious stones which were valued at 20,000 francs.

Preserved at Chartres is a basinet which dates to the end of the fourteenth century, complete with its original aventail and probably made for a boy in his mid teens. The patination on this helmet reveals that at one time it was adorned with a crown in the form of four large *fleurs-de-lys* alternating with four small ones. This crown must have been made of very thin sheet metal and was presumably at least gilded, as it was stolen at the time of the French Revolution in 1792.

As in previous centuries, the sword remained the knight's principal weapon, but from the beginning of the century new varieties started to emerge. These were designed either to deliver a very heavy cutting blow or specifically for the thrust, to deal with the ever-increasing weight and robustness of the knight's armour. Long-bladed swords of war with grips of increased length continued to be popular as they were capable of delivering a blow that could shear off a limb, but an intermediate type emerged which was designed both to cut and thrust. This had a double-edged blade which was wide at the shoulders, but which tapered rapidly to a sharp point for thrusting. The exclusive thrusting swords had stiff, sharply tapered blades of diamond section and by 1360 a portion of the blade nearest to the cross-guard was left blunt, forming a ricasso, so that the index finger could be wrapped over the guard to give more control over the point. These swords generally had elongated pommels of fig or scent-bottle shape, which would allow both hands to be used; a hand placed behind the pommel would give extra impetus to a thrust. The falchion continued to be used widely in this period, mainly due to the weight of the cutting blow it could deliver, but very few examples still exist. This may be because during peacetime a falchion would make an excellent cleaver, hedging

Left: The basinet from the child's armour from Chartres Cathedral, c1390. This basinet is of the very highest quality and retains its original aventail, although the vervelles are missing. It originally had decorative brass borders, and the patination reveals that it was also adorned with a crown.

Below: Statue of Cangrande della Scala, who died in 1329.

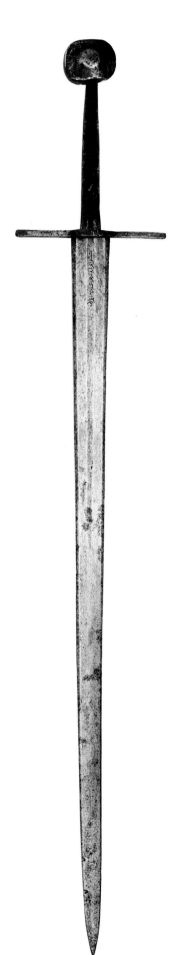

Above: A Great Sword, probably Italian, c 1400.

tool or, indeed, an effective substitute for an axe for cutting wood.

Another characteristic of swords of this period is that they are fitted with flat L-shaped guards just above the cross-guard. This was designed specifically to prevent rain entering the scabbard and rusting the blade. The scabbards themselves continued to be made of wood covered in leather. The Black Prince's scabbard was constructed of red leather sewn over wood and decorated with gilt latten mounts. Unfortunately, the locket and chape are missing, but a sword of similar date, found in the Thames and now in the Museum of London, retains its mounts and gives a clear idea of the form they took.

By the middle of the century, knights are depicted wearing daggers as an accompaniment to the sword. These would appear to have been of three basic forms. The quillon dagger resembled a small sword, usually with a hilt decorated and formed *en suite* with the sword. The ballock dagger, as depicted on the brass of William de Aldeburgh in Aldborough, Yorkshire, had a hilt consisting of a grip, usually of wood, bone or horn, terminating in two kidney-shaped lobes made either of wood, horn or brass, which formed rudimentary quillons. The final form, which appeared later in the century, was the rondel dagger. An early example, dated to the 1350s, appears on an effigy at Clehonger in Hereford, but it is not until the late 1380s that it is commonly illustrated; after 1400 it appears on brasses practically to the exclusion of all other types. It consisted of a blade with a hilt in the form of a grip mounted to either end with a rondel or disk of metal or occasionally wood.

A final type of dagger deserves mention. The baselard was not specifically military but was occasionally found in this context. It had an H-shaped hilt and first appeared about 1370, but continued in use for only about a hundred years. The baselard generally had a longer blade than the other varieties of dagger, and falls almost into the category of a short sword.

At the beginning of the century, as in the thirteenth century, the sword scabbard was hung on the left hip from a broad belt. The buckle end of the belt had been attached to the top of it and the other end about six inches (15cm) below this. However by the late 1350s this was being replaced by a broad and heavy belt worn at hip level and generally decorated

with jewelled and enamelled clasps or rondels hinged together. The belt was presumably laced to the coat armour to prevent it slipping down when the sword and dagger were attached. These were hung from cords or loops attached to their scabbards, the sword being on the left hip and the dagger balancing it on the right.

Besides the sword the knight continued to use the lance, especially when mounted, although, as Froissart records, it was often used in a shortened form on foot, as the French did at Poitiers. By 1300 the lance was about 12 feet (4m) long with a slender steel head. It was fitted with a vamplate (a flat, disc-like hand-guard) and a grapper; when the lance was couched the shaft was gripped between the body and arm, and the grapper would stop it being forced back under the arm. When the lance rest was introduced, the grapper would engage against this instead of merely resting against the armpit. The original shafts would appear to have been made of ash, although Chaucer mentions lances made of cedar wood. The most sought-after steel for lance heads during the fourteenth century was that of Bordeaux. Froissart describes a course run between Jean Boucmel and Nicholas Clifford where they used 'lances well made of Bordeaux steel' and the Englishman's lance head, slipping off his adversary's breastplate, pierced his aventail 'which was made of good mail', entered his neck and cut the jugular vein, thus killing him. In a joust at Badajos in Spain, Froissart furthermore describes Bordeaux lances as piercing the '*pieces d'acier, les plates* and through all the armour right to the flesh.'

In addition to the sword and lance the knight used a number of percussive weapons: the mace, the war hammer and the axe. The mace had been in general use from the twelfth century and early examples are quite often simply bronze heads – either multifaceted, flanged or with a number of projecting studs – fitted onto wooden shafts. However, in the fourteenth century these are increasingly displaced by heavier-flanged steel varieties, capable of inflicting injuries through armour and crushing helmets and body defences. Short war hammers with sharp rear spikes were often carried as a supplementary weapon from the fourteenth century onwards, and a number of skulls from the graves at Wisby exhibit tell-tale square puncture holes, which testify to their effectiveness. War hammers were often illustrated in contemporary illuminations, for example in the Queen Mary Psalter and the *Romance of Alexander*, where they are shown piercing basinets. Froissart recounts the bloody scene at the battle of Roosebeke:

Men at arms set about beating down Flemings lustily. Some had sharp axes with which they split the helms and dashed out brains, others leaden maces with which they inflicted such blows that they felled them to the ground . . . so loud was the clashing of swords, axes, maces and iron hammers on those Flemish basinets that naught else could be discerned above the din.

The axe, which for some time had been relegated to use by the lower orders, once more became popular among the aristocracy and, because of the improvements in the defensive nature of armour, it was often equipped with a long, two-handed shaft to give greater leverage. The axe head was occasionally supplemented by a short rear spike. Such is the weapon that Froissart described at the Battle of Otterburn, where Earl James Douglas 'took a two-handed axe and plunged into the fight . . . none was so well protected by helmet or plate as not to fear the blows he dealt.'

Although not strictly speaking knightly weapons, it is necessary to consider the development of the weaponry of the common soldier, most especially the three types that were responsible for the crushing defeats of the fourteenth century. These were the pike or spear, the especial weapon of the Flemings and Scots respectively, the halberd of the Swiss and the longbow of the English.

The spear had a small diamond-shaped head attached to a long ash shaft of somewhat over 7 feet (2.1m) in length. As the centuries progressed, this shaft was to increase in length until it reached about 16 feet (4.9m), needing both hands to wield it. It was pikes of this length which were so effectively used against cavalry in the fifteenth and sixteenth centuries. The halberd, devastatingly wielded by the Swiss against the Imperial forces at Sempach, consisted of a cleaver-like blade balanced by a rear spike or fluke and topped by a spike. This weapon was said to be capable of splitting a man's head from pate to jaw with one blow even through armour, and a number of the dead from Sempach testify to this most poignantly. This weapon could be used in a number of fashions; the blade could be used for cutting, the spike for

thrusting, and the lug or fluke at the rear was used to hook a knight as he passed and pull him from his mount as an angler might take a fish from a river.

Finally, no survey of fourteenth century weaponry would be complete without mention of the English longbow. This was used as a military weapon in Britain from the Dark Ages to the seventeenth century. It was made of a number of different woods, including elm and ash, but yew was the most favoured. However, so great was the demand that only the best archers were equipped with yew staves and, indeed, for the majority of the reign of Edward III not English yew, but imported Spanish yew. Vast quantities of bow staves were stored in fortresses for use in emergency. So crucial was the supply of wood for bows that in periods of war the makers of pattens (wooden-soled overshoes) were prohibited by law from using bow woods. Not surprisingly, the bow was an expensive item. In the late fourteenth century a painted bow of yew cost one shilling six pence while an unpainted bow cost one shilling (the average daily wage in the latter half of the fourteenth century was between three pence and six pence).

Bow stave bows varied in length from 6 feet (1.82m) to 6 feet 4 inches (1.93m), and had a thick D-section – the back (the edge facing the target) was flat, the belly was rounded. The stave tapered gradually towards either end and was usually tipped with horn nocks. A yarn binding was applied to the middle for about 1 foot (30cm). The bow string itself was of flax or linen and coated with beeswax. When not in use, the bow was stored unstrung in a bag, and the bowstring was commonly kept in the archer's pouch or shirt to keep it dry. The extreme range of a longbow was over 400 yards (365m) and it fired arrows between 30 and 36 inches (76 and 91cm) long. The shafts were made of birch, ash or even oak. They were divided into two types: the heavy sheaf arrow with the deadly bodkin point, or the lightweight flight arrows. Generally goose feathers were used to fletch the arrows. Chaucer mentions arrows with flights of peacock feathers, but an inquest describes a murder weapon as a 'Scottischearewe . . . an ell in length with the red feather of a peacock', so perhaps 'peacock' was used for other birds as well. Experienced archers used bows of upwards of 80 pounds (36kg) pull

Above: The Conyers Falchion, probably English, c1257-72. It has a cleaver-shaped blade; the hilt is cruciform with a straight cross and disc pommel. This is a nearly unique survival of a once-common type of medieval sword.

with an extreme of about 150 pounds (68kg). The secret of success with the longbow was practice, beginning in early childhood and increasing the weight of the bow with age. Compulsory practice was ordered in statute after statute into Elizabethan times.

The *Chronicle of Gerald de Barri* described how a longbow arrow passed through the skirt of a mail hauberk, the gambeson, the chausses beneath that, and pinned the wearer's leg to his saddle. The Chronicler also says that longbow arrows were capable of passing through two inches (5cm) of solid oak. Mail was, in fact, no defence against the heavy bodkin point. The archer usually carried two dozen arrows, and it was a common saying in the Middle Ages that every English archer carried twenty four Scots underneath his belt.

The longbow was rarely used outside England, and in general its position was filled by the crossbow. During the first half of the fourteenth century the most common form of crossbow was fitted with a composite stave of wood, horn and sinew and was spanned with a belt hook as in the thirteenth century. By the mid-fourteenth century the composite bow stave was being replaced by a more powerful one of steel. This needed to be spanned with a mechanical device, either a simple windlass, or a *cranequin* which involved reduction gearing. The arrows used were both shorter and thicker than longbow arrows, and usually had heads of a square section; they were thus called quarrels (a word derived from the French word meaning square, *carré*). Crossbows took longer to load and consequently had a slower rate of fire, but they had a higher penetrative capability. The *Roman de la Rose* described one as 'an arbolast, 'gainst which no armour serves'. The effectiveness of crossbows is borne out by the emergence of armour of proof in the late fourteenth century, which was proved by shooting a crossbow quarrel at it. Crossbows had one great advantage over longbows, they did not need years of constant practice to acquire the necessary skill and strength to use them. As long as a man was capable of standing, he would be able to use a crossbow.

The style of armour in the fourteenth century was predominantly international. However, numerous wills, accounts and inventories attest to the manufacture of weapons in every country of Europe. That

Far left: Five Wallace Collection swords, designed primarily for thrusting. Left, possibly French (1270-1350); second left, European (second half of the fourteenth century); centre, possibly English (late fifteenth century), although similar examples are known to occur in Italy; right, European (about 1380); far right, French (second half of the fourteenth century).

Left: The Westminster Bridge Sword is English and dates to the second quarter of the fourteenth century. It was excavated from the foundations of Westminster Bridge in 1739. The blade is sharply tapered and double-edged, with a hollow diamond section. It has a wheel pommel and slightly arched cross. The silver scabbard mounts are inscribed, 'Wiste I'.

said, as early as 1288 Milan was one of the most active centres of the manufacture of arms and armour, a position which it was to hold for two and a half centuries. In the *Chronicon Extravagans*, Fiamma states that there 'are to be found in our territory huge numbers of artificers who make every type of armour, hauberks, breastplates, helms, gorgets, gauntlets, greaves, cuisses, poleyns, lances and swords, etc. The makers of hauberks alone are 100.' By the fourteenth century Milanese arms were being exported to France and England. Among the armour of Louis X were listed two habergeons and a hauberk of Lombardy and in 1365 Jean de Saffes owned a Lombard sword. Rivalling Milan was Bordeaux, the centre whence came the renowned swords and lance heads so greatly praised by Froissart. As early as the middle of the thirteenth century Henry III of England imported 100 targets and 100 lances made at Bordeaux, for which he paid 40 livres. In Froissart's Chronicles alone there are more than 20 references to the famous swords of Bordeaux. These are described as 'good, light and very stiff'. Sometimes he describes 'short swords' of Bordeaux, but elsewhere he refers to long Bordeaux swords', indicating the manufacture of at least two different varieties. This is corroborated by the will of Sir Thomas Ughtred, dated 1398, in which he bequeathed 'one long and one short Bordeaux sword'. Froissart

records that during the Peasants' Revolt in England in 1381 one Sir Robert Salle of Norwich 'drew a long Bordeaux sword . . . and began cutting and thrusting all round . . . He cut off a foot or a head or an arm or a leg with every stroke.' At the joust at Vannes in 1381 the combatants were armed with 'visor-basinets and glaives of good Bordeaux steel', and the haunted Sir Peter of Béarn was said to have killed a bear with his Bordeaux sword.

Arms and armour were made in several other French towns. The inventory of Louis X listed 17 swords of Bray and 11 of Toulouse, and Chambli, a town near Beauvais, was celebrated for its mail. There was considerable manufacture of helms both in Paris and in Brussels, a fact which Froissart alludes to when speaking of the battle of Roosebeke. There was in fact a Rue de la Heaumerie in Paris.

Throughout the fourteenth century Germany was also producing armour of repute. Thomas Mowbray, Earl Marshal of England, sent to Germany in 1389 for his armour for his abortive duel with the Earl of Derby. Then as now, Germany was famed for the quality of its steel, and from the early thirteenth century Cologne was famous for the manufacture of 'great swords' or swords of war which were highly prized.

There can be no doubt that there were also good armourers in England, and Froissart mentions that there were highly esteemed

Right: An axe head and a mace head, both probably early fourteenth century, found in London.

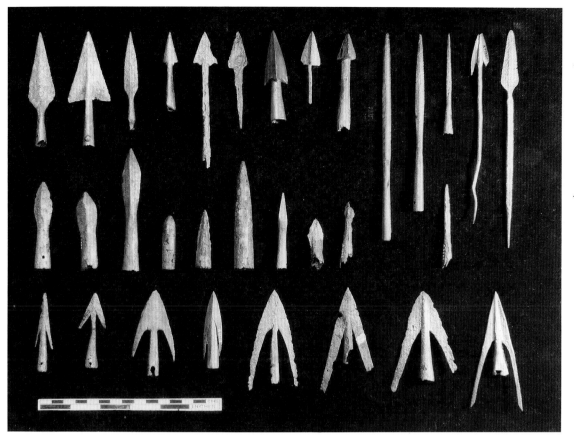

Left: Medieval arrowheads from London, now in the Museum of London. The top row are mostly for the longbow, although those in the centre are usually found on crossbow bolts, like the bodkin types in the middle row. The longbow broad-heads on the bottom row were used for hunting, or in war against horses. The most common 'general purpose' head is the one fourth from left on the bottom row.

Below: The brass of Sir William Bagot, who died in 1407. In Baginton Church, Warwickshire. This brass shows a fully developed fourteenth century armour and has applied decorative borders.

armourers in London. English swords, however, were not highly esteemed, for in 1321 Edward II sent one David le Hope to Paris to learn the secret of the manufacture of swords for battle.

Armour could be bought 'off-the-peg' as well as 'made-to-measure'. The rich could afford to have their armour fitted and elaborately decorated. In 1386 the Duke of Touraine bought three ells of fine linen from Rheims to have a doublet made to serve as a model for a pair of plates. However, we read in the Datini correspondence that, having established himself in Avignon by 1361, Francesco Datini traded widely in arms and armour. An inventory of 1367 lists 45 basinets, three *chapeaux de fer*, ten *cervelières*, 60 breastplates, 20 cuirasses, 12 hauberks of mail, 23 pairs of gauntlets, and so on, which he imported from two Milanese armourers, Basciamuolo of Pescina and Daresruollo of Como. He also assembled the constituent parts of armour and brought large quantities of wire from Milan to Avignon, where he had coats of mail made for him. In 1382, hearing of the rout of a company of free lances in Liguria, he sent his agent in Pisa to Genoa with instructions to buy up as much armour as cheaply as he could for resale on the second-hand market. In 1395 his establish-

ment in Avignon was sending bales of Milanese armour to Barcelona where he considered that they should realize a 15 percent profit. In 1367 the accounts of Leeds Castle, Kent, mentions 'habergeons, bacenettes and pallettes' bought at a fair at Tremhethe in Manor of Charing, near Leeds.

Armour was expensive and only the very rich could afford to keep up with changes in style. Almost to the end of the fourteenth century many knights made do with armour composed mainly of mail, supplemented by a few pieces of plate. Where plate was used, it was forged from billets of metal, which had to be hammered flat by hand or by water-powered tilt hammers. The armour was shaped over stakes or anvils and then polished. It was usually stamped with the mark of the armourer and then individually lined.

The three layers of defence worn by the knight in the fourteenth century – his aketon, his hauberk and his coat of plates – greatly exacerbated the knight's worst enemy, which was not the weight of armour, but exhaustion caused by heat prostration. It was partly to solve this problem, and partly to provide adequate defence against the developing weaponry that the complete 'white armour' of the fifteenth century evolved.

CHAPTER FIVE
Courtesy and Carnage The Fifteenth Century

Right: Sabothai bearing water to King David. Detail of the Heilsspiegelaltar, c1440. This shows a typical German harness of the 1440s. Note the Kastenbrüst breastplate.

Below: A great basinet from Bourg en Besse, c1450. Note the deep fluted brow reinforce.

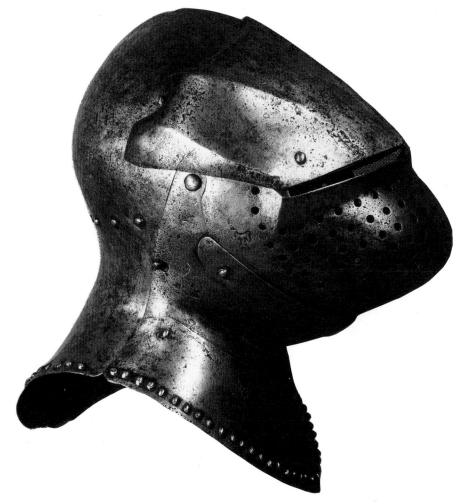

Until the end of the Hundred Years War in 1453, the military might of both England and France had been subsumed in a struggle from which the French were to emerge as a more-or-less professional army. From 1455 until 1485, England was effectively removed from the theatre of European warfare by her internal power struggles of the Wars of the Roses, and for the rest of the century by the Tudors' need to consolidate their regime.

The victories in France and the indenture-contract system of raising troops used by the Crown in the previous century had made the English the premier soldiers of Europe, but by the end of the Hundred Years War England herself was in chaos; the heavy taxes needed to pay for the French adventure had caused violent unrest, and the weakening of royal authority had led to power struggles and rivalry between the great nobles. This weakness led to widespread corruption, especially of the Courts of Law, which meant that the common man could no longer obtain impartial justice. Thus each man turned to his social superior for protection and entered into a contract known as Livery and Maintenance whereby he received the support of his patron in return for his loyalty in both war and peace, and the wearing of his livery.

In this way, the great land owners of England could raise thousands of troops. In 1469 the Duke of Norfolk fielded 3000 men and it is estimated that the Earl of Warwick (The 'Kingmaker') could field between 8000 and 10,000. The situation was only enhanced by the soldiers returning from France who, finding no other employment, were only too happy to take service with a suitable Lord. This system was so widespread that even knights and the lesser nobility contracted themselves to, and wore the livery of, the greater nobility. This system, together with England's virtual isolation from the rest of the Continent, caused the fossilization of the English military system which can be argued to have lasted until the end of the English Civil War.

During the period from the Peace of Tours in 1444 until 1449, Charles VII totally reorganized the armies of France. They were to be led by royal appointees chosen for their military skill and loyalty to the crown and financed by royal taxes raised from the provinces in which they were lodged. Charles forbade the raising of troops without royal licence and by 1445 had created 15 *Compagnies*

d'Ordonnance du Roi to provide a well-equipped mounted force. A further ordinance in 1448 created a permanent force of 8000 infantry but, most importantly, at the same time the royal artillery was reorganized and equipped by the Bureau brothers to become the most advanced in Europe. It was with these troops that Charles was able to defeat the 'English Achilles', John Talbot Earl of Shrewsbury, at the Battle of Chastillon in 1453. So fundamental were these reforms that the French armies were able, nearly half a century later, to effect the invasion of Italy and the conquest of Naples.

This century was also to witness both the meteoric rise to military pre-eminence in Europe of the armies of the Duchy of Burgundy, and their total destruction by the Swiss at the Battle of Nancy in 1476. By his ordinances Charles the Rash, Duke of Burgundy, transformed his army into the most modern in Europe, and it served as a model for the armies of the rest of the Continent for nearly a century. This reorganization into *Compagnies d'Ordonnance*, at first based on the regulations of Charles VII of France, was very detailed and regulated the life of the army in nearly every respect, from pay and equipment to discipline and organization.

In both Switzerland and Bohemia (modern Czechoslovakia) armies composed almost totally of common soldiers were to emerge which were capable of inflicting defeat after defeat upon the still feudally based armies of the Holy Roman Empire. It witnessed the emergence of an independent Swiss Confederation, which saw conflict with the occupying Barons of Austria and Bavaria until the end of the century. In Bohemia there arose a politically motivated religious movement known as the Hussites, the followers of John Huss, a church reformer who was burnt at the stake in 1415. The Hussites aimed to reform the church, by force if necessary, and free Bohemia from the yoke of the Holy Roman Empire. As they could not hope to face the knights of the Emperor in the field, they developed tactics based around the *wagenburg*, a defence similar to the *laager* used in South Africa by the Boers against the Zulus, and in the American West against the Indians of 'drawing the wagons up into a circle'. The Hussite army marched in convoy between two lines of wagons and, whenever threatened by cavalry, simply formed them into a square or circle, chaining them

together and fortifying the gaps. As time progressed specially developed armoured war carts were used, capable of carrying light field pieces. These tactics, used in combination with the increasingly sophisticated firearms of the fifteenth century, met with success after success until 1434.

Throughout the fifteenth century the armies of the various Spanish Kingdoms were either concentrated against the Moors or involved in civil war. It was not until the late fifteenth century, with the uniting of Aragon and Castile by the marriage of Ferdinand and Isabella, that the final reconquest of Granada was attempted. This *reconquista* lasted some ten years, and it was not until 1492, the year of the discovery of America by Columbus, that the Moors were finally expelled from the Iberian Peninsula.

By the fifteenth century the armies of the city states of Italy were mostly *Compagnie de Ventura*, that is *condottieri*. The inter-city wars in Italy were mostly economically based and so, instead of themselves taking arms, the citizens resorted to hiring armies, mostly of heavily armoured cavalry, bound by a *condotta* (contract). Although in the fourteenth century these armies had for the most part been made up of serious fighting men, by the early fifteenth century their confrontations had degenerated into almost hieratic play acting, resulting in little or no loss of life. In the Battle of Zagonara in 1423 there were only three fatalities, and the Battle of Molinella in 1427 resulted in only 300 casualties out of some 20,000 combatants. A major drawback with this system was that while the *condottieri* often had little or no military value, no town could afford to be without them, and so the *condotta* became a self-perpetuating system. The reason for this decline in the military effectiveness of the *condottieri* was that the men of the company represented the captain's capital and therefore any pitched battle could leave him bankrupt. This system was not to be finally eradicated until the end of the century, with the wars of the Borgia Pope Alexander VI and the invasion of Italy by the French.

During the fifteenth century the knight was more and more often confronted by disciplined and better equipped professional soldiers who were armed with a variety of weapons capable of piercing and crushing the best products of the armourer's workshop: the Swiss with their halberds, the English with their bills and long-bows, the French with their glaives and the Flemings with their hand guns. These men were outside the chivalric code and were not considered worthy opponents by the knight; if defeated they were simply cut down. Before the Battle of Agincourt, the Dauphin vowed that he would cut off the right hand of every English archer that he captured and sell their fingers in Rouen at a *sou* (the price of a shirt) apiece. To these men the ideals of chivalry meant little or nothing; their one idea was to defeat their enemy to survive, and from the knight came rich pickings.

The halberd and bill could be used not only to crack plate but to drag a horseman from his saddle, and the use of hand guns provided the final factor in the inevitable process which would render armour obsolete. Gunpowder was to have a similar effect – the knight now stood as much chance of being killed as the ordinary soldier. Gunpowder also helped make the castle obsolete. As the century passed the differences between the arms and armour of the knight and common soldier became less marked, and the richer retainer became almost indistinguishable from the poor knight. The century is marked by the increased use of artillery in the field, and cannon have no respect for rank. Chivalry, when confronted by the reality of death at the hands of a common soldier, could no longer sustain its high ideals and fantasies.

The armies of France had been particularly recalcitrant, although they had three harsh lessons at the hands of the English long-bow-men at Crécy in 1346, Poitiers in 1356, and Agincourt in 1415. These defeats and the subsequent disgrace were a direct result of the failure of the nobility of France to learn from their defeats or to accept the professional foot-soldier as a worthy or even dangerous opponent. It was not until 1437 that Charles VII finally started to raise a more professional army by his *Ordonnance de la Gendarmerie* and abandon the feudal armies based on rank and social status regardless of their military value and necessity.

The fifteenth century saw the reorganization of the armies of France and Burgundy into national and professional fighting forces laid down through ordinances which regulated the life of the army from its composition and armament to its pay, organization and discipline. In the Burgundian army the

Above: A north Italian sallet, c1460. It was probably made for the export market.

Below: A German sallet, c1450 from Rhodes. Now in the Royal Armouries, HM Tower of London.

and dealt with such matters as the plundering of the church or citizens, obedience to officers, divisions of spoils and prisoners, lodgings or the offence of Crying Havoc (no quarter) without orders. Infringement of many of these statutes or ordinances was on pain of death. The least punishment meted out seems to have been the confiscation of harness and horse. At the end of the century the increasing number of Swiss and German mercenaries, the Landesknechts, used in Europe also hastened the end of the chivalric code of honour since they invariably fought without quarter, took no prisoners and slaughtered commoners and nobles alike. Charles the Rash was cut down at the Battle of Nancy and left on the field. His body was found two days later; his head had been split in two by a halberd cut and his body had been stripped and preyed upon by wolves and crows – no consideration of his rank or of the ransom to be had had stayed the hand of the halberdier.

As the ideals of chivalry found less place on the battlefield, they were transferred to the tourney field, and as the reality of warfare became more brutally apparent, the myth of chivalry grew.

Increasingly, the nobility and kings of Europe competed in the opulent splendour of their orders of chivalry, and in following the illusory tenets of the chivalric code. That this code had no practical application in warfare is shown by the fact that even Henry V of England, remembered as one of the most chivalrous and honourable Kings, was content to allow the women and children of Rouen to starve between the city walls and his siege lines, and through military necessity to slay unarmed prisoners at Agincourt.

The internecine struggles in fifteenth century England, known as the Wars of the Roses, produced instances of totally unchivalric behaviour such as Edward IV's violation of the sanctuary of Tewkesbury Abbey after the Battle there in 1471, the wholesale 'heading' of the defeated nobility and virtual vendettas between families. For instance, Lord Clifford was killed at the first Battle of St Albans in 1455 by the Duke of York. Five years later, at the Battle of Wakefield, the Duke of York and his son the Earl of Rutland, a boy of 17, were killed. The Earl of Rutland had fallen into the hands of the then Lord Clifford and on his bended knees begged for mercy. Clifford stabbed him to

Ordinance of Abbeville, dated 31 July 1471, removed the distinction between *Chevalier Baronets*, *Chevalier Bacheleurs* and *Ecuyères*, all men at arms being now paid the same regardless of social status. Discipline was strictly enforced in many armies, especially in the army which Henry V took to France for the Agincourt campaign for which he laid down no less than 34 ordinances. These have been preserved in the *Blacke Booke of the Admiralty*

death and is reported by the sixteenth century chronicler, Hall, to have said as he did so: 'By God's blood, thy father slew mine, and so will I do thee and all thy kin!' The fifteenth century was to witness the final divorce of the romance and theory of knighthood from the cold reality of war.

With the beginning of the fifteenth century comes the emergence of complete 'white armours' and this in turn heralds the extinction of an 'international style' in armour. From this point armour production and design is dominated by two geographically and stylistically separate schools: that of Northern Italy, centred on Milan, and that of Germany. These styles were so all-embracing that they seemed to have totally eclipsed any local schools.

The most important centres for the manufacture of armour in Germany throughout the fifteenth century were Augsburg, Nuremburg, Landshut and, latterly, Innsbruck. The basinet and kettle hat remained popular with German knights during the first half of the century. The great basinet was worn from 1420 at the very latest but was generally smaller and more closely shaped to the skull than those in use in the rest of Europe. The back of the skull and the rear gorget plate were either made in one piece or riveted together. At the front, a similar plate encasing the front of the head and face was pivoted to the back plate. Attached to this front plate was an internal bevor reaching to the wearer's nose. The visor was of a rounded, snout-like form and was detachable by means of the usual pin and hinge arrangement. The pivots, as well as these hinges, were occasionally protected by applied plate rondels.

The basinet illustrated in the *Heilsspeigelaltar* in the Kunstmuseum, Basel, which dates to 1440, has a moderately pointed skull which is closely formed to the wearer's neck, and a deep rear gorget plate. It has a projecting bevor and a rounded visor with horizontal vision slits and circular breaths. At the side are rondels to protect the pivots. While the armet (a term used by scholars to denote a type of visored, close-fitting helmet which has hinged cheekpieces which fasten at the chin and form most of the lower portion of the helmet) was extremely popular with the Italian armourers, it hardly, if ever, seems to have been worn with harnesses of German manufacture.

The kettle hat was an extremely popular alternative to the basinet during the early fifteenth century. It was invariably made of one piece, and the brim was often drawn down all around. Where the brim was turned down evenly, eye slits were cut into it, and in this form the kettle hat was accompanied by a bevor to protect the lower part of the wearer's face. These kettle hats originally had a bell-shaped crown but by 1440 they had developed a low keel-like comb. However, from about 1470 some spirally fluted bowls appear.

Another form of helmet that was common on German armours was the sallet. This appears to have derived from one of the many forms of fourteenth century basinet, and first appeared in Italy as early as 1407, where it was known as a *celata*. From there it was introduced into France and Burgundy by about 1420, reaching England and the rest of Western Europe about a decade later. The original Italian *celatas* were rarely equipped

Above: A German sallet, c 1450-60. It was forged in one piece with a central ridge and long tail.

Below: A German 'black sallet', c 1490, with painted decoration.

Above: A German sallet, made in Innsbruck, c1495. It has a laminated neckguard and visor pivoted high on the skull.

Devil. These sallets were described as 'black' simply because they were left rough from the hammer and were not ground and polished, but they were sometimes decorated, either by being covered in cloth or painted with heraldic designs, as is an example from the Royal Armouries. This type of sallet had an extremely deep skull, with a central ridge which extended from the base of the skull to the point of its very long tail. The skull was bulbous and almost flat-topped, and the bottom ended in a deep convex curve without a turn. It was equipped with a small flat visor pivoted high on the skull with a spring stud on the right-hand side to lock the visor in position. The other form of sallet had a short, laminated neck guard and a bowl modelled to the head, and was equipped with a visor that covered the whole of the wearer's face, making the use of a bevor unnecessary.

Throughout the fifteenth century the sallet, especially in northwest Europe, was accompanied by a bevor. The bevor was a cup-shaped plate shaped to the wearer's chin which covered the front of the face, usually to just below or just above the nose, and was fitted with one or more gorget plates. On German armours these plates were invariably pointed and extended over the top of the breastplate. Bevors were sometimes fitted with a pivoted lame which could be raised or lowered to uncover or cover the lower face and which was often equipped with a spring clip to hold it in place. The bevor was held in place by a strap which passed round the back of the wearer's neck, and fastened either at centre back or at one side of the bevor.

The body defences were at first influenced by those of Italy, and until 1420 there was little to distinguish the German cuirass from those of the rest of Europe. But in 1420 a new type of breastplate appeared, known today as the *Kastenbrust*. This was boxed in appearance, and the top of the breastplate sloped outwards and downwards from the chest, angling in sharply to the waist to form a deep undercut. The *Kastenbrust* was fitted with a stop rib below the neck, a lance rest on the right hand side and a deep, hooped fauld, and was often decorated with radiating flutes. This was to be the characteristic German breastplate until the second half of the fifteenth century.

Shortly after the appearance of the *Kastenbrüst* a one-piece back plate decorated *en suite* with a deeply hooped culet also

with visors, but those common in Western Europe were at first short-tailed and visored, with deep, rounded bowls. This visored form found little favour in Italy, but was extensively copied by Italian armourers for export. At first the lower edge of the visor reached only far enough just to cover the wearer's nose, yet the tail reached almost to the shoulders. By 1450 the depth of the bowl had been reduced to the same level as that of the visor; it was shaped to the head and nape of the neck, finishing in a medium-length tail, and provided with a prominent keel-shaped central ridge. It was equipped either with a half visor and a cusped reinforce for the brow, or with a full visor which covered the front of the skull.

The typical German form of sallet probably evolved from a combination of the native German kettle hat and the Franco-Burgundian development of the Italian *celata*. Sallets were rare in Germany until 1460 and at first were of the typical form used in the rest of Western Europe. The German form was generally larger and deeper than the earlier types, with a long tail sloping downwards at the rear, and can be divided into two distinct groups: either with a small, half visor which formed a sight between its upper edge and the outwardly turned edge of the helmet itself; or, finally, made in one piece with a slit for the eyes.

By about 1490 two new types of sallet had appeared in Germany. One type is the so-called 'black sallet', depicted in Dürer's famous copperplate *Knight, Death and the*

appeared. These at first fastened to the breast plate by hinges on the left and straps on the right, like Italian armours, but this system was later replaced by a waist belt and straps and buckles at the shoulder. In about 1450 the breast plate became flatter, with a medial ridge, and the fauld became shallower; the cuirass ended at the waist and overlapped a deep waist lame. This plate itself was overlapped by the fauld.

By 1460 a new type of breastplate, exhibiting a new type of construction, had started to appear. It was made in two pieces – an upper breastplate and a low plackart flanged at the waist. To this flange was attached a fauld, which overlapped the breastplate and was attached to it by a system of sliding rivets. From this period the stylistic tendency in German armour manufacture was to produce long, gracile forms, emphasized by fluting and cusped decoration to the main edges. The waist became very slender and the fauld barely covered the hips; this was often, but not always, accompanied by one-piece spade-shaped tassets to guard the top of the thighs. The back plate consisted of an upper plate and a plate to defend the join of the base of the neck and shoulders, riveted to the inside of the upper plate. This back plate overlapped a deep waist lame, to which was attached a culet of three overlapping lames. At the rear the culet sloped to form a tail-like projection. This type of armour typifies the high German Gothic and lasted until the end of the century. Perhaps the most well-known examples are two armours made by Lorenz Helmschmied in the Waffensammlungen, Vienna, for the Archdukes Sigismund the Wealthy of the Tyrol and Maximilian (later Holy Roman Emperor). Both armours are fluted and cusped and have applied brass borders at their main edges and shell-like piercings at their subsidiary borders. The breastplates have two plackarts and a short fauld, which reaches only to the hips. These armours were designed for use without tassets.

Shortly before the last decade of the century one-piece breast and back plates made a reappearance. These were manufactured chiefly by the smiths of Innsbruck and had waist flanges to which the culet and fauld were riveted.

From about 1420 the German knight would have worn simple laminated spaudlers, consisting of a domed plate for the point

of the shoulder, supporting a number of laminations down the arm. Below these were worn simple gutter-shaped upper and lower cannons joined by leather straps, and a moderately sized shell-shaped couter which was laced to the arming doublet. These were accompanied by a besagew to protect the gap between arm harness and breastplate and remained in common use until the second half of the next century. From about 1450 onwards it was common for the spaudler to be riveted to the upper cannon.

At this time appeared a type of shoulder defence where the main plate of the spaudler was enlarged to wrap round the front and back of the armour, to form a rudimentary pauldron. After about 1470 this became more Italian in its form: the rear portions were enlarged to form wing-like projections and, in the last quarter of the century, gard-braces (extra external plates attached to the front of the pauldrons) appeared. The upper edges of these plates were sometimes flanged to provide low haut pieces to protect the neck. The very simple vambrace consisting of gutter-shaped upper and lower cannons and couter,

Above: A German bevor (chin piece), for wear with a sallet, made in Landshut by Matthes Deutsch, c1480. It has a pivoted upper lame retained by a spring catch.

Left: The armour of Archduke Sigismund of Tyrol, by Lorenz Helmschmied of Augsburg, c1480. This armour represents the apogée of the armourers' art, and is typical of the late German Gothic with its fluted surfaces and gracile lines.

all attached by points to the arming doublet, was extremely popular. It was known in England as a 'splint', and was often worn by the common soldier of the period. However, by the 1470s expensive armours commonly had closed upper and lower cannons, with an enlarged couter which was extended to cover the bend of the elbow and often drawn out to form quite a sharp point over the joint of the elbow.

To complete his arm defences the German knight wore gauntlets. Until about 1430 these had been of the typical hour-glass form of the fourteenth century, but at this time a new form made its appearance: this was a mitten gauntlet with a one-piece main plate

Far left: Saint George and the Dragon by Roger Van der Weyden, Flemish, c1432. It shows the saint wearing a German armour, c1432, with a Kastenbrust breastplate with a deeply hooped fauld.

*Far right: An Italian armet,
probably Milanese, c1500. It is
composed of five parts; the skull,
a brow reinforce, the visor and the
cheekpieces.*

*Far right, above: The same armet
with its visor open, showing how
the cheekpieces fix together at the
front.*

which was shaped to the base of the thumb
and had a slight bend along the line of the
knuckles, or occasionally an articulation.
Although this gauntlet was designed to protect the back of the hand, it had a narrow
plate encircling the wrist, and the thumb and
occasionally the fingers were protected by
small laminations riveted to leather strips. In
conjunction with the High Gothic styles of
armour, the gauntlet form also underwent a
metamorphosis to produce a long, narrow
outline. The wrist plate was embossed for the
ulna, and the main defence for the back of the
hand consisted of separate laminations and
terminated in a spiked knuckle piece. The
cuff was sharply pointed and there was a
separate thumb defence hinged to the main
body. The whole gauntlet was fluted with
ribs, as were the finger lames to define the
fingers. Occasionally gauntlets had separate
fingers, as on the armour of Archduke Sigismund. By the end of the century, a variety
had appeared with a cuff so long that it
reached the elbow, where it was attached to
the arming doublet with a point.

The leg harness was late in developing a
distinctive German character. By 1430 an
additional articulated plate had been added to
the top of the concave upper plate of the
cuisse, and the hinged side extensions
divided vertically. The cuisse was articulated
to the poleyn by a single lame; the poleyn
itself had small, fan-shaped side wings. The
greaves, over which the poleyns were
strapped, remained virtually unchanged
throughout the century and the leg defence
was completed by sabatons of graduated,
curved lames, lying horizontally down the
front of the foot and ending in a sharply
pointed toe cap. The fluted decoration of the
1460s was also applied to the cuisses,
although never to the greaves. From 1460 the
cuisses themselves were extended upwards
by increasing the number of laminations, and
those armours made by Helmschmied
around 1480 have cuisses which extend to the
hip and obviate the necessity for tassets. By
this point, in accordance with contemporary
German fashion, the pointed toes of the sabatons had become so exaggerated that additional pieces were added which could be
removed for fighting on foot.

The other great centre for armour manufacture in the fifteenth century, and indeed
perhaps the most important in terms of
volume, was Italy, especially Lombardy, and

in Lombardy the most important of all was the great city of Milan. Throughout the four-teenth century there are references in English and French texts to Italian armours, espe-cially those of Milan. It was to Milan that in 1389 the Earl of Derby, afterwards Henry IV, sent messengers to Gian-Galeazzo Visconti, to request an armour for his projected duel with Thomas Mowbray; as well as supplying this armour, Visconti sent four of the best armourers in Lombardy to arm the Earl. Per-haps the most famous family of merchant armourers of Milan was the Negroni da Ello detto Missaglia.

Italian armours were worn widely throughout Europe and in fact gained more popularity than did those of Germany, from which they differed in a number of very im-portant ways. Instead of the attenuated 'Gothic' lines favoured by the German crafts-men, the Italian armourers produced much plainer, more rounded designs which gave their armour a utilitarian and robust appear-ance. This impression was heightened by the fact that the armours were more heavily defended on the left side. The basinet was rarely, if ever, seen in Italy after 1420, nor was the kettle hat ever popular. Those that were used were of the variety with the brim bent down all round, with a keel-shaped comb. These were often covered with cloth but were used for the most part by the com-mon infantryman and were rarely, if ever, worn with bevors.

The two most important types of helmet manufactured in Italy were the armet and the *celata* or sallet. The armet was derived from the basinet and consisted of a one-piece hemispherical skull truncated at the level of the tops of the ears except at the rear, where there was a narrow tail of steel shaped to the head extending as far as the nape of the neck. Cheek pieces were shaped to the wearer's jaw and lower face and fastened at the chin by a stud. They were hinged to the lower edge of the skull and overlapped the central strip at the back. The resulting face opening was closed by a pivoted visor, which was detach-able and bluntly pointed and passed over the sides of the cheek pieces.

The early form of armet was equipped with vervelles around the base for the attach-ment of a mail aventail. By the early 1440s, the skull had developed a slight medial ridge and a cusped brow reinforce had been added. At the rear projected a short stem to which

Far right: An Italian celata (sallet), second half of the fifteenth century.

Right: A pair of German mitten gauntlets, c1490, made in Landshut. Now in the Royal Armouries, HM Tower of London.

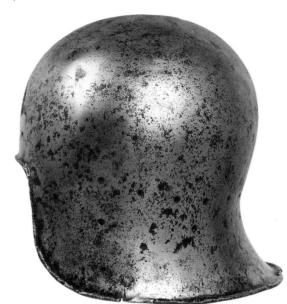

was riveted a rondel of steel. The sight was formed by the turned edge of the top of the face opening and the turned edge at the top of the visor. The stem and rondel at the rear of the helmet were probably intended to support and protect a strap for an additional defence for the front of the helmet, known as a 'wrapper'. This covered the lower half of the chin and visor and was notched on its right side for the visor's lifting peg. The wrapper was fitted with two or more gorget plates and extended onto the chest. After 1460 the ridge of the armet became more pronounced to form a keel-shaped comb and the mail aventail, where worn, was now riveted to the helmet with a steel strip. Cheek pieces became increasingly shaped to the line of the jaw. The armet was to remain popular well into the sixteenth century.

The other form of helmet commonly used in Italy, and which was perhaps even more widespread abroad, was the *celata*. There are two types referred to in contemporary documents: the *celata* itself and the *barbuta*. The terms are used quite indiscriminately and in fact these helmets are almost indistinguishable except in the shape of their face openings. Both had rounded skulls with a keel-shaped comb, were fitted to the nape of the neck, and had an everted edge at the rear. They reached almost to the shoulders at the back and sides. The face openings differed in that the *celata* had a wide, arched face opening while the *barbuta* had a T-shaped opening, often bordered by an applied stop rib. However, examples of *barbutas* in the form of the classical Greek Corinthian helmet are

quite common. The Venetian sallets found at Chalkis, which are constructed of two pieces, would seem to derive from this. The *barbuta* itself does not seem to have survived the 1470s, and by 1480 a new form of *celata* had started to appear, which had a laminated neck guard and a brow reinforce like the armet. Finally, another form appeared in the

Right: The Garter Portrait of Frederigo di Montrefeltro, Duke of Urbino, attributed to Pietro Berguete. It shows the Duke wearing full armour with his armet, fitted with its wrapper, at his feet.

closing years of the century. This was fitted with what is known as a 'bellows visor', which enclosed the whole face.

From the early years of the century until around 1420 the full 'White Armour' in Italy was slowly evolving. An example preserved at Churburg, which dates to about 1420, consists of a globular breastplate which reaches to the waist and is overlapped by a plackart attached by straps and buckles and carrying an internally leathered fauld of three lames. On the right side it has four staples to which the lance rest is attached, and just below the neck is the usual stop rib. The back plate is composed of an upper and lower plate and a culet, and is strapped to the breastplate at the shoulder and waist.

As early as 1425 the centre of the lowest lame of the fauld was cut into an arch which, by 1430, was divided in two to form rudimentary tassets. These were matched by a rump guard leathered to the base of the culet. From about 1440 the tassets were triangular or spade-shaped, and small side tassets were used to supplement them. After about 1425 the cuirass was hinged on its left and fastened by straps on its right, and the lower back plate and enlarged plackart were suspended by a single strap and buckle. In the second half of the century the plackart had expanded to reach just below the neck and became wider and wider until 1490, when it almost totally covered the breastplate. From then on it was increasingly replaced by a single-piece breastplate.

One of the main differences between Italian and German harnesses was the form of the arm defences, in particular the use of pauldrons. Until the 1420s, the main shoulder defence was generally mail, but by the end of the second decade of the century laminated pauldrons appear for the left arm, with a smaller one being worn on the right arm. Large pauldrons remained in use throughout the fifteenth century, but became more rounded after 1440 and spread out across the wearer's back to overlap. As early as 1420 gard braces or reinforcing plates were added to the pauldrons; at first these were circular but later followed the contours of the pauldrons and were attached by staples and a pin. The upper edges of the pauldrons were flanged to form haut pieces to protect the neck. On the whole, vambraces on Italian armour defended much more of the arm than did the German variety, and by 1430 the

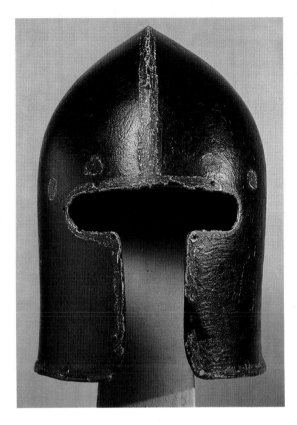

Left: Milanese barbuta, c1445. It has been painted black and the edges, rivets and ridge have been painted white.

upper cannon almost encircled the arm, and the side wing on the right couter had been enlarged and extended over the elbow joint to defend the tendons. The left couter itself was supplemented by a large shell-shaped guard attached by a staple and pin. The lower cannons were hinged and strapped together. At first they were tulip-shaped but after 1450 this was less accentuated. The upper and lower cannons and couters were articulated

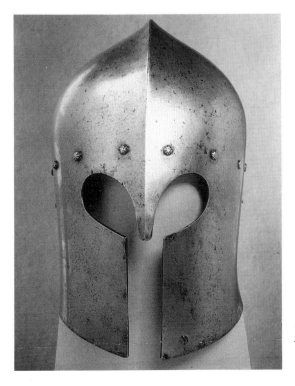

Left: An Italian barbuta, probably Milanese, c1445. This form of helmet closely resembles the Corinthian helmets of Classical Antiquity.

Right: An Italian sallet with a deep skull and bellows visor, Milanese, c 1500.

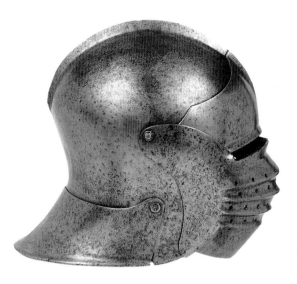

Below: Part of the Rout of San Romano *by Paolo Uccello, c1450. Niccolò Mauruzi da Tolentino (in the centre foreground, carrying a commander's baton) leads the Florentines in their victory over the Sienese in 1432. Note the shattered lances and discarded pieces of armour strewn upon the ground.*

by rivets and ·small laminated plates, and fastened to the arming doublet. The pauldrons were put on over the vambraces and buckled round their upper edges and then laced to the arming doublet near the neck. As in the rest of Europe, hour-glass gauntlets were worn until about 1420, but by 1440 mitten gauntlets had totally superceded them. The metacarpal or main plate extended as far as the fingertips; the right gauntlet was articulated twice over the fingers and once over the wrists, but the left only over the fingers. The cuffs of these gauntlets were at first rounded but became leaf-shaped as the century progressed.

Right: An Italian mitten gauntlet for the left hand, Milanese, c1470.

As with the rest of the armour, the leg harness demonstrated little development before 1420. At this date the top of the cuisse became concave and its upper edge was turned outwards. It still retained its hinged side extensions, which were vertically divided. From the third decade of the fifteenth century an additional top plate was inserted, which had a convex top with a strong outward turn. The poleyn was articulated to the cuisse by a single lame and from very early in the century was accompanied by a mail fringe attached to its bottom lame. In addition, from this time the side wings of the poleyn were enlarged and curved into the back of the

leg to protect the tendons. This curve was given a V-shaped flute or pucker, thus producing what is regarded as the typical Italian form. After about 1450, the lame below the poleyn became pointed unless it was to be worn with the fringe of mail, and a number of Italian leg defences survive that were never intended to be worn with greaves. The greave, however, changed hardly, if at all, in the fifteenth century and the leg defence was most commonly completed by a mail covered shoe.

Besides producing armours of an entirely Italian nature for export, the Italian armourers produced vast numbers of armours, basically of Italian form, but with certain variations in detail; for example the armour from Swabischgemund in the Heilegenkreuzkirch has a breastplate with two plackarts riveted rather than strapped into position, with cusped upper edges like those on armours produced by Helmschmeid. It has arm defences of Italian form but with a degree of fluted decoration, and is completed by a German style bevor and sallet. Its back plate is constructed in a typically Germanic fashion and its tassets are fluted.

Above: St George and the Dragon *by Friedrich Herlin, c1460. St George is wearing a typical Italian 'export armour'.*

Right: The great helm of Henry V, c1422, forming part of his funerary achievement.

Far right: An armour belonging to a member of the Von Match Family, Milanese, c1450, from Schloss Churburg.

Ghent and Tournai) under the protection of the Dukes of Burgundy, or by local armourers working in the Italian style. The plates of these armours were usually fluted, sometimes cusped and rather spiky after the fashion of Germany, but the pauldrons, tassets and couters are of Italian form, as in the painting of St George by Friedrich Herlin in the Statdmuseum, Nordling, or in the Caesar Tapestries in the Bern Historical Museum. Armours of this type are commonly depicted in English monumental effigies from the middle of the century and may either represent English-made armours, or imported Flemish products. It was in armours such as these or armours of a purely Italian fashion that the nobility of England fought and died in the Wars of the Roses. This is confirmed in a letter written to Sir John Paston on 28 August 1473 by one Martin Rondelle, who signed himself as *Armurier de Monsire le Bastart de Bourgogne*, written from Bruges, where he discussed '*unne armura de unna sella . . . et . . . una barbuta*' in which the said John Paston was interested. Martin could not state prices until he had further details of his customer's requirements but, in the fashion of salesmen everywhere, assured him that he would be only too happy to pay for the quality of work he would receive. Whether this transaction was completed is not known, but on 10 August 1483 Lord Howard paid six shillings and fourpence to the 'armerer of Flanders apon his leger harnes'.

Throughout the fifteenth century English knights wore armours which followed

Throughout the fifteenth century the Italians supplied sallets to the rest of Europe. These took the form of *celatas* with full visors. At first the lower edge of these visors reached only halfway down the face opening, but by 1450 sallets were being made in a shallower form so that the lower edge of the visor was level with the lower edge of the sallet.

The trade routes from Germany and Italy met in Flanders. Here one finds armours being produced of a hybrid form blending aspects of both Germanic and Italian armours, much like the armour from Swabischgemund mentioned above. These were probably made by Italian armourers who are known to have been working in Flanders (especially in Antwerp, Bruges, Brussels,

Right: The brass of Sir Peter Halle and his wife, c1430, in Herne Church, Kent.

Italian fashion in many respects. Monumental brasses of the first three decades of the century show one-piece breastplates ending at the waist with a deep fauld of six or more lames, matched at the rear by a similarly formed back plate and culet. These were accompanied by the great basinet, and arm harness very similar to that of the end of the fourteenth century with the addition of a besagew. The wings of the couter and poleyn were either heart-shaped, or fluted and shaped rather like a cockle shell. These armours are typical of those worn at the Battle of Agincourt.

By the 1440s English wills and inventories commonly mentioned imported armours, most especially from Lombardy; a fine example is depicted by the effigy of Richard Beauchamp, Earl of Warwick, in St Mary's Church, Warwick. This is cast in latten and was made about 1450. The contract for its manufacture states that it was 'armed according to patterns', but even this has a number of flutes in the Germanic style. Throughout the rest of the century, English armours, although generally Italianate, showed a

desire for certain Germanic features; for instance, besagews were commonly worn and couters were often symmetrical and attached by points in the Germanic fashion. The plackarts of the breastplates were invariably riveted rather than strapped on, and it was common to wear the tassets of the armour riveted halfway up the fauld. The poleyns had heart-shaped wings, smaller than their Italian counterparts.

Up until the 1450s it was very common for the English knight to continue to wear the great basinet and indeed depictions of the armet are rare, although Richard Beauchamp's effigy is equipped with one. From 1450 the most common form of helmet in England was the sallet. These often have a high, pointed skull and a brow reinforce, as does the St Mary's sallet at Coventry.

In addition, English armour, typified by the effigies of Sir William Harcourt in Aston Church, the FitzHerberts in Norbury Church, and Lord Hungerford in Tewkesbury Abbey, includes a gauntlet that was certainly not mainstream Italian. This had a long pointed cuff, articulated to two or three

Below: A reconstruction of an Italian armour, c1450, based on the Churburg armour in the Scott Collection, Glasgow.

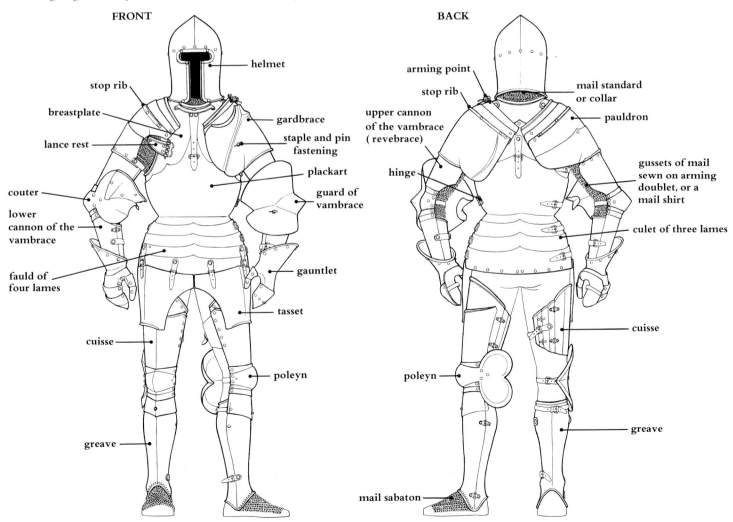

FRONT

helmet
stop rib
breastplate
lance rest
couter
lower cannon of the vambrace
fauld of four lames
cuisse
greave

gardbrace
staple and pin fastening
plackart
guard of vambrace
gauntlet
tasset
poleyn

BACK

arming point
stop rib
upper cannon of the vambrace (revebrace)
hinge
poleyn
mail sabaton

mail standard or collar
pauldron
gussets of mail sewn on arming doublet, or a mail shirt
culet of three lames
cuisse
greave

113

Above: The Coventry sallet, c1460, possibly English.

Right: The gilt-bronze effigy of Richard Beauchamp, Earl of Warwick, c1450 (after Stothard). The Earl wears a Milanese harness, typical of those worn in the early part of the Wars of the Roses.

Centre right: The tomb effigy of Sir William Harcourt, who died in 1482. This armour exhibits a number of features particular to armours worn in England. In Aston Church, West Midlands.

Far right: The brass of Sir Anthony Grey who died in 1485. In St Albans Cathedral, England.

heavy lames which protected the fingers. These were often ridged to delineate the fingers and were worn over bare hands or leather gloves. The lame nearest the fingers was embossed for the thumb, which was itself protected by a small lamination. This was often worn with a reinforcing plate strapped to the left hand, as is shown on the effigy of John Fitzalan, Lord Maltravers, Earl of Arundel, which dates to around 1435. Presumably it is gauntlets of this style that Duke Philip the Good of Burgundy commissioned in 1438, describing them as of the 'façon d'Angleterre' (in the English fashion).

Although the bulk of fifteenth century armour that has survived is said to be Italian or German, a number of national centres within other European countries were still producing armour. For instance, Tours and Lyons in France had, by the fifteenth century, superceded Bordeaux. However, the armourers working for the French King appear to have been Italians and the armour produced in these centres followed mainstream Italian fashion. In Spain there were a number of important armour-producing centres; in Burgos and Seville the cuirass and pauldrons on a number of armours were constructed of plates riveted to a cloth covering (that is, of 'brigandine work'), and a special form of kettle hat, known as a *cabacete*, was favoured by all warriors. It had an almond-shaped skull with a small stalk at its apex and a turned-down brim which curved up at the front and back to form a point. This was accompanied by a special prow-shaped type of bevor known as a *barbote* which had a pivoted lame at its upper edge with horizontal sights cut for the eyes; bevor and lame together enclosed the face.

Throughout the fifteenth century the knight wore a padded garment beneath his armour. This was a development of the aketon known as the 'arming doublet'. Unfortunately no undoubted examples survive from the fifteenth century and what form these garments actually took is open to debate. However, it would seem likely that they were similar in many ways to the extant linings in a number of fifteenth century pieces of armour which are made of quilted linen and padded with tow, wool or some other similar stuffing. These were long-sleeved garments, probably with a collar, which reached to just below the hip, depending on the type of armour with which they

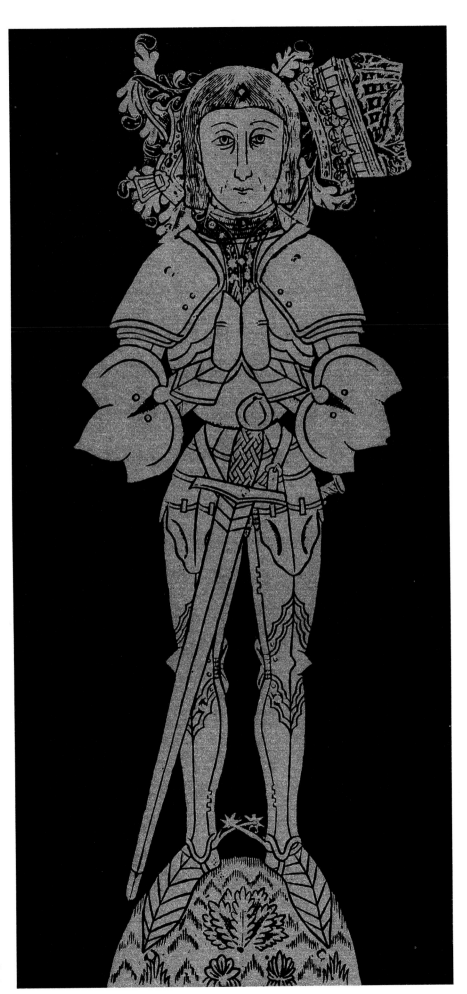

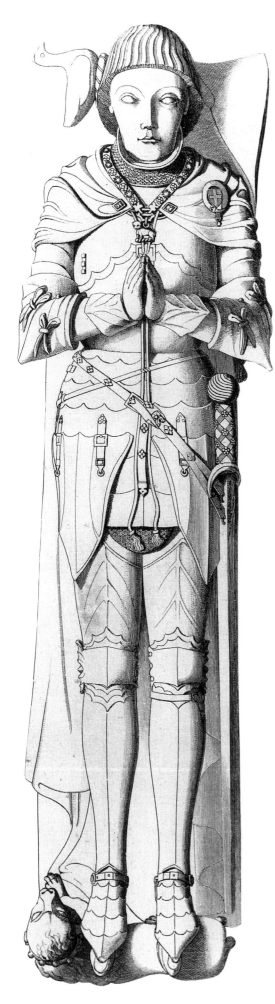

were to be worn. An English manuscript, now in the Pierpont Morgan Library and dated to the mid-fifteenth century, describes 'how a man schall be armyd at his ese when he schal fighte on foote'. The garment is described as being of fustian lined with satin and cut full of holes, and the points by which the mail and body armour were attached were of fine twine, waxed so they would not stretch or break. Since this is such an excellent description, it seems worthwhile quoting in full:

He schal have noo schirte up on him but a dowbelet of ffustean lyned with satene cutte full of hoolis. The dowbelet must be strongeli boude there the pointis muste be sette aboute the greet [bend] of the arm and the b ste [sic] before and behynde and the gussetis of mayle muste be sowid un to the dowbelet in the bought of the arme and undir the arme the armynge poyntis muste ba made of fyne twyne suche as men make stryngys for crossebowes and they muste be trussid small and poyntid as poyntis. Also they muste be wexid with cordeweneris coode, and than they will neyther recche nor breke. Also a payr hosyn of stamyn sengill and a payre of shorte bulwerkis of thynne blanket to put about the kneys for chawfynge of his lighernes. Also a payre of shone of thikke Cordwene and they muste be frette with smal whipcorde thre knottis up on a corde and thre cordis muste be faste swoid on to the hele of the shoo and fyne cordis in the mydill of the soole of the same shoo and that ther be betwene the frettis of the hele and the frettis of the mydill of the shoo the space of three fungris.

From inventories or letters of this date it is obvious that the knight and the great nobles vied in covering their arming doublets in fine, rich materials. In a letter written from Calais by Sir John Paston to his brother John in the year 1473, he says, 'I praye yow sende me a newe vestment off whyght damaske . . . I wyll make an armyng doblett off it, thow I sholde an other tyme gyff a longe gown of velvett ffor another vestment.'

Left: An incised tomb slab of a Burgundian noble, Sir Dierick Van Der Merwede, from Brabant, Holland.

Far left: The tomb effigy of Sir Robert Harcourt KG, who died in 1471. In Stanton Harcourt Church, Oxfordshire.

Right: The brass of a French knight and his wife, c1421, from St Alpen Châlons sur Marne, France.

Right: 'How a Man Schall be Armyd at his ese when he schal fighte on foote.' This English manuscript, c1450, shows a knight being armed for combat.

From about 1430 it became increasingly rare for a complete habergeon of mail to be worn under armour; instead small pieces were attached by points to the arming doublet. These usually consisted of a standard or standing collar of mail, voiders or gussets which covered the armpits, elbow joints or complete sleeves, and a skirt which could reach anywhere from the top of the thighs almost to the knees, most especially in Italy where mail often extended far beneath the armour. It was also a common practice in Italy for the gussets or sleeves of mail to be worn under the pauldrons, yet over the upper cannons of the vambraces. In Germany the skirts of mail were often replaced by mail breeches shaped like a pair of modern boxer shorts.

Although brigandines had first appeared in the latter part of the fourteenth century, by the mid-fifteenth they were extremely common and worn by all classes of soldier. From Lord Howard's Household Accounts for the years 1461-70 it is clear that the majority of his retainers and tenants were issued with brigandines from his own personal armoury and in fact even the very highest in the land wore them, often in preference to plate as they were lighter and much more flexible. The Scottish kings of the fifteenth century imported French craftsmen skilled in the manufacture of brigandines, and even emperor Maximilian I commissioned a brigandine by one Bernardino Cantoni of Milan. In 1465 one J Payne wrote to John Paston (as heir of Sir John Fastolf) requesting reparation for losses he had suffered while engaged upon Fastolf's business during the Cade Rebellion in 1450. The 'commons' had gone to his lodgings at the White Hart in Southwark in south London, and had taken, among other goods, 'i. (one) peyr of Bregandyrns kevert with blew fellewet and gylt naille, with leg harneyse, and i. harneys complete of the touche of Milleyn (bearing the touch mark of a Milanese armourer)'.

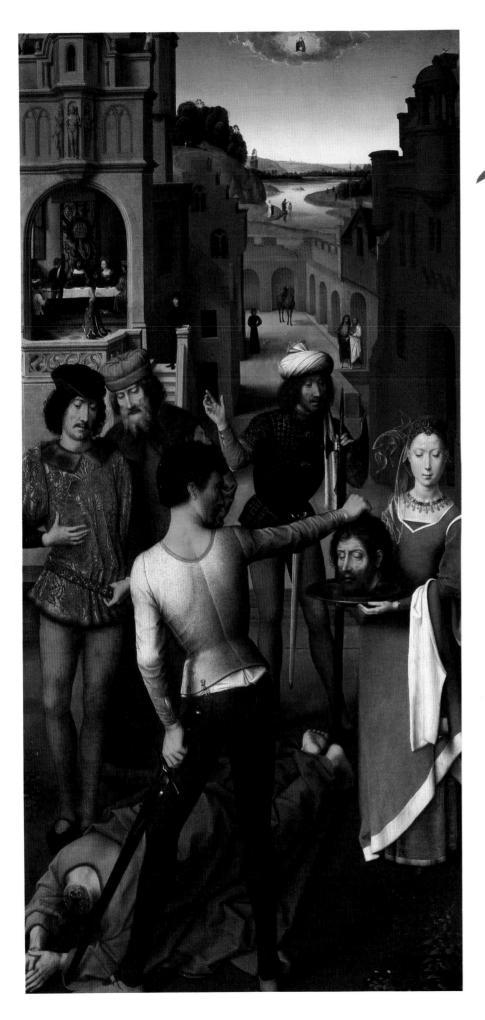

Left: The beheading of St John the Baptist, a detail from the Mystic Marriage of St Catherine, *by Hans Memling, c1470. The figure in the centre background holding a pollaxe is wearing a brigadine. Note the arrangement of the rivet heads, in threes.*

Below: A billman, c1480. He wears equipment typical of a retainer of the period of the Wars of the Roses – a sallet, mail standard and gussets and a brigandine.

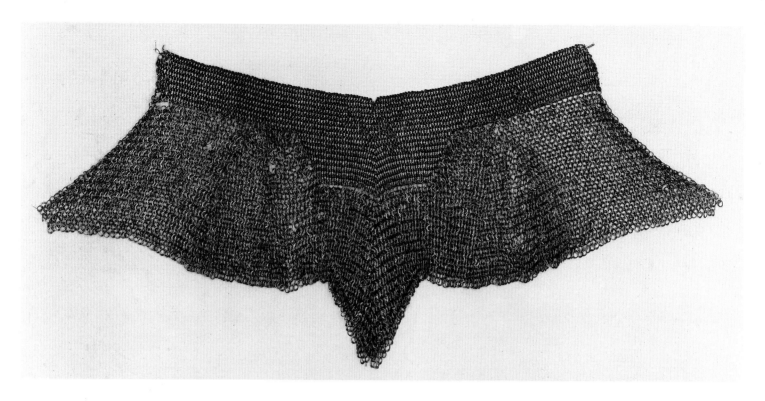

Above: A mail standard (collar), late fifteenth century.

Brigandines were also worn as a light armour by men who did not expect to go into battle, or who might be travelling in unfriendly but not openly hostile country. Comines says that while the men of Charolois and Calabria were fully armed, the troops of Berri and Brittany who marched into Paris in 1465 wore only light brigandines or, some said, garments with gilt nails sewn onto satin, 'that they might weigh the lesse'.

The brigandine of the fifteenth century was for the most part a front-opening, slightly waisted garment which reached the top of the hips. It was constructed by riveting overlapping plates through a cloth covering and canvas interlining. These rivets formed decorative patterns and were arranged either in horizontal lines or, more commonly, in groups of three. There are a number of extant fifteenth century brigandines, the most complete of which is a garment for a boy of six to eight years, which dates to the third quarter of the century, and is preserved at Chartres. There is a fine example in the Waffensammlungen, Vienna, and a group in the Royal Armouries at the Tower of London.

The brigandine was sometimes constructed with two large, L-shaped plates on the chest to protect the lungs. From this columns of smaller, oblong plates overlapped upwards towards the neck and downwards towards the waist. This construction is a direct survival from the coat of plates, and examples preserved in the Royal Armouries

and in Vienna are made in this way. However, more commonly the front of the brigandines were simply constructed of overlapping oblong plates, like one in the Historisches Museum, Bern, reputedly taken at the Battle of Nancy. At the rear the plates were arranged with a central row of plates tapering towards the waist and flaring towards the base of the skirts. The junction between body and skirts was effected by a row of plates which curved both outwards and round the waist. The fastenings at the shoulders and down the front were usually straps and buckles; however, the armour from Chartres is laced with points and eyelets reinforced with metal rings. The outer layer of cloth was commonly of very expensive material. The Household Accounts of Edward IV records gifts to a number of his Knights of the Body (Sir William Parr, Sir Thomas Montgomery and Sir Thomas Borough). Lord John Howard received a purple velvet-covered brigandine with gilt headed nails and Lord of Audeley received 'the gift of oure said Souverain Lorde the Kyng for covering a peire of brygandyns . . . clothe of gold ii yerds crymsyn uppon satyn grounde'. In the fifteenth century brigandines were often depicted with what appear to be sleeves, as shown in the Arzila Tapestries, and in a Franco-Burgundian tapestry now in the Burrell Collection which depicts Hercules initiating the Olympic Games. However, these would seem to be spaudlers constructed in brigandine form but attached to the main part of the brigandine by points. Brigandines were a cheaper alternative to a plate cuirass for the poorer knight, and were often worn with a plackart without fabric covering. Indeed, Charles the Bold, in his Ordinance of Saint Maximin de Trèves of October 1473, required them as part of the equipment of *coustelliers*.

By the fifteenth century the armourer's craft had advanced to such an extent as to make the shield an unnecessary encumbrance, and it ceased to be carried by knights for purposes other than the joust. It was used only by infantrymen who carried small bucklers (round shields) which were used in conjunction with swords, a style of fighting which survived in England well into the Elizabethan period. Crossbowmen, hand-gunners and occasionally archers used pavises, large rectangular shields which could be supported by a prop during siege operations. Alternatively, they could be carried by individuals known as 'pavissiers', whose duty it was to provide protection when and where it was needed.

As in the fourteenth century, the knight expended vast sums of money on his appearance, and to this end he required his armour to be both functional and decorative. In German and Italian export armours this decoration took the form of shell-like flutes and pierced and cusped borders. This fluting, particularly on German armours, and especially on the back plates, echoed the pleating of the gown which the knight would have worn as part of his civilian dress. Applied decoration, usually in the form of gilt latten borders, was fairly common on German armours up to 1500 and, as mentioned above, appears on the armours of both Sigismund and Maximilian, but was increasingly rare in Italy from the beginning of the century. In the Household Accounts of Lord John Howard we find payments to a goldsmith who made buckles, pendants and 'barrys' for his sallet and an inventory of his goods lists two sallets garnished with gold.

A few good-quality armours were painted, usually with depictions of saints or coats of arms. From the beginning of the fifteenth century, engraving was used to decorate armours. It was simple and confined to the borders. A pair of spaudlers with integral besagews at Churburg are decorated with *pointillé* work showing the word 'urs' on one

Left: An Italian sallet with a red velvet cover and gilt copper mounts, c1480.

and a crouching bear on the other. Another armour from Churburg, now in the Glasgow Museum, has the letters 'YHS' and the motto 'Avant' engraved about its borders.

Helmet crests had fallen from favour by the beginning of the century and were increasingly replaced by a plume of feathers

Below: An English brass showing a heraldic tabard worn over armour.

Above: A fifteenth century Franco-Burgundian tapestry depicting Hercules initiating the Olympic Games. The central figure at the back appears to be wearing arm defences in the form of sleeves constructed in the same way as his brigandine.

issuing from a large, spherical ornament known as a *pomme*. However, a number of heraldic crests are illustrated being worn in battle in the Beauchamp Chronicle.

Armours, especially helmets, continued to be covered in rich material and garnished with jewels and gold. Although from the second decade of the fifteenth century armours were worn without any cloth covering at all, there are still a good many examples of knights wearing cloth overgarments, some of which were heraldic, while others were simply of some costly fabric. These took the form of loose robes or heraldic tabards; many are illustrated in the Beauchamp Chronicle and on contemporary brasses. An early example is to be seen on the *Goldenes Rössel*, a New Year's gift in 1403 to

Charles VI of France from his Queen, which shows the King and his Marshal, who bears the King's helmet, kneeling before the Virgin, Child and Saints. Over his armour Charles wears a flared, knee-length garment with short side slits and fashionable houppelande sleeves. The garment is worked in blue enamel powdered with gold *fleurs-de-lys*. In Italy it was quite common to wear a short cloak slung from the shoulders, or an open-sided tabard-like garment called a *giornea*, which was also a common civilian overgarment, an example of which can be seen in the painting of St George by Pisanello.

As part of the spoils after the Battle of Nancy in 1476 the Swiss took the silk coat of Charles the Rash, which is now preserved in the Historisches Museum, Bern. This is a

when captured he was not recognized, and was killed with the other prisoners.

The late fourteenth century types of shaffron continued to be used into the early fifteenth century and can be seen on two bass-reliefs of Henry V from his tomb in Westminster Abbey. These are represented by the extant Warwick shaffron which is characterized by bosses for the eyes and a bulbous projection for the nose, and rigidly riveted extensions to envelop the rear of the head. By this time, however, they were being rapidly superceded by a type where the

Left: A crossbowman's pavise, Bohemian, c1480, bearing the arms of a town called Zwickau, Saxony.

Left: St George, by Antonio Pisanello, c1450. St George wears a typical Italian armour of the mid-fifteenth century and a giornea.

circular-skirted garment made of red silk satin, with a two-part sleeve incorporating a puff at the shoulder to allow ease of movement, and a straight, loose section to the wrist. The garment may or may not have been intended for wear over armour, but it is an interesting survival, especially because of its association with the Duke of Burgundy.

As the century progressed and fewer knights bore their heraldic devices on overgarments, it became more difficult to identify individuals in battle; this would seem to be related to the fact that as warfare became less chivalrous, ease of identification was no longer a particular advantage, and could possibly be a disadvantage. However, from the early part of the century comes the sad story of the Duke of Brabant, the younger brother of the Duke of Burgundy who, against his brother's instructions fought in the Battle of Agincourt. He arrived to the field late, and in his hurry left his armour and surcoat behind; he borrowed the harness of his chamberlain and improvised a tabard from a banner, but

Above: A detail of a knight mounting his horse, an illustration from the poems of Christine de Pisan, written in the fifteenth century.

nose defence was more gutter-shaped, as can be seen in the fifteenth century manuscript of the Poems of Christine de Pisan in the British Library. These are accompanied by short peytrals and cruppers of mail with strongly dagged lower edges. However, until about 1450 horse armour was for the most part similar to that of the late fourteenth century, but usually did not have a crupper and flanchards. In 1445 the Duke of Burgundy commissioned for himself a complete bard of brigandine work. The earliest complete fifteenth century harness to survive is that made by Pier Innocenzo de Faemo of Milan, now in the City Museum in Vienna. It has a deep crupper and peytral composed of large plates riveted together, and joined by flanchards. It has a laminated crinet or neck defence which completely enclosed the horse's neck. The shaffron is gutter-shaped with two hinged side plates on each side and it no longer has the bosses to protect the eyes but has a semi-circular outwardly projecting plate riveted over each eye opening.

The majority of surviving later fifteenth century horse armours are German. These

have small peytrals and cruppers with separate small flanchards; the laminated crinet covers only the top of the horse's neck, and the small shaffron covers just the front of the head and nose. These shaffrons have applied ear-guards, eye flanges and side plates.

The sword remained the favoured side arm of the knight throughout the fifteenth century. The 'cut and thrust' variety which had been popular in the fourteenth century remained in vogue and varied in length between 28 and 40 inches (70 and 100cm). However, in order to lighten the blades, these were either hollow-ground or ground to give a central ridge with a parallel-sided blade. The cross guards were generally more attenuated and often inclined downwards towards the point, and the grips short and single-handed with pommels of either wheel, pear or kite shape. Hand-and-a-half purely thrusting swords with elongated pommels and blades of narrow, diamond section were extremely popular and were intended to thrust into the gaps in the increasingly sophisticated plate of the fifteenth century. For fighting at close quarters they were given a long *ricasso* (that is, the upper 6 inches or 15cm of the blade was blunted to allow a grip for the left hand so that the sword could be used in a shortened form).

The fifteenth century also saw the appearance of shortened swords to replace the long knives of the infantry. In Italy this type of sword had an extremely broad blade and was known as a *cinquedea* since it was supposedly five fingers wide at the top. These tapered sharply to provide a point for thrusting. In England a specific short sword with a single edge and sharp point was developed for the use of infantry. Instead of a cross hilt the rear quillon was bent upwards and backwards to meet the pommel, thus providing a rudimentary knuckle-bow, and the front quillon was bent towards the blade, giving an S-shaped guard. On the Continent additional guards were added to the sword hilt specifically for those not wearing steel gauntlets. In Spain hemispherical arms or loops were added to the base of the cross guard to give protection for fingers looped over the cross guard. Towards the end of the century in addition to this, a side ring which joined the ends of these arms together was added, and it is from hilts of this form that the swept-hilt of the rapier of the sixteenth and seventeenth centuries developed. Falchions do not seem to have been popular in the fifteenth century, probably because of the increasing perfection of the plate armours; however, they make an appearance once more at the very end of the century, but as elaborately decorated weapons for the nobility.

From as early as 1420 the hip-belt popular in the fourteenth century was gradually replaced by a diagonal sword belt, although the tomb of Lord Hungerford (1455) still shows the jewelled hip-belt in use. This diagonal belt divided at the rear where one strap was attached to the top of the locket mount at the top of the scabbard, and the second strap attached to a mount a foot or so below. The other end of the strap passed round the wearer's waist and was attached to the front of the locket on the opposite side.

The sword continued to be balanced on the right hip by a dagger, but these now seem to have been almost exclusively of the rondel or ballock form. The blades of these daggers tended to be of a strongly triangular cross-section, designed principally for punching through armour and mail and not for cutting. The dagger was reserved primarily for administering a *coup to grâce* or was used *in extremis* and for this reason is sometimes referred to as a *miséricorde* (mercy).

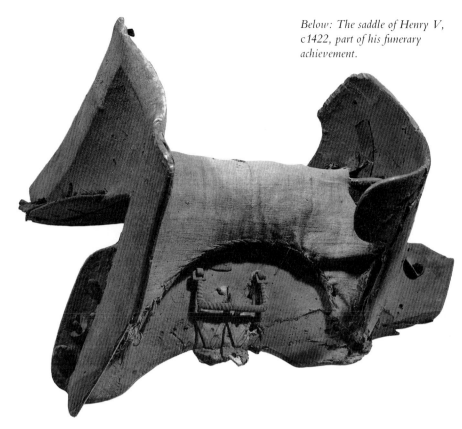

Below: The saddle of Henry V, c1422, part of his funerary achievement.

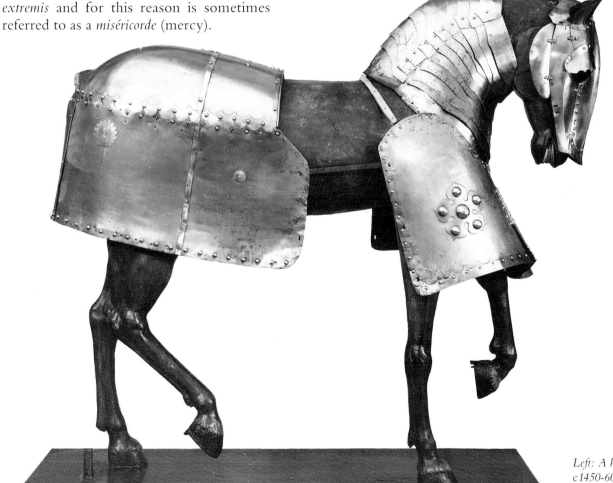

Left: A horse armour, Italian, c1450-60, by Pier Innocenzo da Faerno.

Right: A late fifteenth century German horse armour, possibly made for Waldemar VI of Anhalt-Zerbst. The armour for the man is also German, but composite.

The lance remained popular for mounted combat but it was larger than its fourteenth century counterpart and swelled both in front and behind the hand and then tapered towards both ends. It was equipped with a large vamplate of steel in front of the hand. During this century it became increasingly common for men-at-arms to fight on foot and since by the end of the fourteenth century shields had gone out of use, both hands were

Left: A German composite war harness for man and horse, c1480.

free to wield weapons. During the fourteenth century the two-handed axe had been particularly popular and the halberd had evolved; from a combination of these weapons a knightly weapon developed. This was the ravensbill or pollaxe, ('poll' was the contemporary word for a head and the term had no reference to the shaft of the weapon), which was capable of piercing and shattering the best plate. Pollaxes consisted of many different combinations of beak, hammer or axe head mounted on a 4 to 6 foot (1.2 to 1.8m) shaft, with a diamond section spike at top and bottom. Small rondels or disc-shaped guards were fitted to protect the hand from weapons sliding down the shaft, and tongues of steel

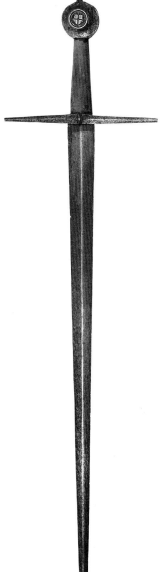

or latten were nailed between the head and this guard to stop the shaft being lopped in two. Pollaxes were far from clumsy and could be wielded with great speed and effect to hack, thrust and parry. They were used both for battle and in foot tourneys, where fatal or near-fatal injuries were commonly inflicted with them. Richard Beauchamp, Earl of Warwick, is recorded in the Beauchamp Chronicle as severely wounding Sir Pandolpho Malatesta with a pollaxe at a friendly contest in Italy.

The mace and war hammer remained extremely popular secondary weapons. These were often slung from the saddle by a leather thong and weighed between 2 and 5 pounds (0.9 to 2.2kg). By the early fifteenth century maces were made entirely of iron and steel and were equipped with a disc to protect the hand. These maces were between 20 and 24 inches (50 and 60cm) long and were much lighter and more elegant than their fourteenth century counterparts. In keeping with the Gothic feel of the period, they often had sharply pointed flanges pierced to look like Gothic tracery.

Above: The Sword of Tenure of Battle Abbey, c1420-30.

Right: An Italian sword, possibly late fourteenth century but before 1432, from the Arsenal at Alexandria.

As with maces, war hammers usually measured some 24 inches (60cm) in length and were used to pierce and crush plate. The war hammer quite closely resembled a miniature version of the pollaxe, except that the axe blade was replaced by a hammer head and the spike at the base was omitted. Single-handed axes remained in use, although they were never very popular.

The armour of the common man varied greatly throughout the century and with the wealth of the village, town or lord which provided it. At the beginning of the century the vast majority were equipped with aketons or multi-layered jacks of linen. These were long sleeved and had deep skirts, and were usually worn with open-faced basinets, sometimes accompanied by aventails. As in previous centuries the common man made do without the leg harness, but occasionally separate poleyns were worn. Indeed, at Agincourt the English archers wore no armour at all except for helmets of leather or basketwork reinforced with iron bands.

By the middle of the century, although jacks continued to be worn, the basinet had been replaced by the sallet and the jack shortened to reach just below the hips. The aketon or jack was sometimes accompanied by a short-sleeved mail shirt, but from the 1450s onwards the professional infantryman was increasingly well armed. From this time the jack was more and more often accompanied by a brigandine, a mail standard and splint arm defences or gussets of mail. Additional protection was sometimes provided by mail breeches or *brais d'acier*. Indeed, the household accounts of Lord John Howard, later Duke of Norfolk, show that out of a body of troops equipped in the year 1481, 85 per cent were issued with brigandines, standards, splints and sallets. However, these did not totally supercede the multi-layered jack, especially in England where they are described as being worn by troops of Richard Duke of Gloucester (later Richard III) by Dominic Mancini in 1483:

There is hardly any without a helmet and none without bows and arrows, their bows and arrows are thicker and longer than those used by other nations just as their bodies are stronger than other peoples' . . . the range of their bow is no less than that of our arbalests; there hangs by the side of each a sword no less long than ours but heavy and thick as well. The sword is accompanied by an

iron buckler . . . they do not wear any metal armour . . . except for the better sort who have breast plates and suits of armour. Indeed, the common soldiery have more comfortable tunics that reach down below the loins and are stuffed with tow or some other soft material. They say that the softer the tunics the better do they withstand the blows of arrows and swords.

This improvement in equipment went hand in hand with the increasing professionalism of the foot soldier and the payment of wages. In the professional army established by Charles the Rash of Burgundy, he laid down the specific requirement for each class of soldier in terms of arms and equipment. In the Ordinance of Bohain en Vermandois dated 13 November 1472 he decreed the following equipment: the hand gunner was to be equipped with a sleeved mail shirt, a mail or plate armour defence for the throat and neck, a sallet and a breastplate, a sword and a dagger and his hand gun; the archer was to have a brigandine over an aketon, splints for his arms, a gorgerine or neck defence, a sallet, his bow and a long dagger; the pikeman likewise was required to wear a padded jack, a right-arm defence, a sallet, and carry a targe and his pike. The use of this type of equipment is further confirmed by Lord John Howard's Household Accounts. In 1481 he lent to one Harry Mainwaryng 'a peir of brigandines keuvred with purpil velvet, a salate, a standart, a chief of arrowes, a peir of splentys and his jackette and a gusset.' In the same year he equipped one Thomas Cooke with 'a peir brigandines, a standart of the best, a salate, a cheff of arrowes, a peir splentes, his jackett, a gusset.'

Towards the end of the century breastplates specifically designed to be used by infantrymen or retainers, usually constructed in the German fashion with a riveted plackart, started to be manufactured on a large scale. These were designed to be worn without a back plate and were strapped on over the aketon, brigandine, and so forth by cross straps which fastened across the back. Quite often brigandines were accompanied simply by the plackart on its own. Particularly in

England, the defensive arms were completed by a small round buckler.

The long-bow retained its pre-eminence among the armament of the English infantry to the end of the fifteenth century. However, archers were increasingly supplemented by well-armed billmen; the long-bow and the bill were to characterize English armies until

Above: An early fifteenth century hand-and-a-half sword, possibly English.

Top: A south German mace, c1470.

Left: Two pollaxes dating to the second half of the fifteenth century.

Right: A mail shirt, German, c1450.

Far right, above: The Battle of Crécy, from a late fifteenth century copy of the Chronicles of Froissart.

Far right, below: Earl Richard defeating the Dauphin. A detail from the Beauchamp Chronicles, c 1485. *It shows English archers and French crossbowmen in action.*

Below: An iron hand gun, c 1500.

Bottom: A Bavarian crossbow c 1450-70. The tiller is overlaid with carved staghorn to resemble ivory and the steel bow with painted parchment.

almost the end of the reign of Henry VIII.

The bill was mounted on a shaft between 5 and 7 feet (1.5 and 2.1m) long, and the heavy cutting edge of the hedging bill remained predominant, and a spike was added to the top and a lug to the rear. This weapon was popular both in Italy and France, but in Italy it became more attenuated. The glaive, a single-edged blade mounted on a long shaft and fitted with a circular steel plate just below the head, was extremely popular in France

and was the characteristic weapon of the Scots Guard of the Kings of France. It was well suited both to cutting and thrusting. The halberd continued to be used throughout the fifteenth century and its use became more widespread, but at the end of the century it was ousted in its native Switzerland by the pike. The final form of staff weapon used by infantry was the *ahlspeiss*, which consisted of a long steel square-section spike mounted on a shaft equipped with a rondel to protect the user's hand. It was designed specifically for a thrust which could pierce armour. Although essentially a weapon of war, it was often used in foot combats.

The infantryman's arsenal was completed by the hand gun. Although these had appeared in the fourteenth century, indeed the town of Perugia bought some 500 in the year 1364, it is not until the fifteenth century that they truly made themselves felt. In the early part of the century they were much like miniature cannon; the barrels were either of bronze or iron mounted onto a shaft. To fire, the shaft was tucked beneath the arm and the powder was ignited with a hot wire or slow match held in the other hand. By the middle of the century this system had been improved: the barrels of the guns were lengthened and their bore reduced; the stock was bent at the rear so that it could be rested against the chest; and the touch hole which

Battle of Stoke. But as early as 1411 Duke John the Good of Burgundy possessed no less than 4000 hand guns in the Ducal Armoury. Their extreme range was probably some 200 yards, and even the best armour was vulnerable to these weapons at close range, but they could not match either the long-bow or cross-bow in either accuracy or rate of fire. These factors, in conjunction with the cost of gunpowder, which was 18 pence per pound in England in 1346, conspired to inhibit their development.

Whereas accuracy and rate of fire were important on the battlefield, they were not so essential in siege operations, and it was here that cannon first made themselves felt. They more than amply repaid the cost of the powder used by the panic they inspired and the destructive power they had when they hit their target.

Gunpowder had been known in Europe as early as 1260. It is recorded in the writings of Roger Bacon, a Franciscan scholar who

had previously been at the top of the barrel was moved round to one side. A serpentine or pivoted Z-shaped lever to hold the match was attached to the stock on the same side. The gun could then be fired two-handed simply by bringing this lever upwards, which deposited the slow match into the pan. By the end of the century the ignition system was further improved by the introduction of what is known as a lock. An advanced form of the serpentine, this worked by a sear-lever which was connected by a spring-loaded and pivoted bar which was attached to the serpentine. These workings were attached to a steel plate known as the lock plate. Pressure was applied to the sear-lever which, when squeezed against the stock, worked on the pivot. This in turn brought the serpentine into contact with the pan and fired the gun. These weapons had a bore of between ⅝ and ⅞ inches (1.6 and 2.2cm) and fired either lead or cast-iron shot; the latter was prized for its ability to pierce even the best plate armour.

As the century progressed and firearms improved, their effect became more noticeable on the battlefield, and all self-respecting armies contained large numbers of hand gunners, usually Flemings, Burgundians or Germans. In 1471 Edward IV had a company of 320 hand gunners when he landed at Ravenspur to retake his kingdom, but just 16 years later the Earl of Lincoln had some 2000 at the

Right: Burgundian infantrymen, c1480, by the Master of the WA, Bruges.

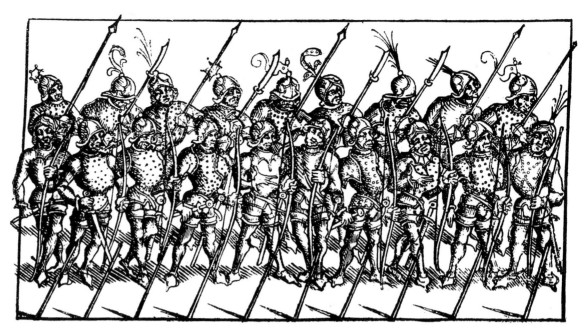

viewed it simply as an instrument of amusement. However, by the second half of the fourteenth century, this mixture of four parts saltpetre to one part carbon and one part sulphur was being applied to more sinister purposes. As early as 1326 the great city state of

Right: The Battle of Shrewsbury from The Beauchamp Chronicles, *c1485. It shows archers equipped with sallets, standards and brigandines, and a billman in a munition half armour.*

Florence was ordering guns and a contemporary manuscript by Walter de Milmete depicts an early cannon in use. It is vase-shaped, made of bronze and is apparently lying on a table. An almost identical gun was excavated at Losholt in Sweden. These early guns were made of cast bronze and were ignited by a piece of red-hot wire, so they could not be moved far from a heat source: the proximity of gunpowder and fire had an obvious potential for disaster. They fired balls and dart-like missiles, but had little or no application in the field, although Italian writers maintained that the failure of the Genoese cross-bowmen at Crécy was due to their being disordered by the English guns.

By the last quarter of the century, huge iron guns had started to appear; these were constructed on a hoop-and-stave principle, like contemporary barrels. The staves were arranged around a wooden former, the hoops were heated until they were red hot and were then slipped into place over the staves. They contracted as they cooled and compacted the staves together. Finally, the whole barrel was heated in a furnace, until the former burnt away, and the staves and hoops fused together. A breach block was made to fit one end of the barrel. These guns, or bombards, were so heavy that they were fired lying on the ground, with the breach end butted against vast baulks of timber driven into the earth. Bombards were muzzle loaded and used only in sieges. They could measure anywhere between 12 and 18 feet (3.65 and 5.49m) in length and had a bore between 15 and 18 inches (38 and 46cm). The Great Ghent Bombard, also known as 'Dulle Griet', built by the Duke of Burgundy, was 18 feet (5.49m) long, could fire a projectile weighing somewhere between 800-900 lbs, with a charge of powder of around 70 lbs. Perhaps a better known gun called Mons Meg, now in Edinburgh Castle, was also made in Burgundy around 1450; it is 13 feet 2 inches (4.01m) long, has a bore of 19½ inches (50cm) and is reputed to have fired a ball some two miles.

Cannon could fire either stone or iron shot. Stone shot was cheaper to produce and required less powder to fire, as it was lighter, but was less effective against fortifications. Bombards required their own wagons and usually a crane to load them, and a vast baggage train to transport their ammunition and powder. During the fifteenth century smaller

and more effective cannon were developed. By the middle of the century light breech-loading field artillery was well advanced and was used to great effect by the French against the English at Chastillon. Soon every army of any pretension had a large number of guns.

The trunnion, two lateral lugs, one projecting from either side of the barrel at the point of balance, had been introduced by 1470. This made the field gun a more practical proposition since it allowed the range to be adjusted by the use of an elevating quadrant. The introduction of wheeled carriages made artillery truly mobile. The barrel lengths and calibres of medieval cannon were by no means standardized, and there are a bewildering number of different types which are known in different countries by different names. In England there were bombards, falcons, sakers, culverin and basilisks; in the Burgundian army there were *bombards*, *veuglaries* (siege guns with a barrel length of up to 10 feet [2.54m] and a calibre of 2-10 inches [5-25cm]), and *couleuvrines*, which were guns of cast bronze or wrought iron which were usually breech-loading, had a

Above: The Siege of Caen, from The Beauchamp Chronicles, *c1485, shows an early cannon and crossbowmen using pavises.*

Right: An armourer making mail. Detail from a French book of proverbs, c1470.

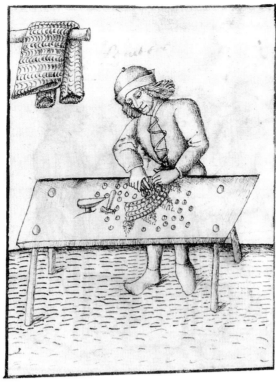

Right: An armourer making mail. Detail from a French book of proverbs, c1470.

their discharge and the fume and stink of the powder must have had a very demoralizing effect on an enemy who had perhaps rarely, or never, encountered such devices before. However, guns could be dangerous servants; they could explode or recoil and kill or maim the gunners, and it was not unknown for an over-enthusiastic observer parading in front of his prized artillery to fall victim to his own guns. It was in this way that King James II of Scotland was killed by his own cannon at the Siege of Roxburgh in 1460.

King James was not the only prominent fatality attributable to gun fire at this early date. John Talbot Earl of Shrewsbury, known as the 'English Achilles', was killed at the Battle of Chastillon in 1453; the Chevalier Bayard (*Sans Peur et Sans reproche*, without fear and without reproach) died in 1524 from an arquebus injury, and Giovanni de Medici, the famous *condotierre* called 'Of the Black Bands', was killed by cannon fire in 1526.

If the names of these early guns, many of which were the names of hunting hawks or fabulous fire-spitting monsters, are echoed in the names of our modern guided missiles, their cost is no less closely paralleled. Kings plunged themselves into debt to finance this arms race and to equip themselves with fire-power equal to that of their friends, enemies and neighbours.

barrel of about 4 feet (1.22m) long and were mounted on carriages. Another type was the *serpentine*, which was similar to the *couleuvrine* but slightly larger. It is these two latter types which formed the field artillery of most armies. The final type of cannon was the *ribaldequin*. It appears in Accounts of the City of Bruges as early as 1339. This consisted of a number of barrels clamped together on a wooden base, often on a wheeled carriage, which could be discharged individually or all at once. Such a volley could often break any attack on the gun and so these were much used to command breaches.

Medieval cannon had huge destructive power, but a major part of their effectiveness lay in their fearsome reputation. The noise of

Arguably the art of the armourer reached its zenith in the fifteenth century. Its greatest exponents were the Missaglia Negroni of Milan, with their stamp of crossed keys, and the Helmschmeid family of Augsburg, with their mark of a helmet surmounted by a cross. The greatest care was taken in the production of fine armours so that not only were they fitted to the individual wearer, but the metal itself was thickest over the most vulnerable points; generally a good armour was heavier on the left-hand side. The breastplate is invariably thicker than the back and the front of the helmet skull is likewise thickened at the front. Modern metallurgical tests have shown that the steel was often harder on the outside than it was on the inside. 'Armour of proof', which is known from the fourteenth century, was very common in the fifteenth. Quite often, when a great lord could not attend for fittings, he would have a suit of his clothes sent to the armourer to help in the manufacture. Obviously only the very rich could afford armour of such a standard and we know that armour could be bought either

Below: Not sword to ploughshare, but kettle hat to cauldron. A helmet re-used as a cooking pot.

'off-the-peg' or 'made-to-measure' from armourers of lesser standing. We know, for instance that in 1441 Sir John Cressy bought a ready-made Milanese armour for eight pounds six shillings and eightpence, and in August 1469 Lord John Howard paid to one Thomas Armerer of London, 'foure II harneyses be My Lordes desynenge, for xx marks.' However, on the last day of July 1463, he had paid only five marks for a harness which was complete except for sallet and greaves. On 30 September 1468 he bought a 'harnes complet fore hym and an estriche fether' for six pounds sixteen shillings and eightpence for Master Nicholas Howard.

Armour could also be bought at fairs (in those days places of serious commerce as well as enjoyment). In 1435 Philip the Good, Duke of Burgundy, bought 48 mail hauberks for the Ducal Armoury at the Great Fair at Antwerp. It was common for nobles and kings to stockpile arms and armour to equip their retainers; the various items of armour were acquired piecemeal and distributed in the same manner, no attempt being made to match any separate item with another. The Burgundian Ducal Accounts for 1449 include the purchase of 649 helmets, 33 arm harnesses and 146 brigandines. Likewise, on his death the inventory of the goods of John de Vere, 13th Earl of Oxford, lists objects 'in the armery house' which consisted wholly of armour and weapons, mostly for foot soldiers. Included are 175 sallets, 101 brigandines, 77 pairs of splints, 16 corsets, 84 pairs of mail gussets (for the arms), 18 gorgets, 24 aprons of mail, 120 of halberds, 140 bills and 120 bows. As mentioned above, this type of equipment was also issued by Lord John Howard to his retainers.

Besides the great armour producing centres of Milan and Germany, no less than 73 armourers are known from Brussels, in Ghent there were 32 specialized weapon smiths, and if the Bastard of Burgundy's armourer came from Bruges, there must have been good armourers there as well. In 1461 Charles the Rash, as a precautionary measure, forbade the manufacture of armour in the city of Liége, which had rebelled against him. There can be no doubt that all the main centres for the production of armour in the fourteenth century continued to prosper well into the fifteenth. Lord Howard bought armours both from London and from one Robyn 'the Armurer of

Above: A marketry frieze from the Ducal Palace at Urbino, Italy, showing armour stored in cupboards.

Gipswich'. Brigandine manufacture was also a separate trade – the Household Accounts of Lord Howard are full of payments made for brigadines at the apparently standard price of sixteen shilling and eightpence in London, Southwark and Ipswich.

Armour needed a good deal of maintenance and cleaning. The points on an armour obviously would not last forever, and in 1463 one dozen arming points cost threepence. Arming points were commonly red in colour, and straps shown in contemporary sources, especially in Italy, also seem to have been red. To avoid rust, armour needed to be kept scoured or at least oiled, and we know from household accounts that olive oil was deemed best. When not in use armour was stored in a number of ways. It could be hung up in cupboards, as can be seen in the Ducal Palace in Urbino, where a marketry frieze depicts Federigo Montrefeltro's armour. However, in England in 1463 a 'harness barrel with a lock for the same and hay to truss the harness with' were purchased for fifteen shillings and ninepence.

CHAPTER SIX
The Sixteenth Century
The Final Flowering

The date at which the European High Middle Ages is said to give way to the Renaissance is somewhat arbitrary. It is rarely the case that contemporaries felt any change of epoch, and the evolution from one phase of social and cultural development to another was usually gradual and fragmentary. Similarly, it is perhaps unrealistic to attempt to pinpoint the culmination of the power, influence and prestige of the knight in Europe, or to say when the medieval knight gave way to the Renaissance man.

Militarily, it has been suggested that 1494 (the commencing date of the Italian wars precipitated by the dynastic rivalry between the Habsburg and Valois ruling houses) marks a feasible starting point for the rise of 'modern' warfare and the beginning of the end for the medieval ideals of chivalry and knighthood on the battlefield. In England, the change of royal house from Plantagenet to Tudor in 1485 is often regarded as a convenient watershed; alternatively, to take the most simplistic view, the year 1500 (the end of one century and the beginning of another) is as good as any to draw the history and development of the medieval knight in Europe to a close. Whatever one's preference, the fact remains that the decline of the feudal order of society, and the obsolescence of the knight's mode of warfare combined to render his military role increasingly anachronistic in the New Age.

This is not to say, however, that the old medieval knightly ideals were not continued and upheld in the Renaissance. The social, political, military and Romantic importance of the knight to European society did not suddenly cease on 1 January 1500; despite the precepts set out for the benefit of the 'modern' ruler in Machiavelli's *The Prince* (1513), and despite the increasing use of 'levelling' weapons of war and tactics, the ideals of the knight (including his often hopelessly outmoded code of chivalry) were inevitably carried forward into the next century and beyond.

The decade 1509-19 saw three new monarchs, all of them young 'universal' men after the Renaissance ideal, ascend to the thrones of Europe's major powers. These were Henry VIII, his rival Francis I of France, and his rival in turn, Charles V of Spain, initially the ally of England against the French. Each of these men took a keen interest in the religion and politics of their age, together with philopsophy, history, science and the 'new' learning; they kept abreast of modern developments and inventions such as the printing-press, or the increasingly rapid evolution of weapons such as the early 'dead-fire' guns and other forms of weaponry (with the new tactics and strategy that their use often required), and yet through all this they also retained many traditional medieval attitudes. In particular, all three looked to the glories of the past to enhance their position in the present; all three loved the pageantry and chivalry of the tournament and excelled in its feats of arms, seeing themselves as 'warrior kings' in the medieval tradition and modelling themselves on Romantic chivalric heroes, pursuing glory in war as an end in itself. As a result, until the experience of age and the political realities of statecraft in the sixteenth century finally exerted themselves, they often pursued impractical political or military ideals that often had serious political and financial consequences for their realms.

Henry VIII's wars in Scotland were clearly a domestic issue, and justifiable on that ground; on the other hand, his ruinously expensive military 'adventures' on the continent were just such a false ideal. Mesmerized by England's past military victories and the territorial acquisitions of Edward III, many Englishmen, the king among them, still felt they had a right to certain parts of France and a duty to regain this lost inheritance. Valid political reasons for periodic involvement on the Continent certainly existed, but one receives the distinct impression that England was being drawn into such conflicts as a result of much wider political movements; in particular, the dynastic and territorial rivalry between the Habsburg Emperors and the emergent power of France, which dominated much of the century. Henry VIII's invasions of France in 1512, 1523 and 1544 constituted a small part of this struggle; they were not, perhaps, in the best political interest of England itself. By the second half of the century it was apparent that the *chevauchée* style of warfare prevalent during the first half of the Hundred Years War had little place in the Renaissance world, where political and territorial consolidation would decree the shape and form of Europe for centuries to come. The early sixteenth century thus saw the confused blending of medieval tradition and ambition with the new political thought and rationalization of the Renaissance.

Although he probably did not realize it, the role of the knight in this changing world was even more confused and uncertain than that of his monarch; at least the latter's divine right to rule was still largely unquestioned. The military status of the knight as a functional unit on the battlefield had, however, been subject to a process of slow, spasmodic, but nevertheless steady erosion since the middle of the fourteenth century. Since this status was the basis of his ancient superiority over all other types of soldier, and the foundation of his consequential social pre-eminence in feudal society, its undermining was a serious threat to the supremacy of the knightly aristocracy of Europe, both on and off the field of battle.

The knights as a class looked to the past for their standards, aims, ideals and aspirations. The chivalry and military glory of past ages was admired and emulated, if not in war then at least in the tournament. Warfare in the fourteenth and fifteenth centuries, as has already been shown, was often far from chivalrous or noble; it was more a matter for sheer survival. Towards the end of the military era of the knight in Europe, this blurred line between romance and reality was to

Above: Franco-Flemish tapestry, c1525-35, depicting Alexander the Great as a European knight on horseback, with armed retainers on foot. One of the latter is carrying a hand-gun, the weapon which eventually was to render full armour obsolete.

Above: Maximilian I presented a 'grotesque' parade armour to Henry VIII early in his reign. Only the helmet survives.

Below: The Field of the Cloth of Gold depicts Henry VIII's historic meeting with Francis I in 1520.

man the Magnificent in a league against the Habsburgs. Since the fourteenth century, the knight's chivalric code and military utility had also been undermined on the battlefield by increasingly effective forms of opposition from the lower orders. Initially, it was archery; then, disciplined bodies of infantry with staff weapons such as pikes or halberds. The response to such weapons had been the development of sophisticated forms of plate armour designed as much to deflect blows as to prevent penetration; such was the cost and the visual impact of the harnesses that they had become a knightly status symbol in themselves, to be worn not just in battle but in parades, tournaments and other similar grand occasions.

It was gunpowder, of course, that eventually toppled this image of the knight. The first significant victory due to the use of hand firearms was perhaps at the battle of Bicocca in 1522, in the first of the Habsburg-Valois wars that were to tear Europe apart for the first half of the sixteenth century. The defeat of the French at Bicocca was followed by their even more disastrous defeat at Pavia three years later; again, Burgundian hand-gunners contributed much to the rout which finally led to the capture of Francis himself. Armour could be made of sufficiently heavy weight to be proof against shot, but was then too heavy to wear; the only alternative defence was mobility, and this required the discarding of surplus armour. By the middle

exact a dreadful toll. The wars of the fourteenth and fifteenth centuries saw the virtual extinction of 'chivalry' as a practical code for the knight in battle; this trend was to continue in the sixteenth century, with such horrors as the sack of Rome in 1527 by both the Protestant and Catholic forces of Charles V. Political expediency was everything. Whereas in previous centuries the kingdoms of Europe had combined, albeit uneasily, to launch Crusades against the Saracen Turk, Francis I actually allied himself with Sulei-

Left: An Italian painting of the Battle of Pavia (1525) showing the triumph of the Habsburg forces over the French, led in person by Francis I.

Below: An Almain Rivet (munition armour) from Winchester City Museum. The darkened plates have been restored, and the left arm has been turned to show the inside. A simple iron skull cap would have completed the outfit.

of the century, it was clear that the era of the mounted 'knight in armour' was over.

The sixteenth century saw perhaps the finest achievements in armour design and decoration, but in many cases this was to be at the expense of the 'beauty in function' ideal attained by armour of the late fifteenth century. The characteristic styles of the German and Italian armourers tended to be no longer so clear-cut and immediately recognizable; the Germans adopted rounded profiles reminiscent of Italian armour while the Italians began to employ structural features and technical innovations hitherto the province of their German rivals. Vast quantities of armour (not only of the best but also of the worst quality) were produced for export, the trade routes across Europe serving to disseminate and stimulate armour design and development still further. Much of this armour was not for noble clientele, but was intended to equip the new modern armies of the age; armies increasingly reliant upon the 'staying power' of armoured infantry, rather than the cavalry charges of the knights.

On his accession to the throne, one of Henry VIII's first self-appointed tasks was the reorganization and restocking of the national arsenal in the Tower of London; to this end he purchased in 1512 a total of 2000 light armours from Florence, at sixteen shillings each, and in 1513 a further 5000 from Milan. The threat of a French invasion in 1539 prompted the purchase of another 1200 armours from Cologne and 2700 from Antwerp, one of the largest centres in Europe

for the manufacture of low quality 'munition' armour intended for the common infantry. If one considers that the other myriad rulers, kingdoms and principalities in Europe were also buying armour of this sort

in quantity, one begins to realize the extent of armour production in the early sixteenth century.

These were for the most part 'half-armours', that is, they were relatively light armours without plate defences for the legs. Often such an armour was termed a 'corslet'. This consisted of an infantry cuirass (often recognizable by its lack of a lance rest, or any provision for the same), gorget, full arm harness including gauntlets, a pair of tassets and an open-faced helmet. The 'morion' helmet (frequently called a 'pot') was very popular for infantry use; the most common types were the 'Spanish' morion ('cabasset', probably Anglicized from the Spanish 'cabacete'), or later in the century the 'comb' morion. Lighter, and correspondingly cheaper, armours were called 'Almain rivets'. Henry VIII's first purchase of armour in 1512 was of these; each set comprised a sallet, gorget, breast and back (usually furnished with short laminated tassets), and a 'pair of splints' (arm harness). The latter were very simple, crude defences for the outside of the arm; they were usually of relatively thin metal, with laminated vambraces made in one with the spaudlers (which covered the top of the shoulders), and with a couter to protect the joint of the elbow. Gauntlets were not usually worn, but instead there were laminated projections extending over the backs of the hands from the splint covering the forearm. Such light armours were sometimes worn with a broad collar or mantle of mail and an iron skull cap or broad soft hat or both. They were habitually worn by the German Landesknechts, who in the early sixteenth century achieved an impressive reputation as fearless mercenary soldiers. They were invariably infantry, and fought primarily with the two-handed sword, the pike and occasionally other staff-weapons such as the halberd, and eventually the hand-gun. In Germany especially, they affected an outlandish, variously-coloured 'puffed and slashed' mode of dress.

Similar half- or three-quarter-length armours were popular for light and medium cavalry. Paintings dating from the first few decades of the sixteenth century, such as the *Battle of Alexandria* (1529) by Albrecht Altdorfer, show not only the squadrons of heavily armoured knights on fully barded horses, but also large units of much lighter, less armoured, more manoeuvrable cavalry. These were known as 'demi-lancers' or 'lancers', from their use of a light lance which did not require a lance rest bolted to the breastplate. They constituted medium-weight cavalry and generally wore three-quarter-length armour incorporating leg harness only to the knee, and heavy leather boots instead of greaves and sabatons. Their helmets were closed, like those of fully armoured knights. The 'javelins' or light horse (the latter term dating from the middle of the century) were equipped with cuirass and tassets, gorget, simple spaudlers instead of full pauldrons, and no arm harness other than, occasionally, mail sleeves. Their headpieces were invariably open-faced, often the type known as a 'burgonet'. This was an open helmet with a peaked brim over the eyes, cheek-pieces, and a skull having a central ridge or comb and fitting relatively closely to the nape of the neck. This could be converted into a closed helmet by the addition of a wrapper or 'buff' covering the face. As armour became less practical on the battlefield or in the hot climate of southern Europe, the light cavalry frequently wore even less than this, relying upon mobility for defence and commonly wearing only a hel-

Right: An early sixteenth century woodcut after David de Neckar of a German Landesknecht. Note the 'splint' arm harness with its projecting plate (visible over the back of the hand holding the sword), worn instead of gauntlets.

met, light cuirass or mail shirt, and gauntlets. Brigandines remained popular for all classes, their shape following the styles of civilian fashion; they were worn by both light cavalry and infantry. Men of knightly rank increasingly joined the lighter forms of horse in preference to the more and more expensive and anachronistic heavy cavalry, without seeing any dishonour in this.

Full armours of heavy plate continued to be produced throughout the sixteenth century, but increasingly their use became restricted to the tournament rather than the battlefield. At the beginning of the century the most common headpiece for such armours was the armet, but this was rapidly overtaken in popularity by the close-helmet, itself a derivative of the former type. At the time, little distinction seems to have been drawn between them, and the terms were often used synonymously. For the sake of convenience, however, this terminology was later clarified to the extent that we now regard the armet as a form of close-helmet, front-opening with two hinged cheek-pieces overlapping for fastening at the chin, the visor then pivoting at the sides. The close-helmet itself opened entirely from the sides; the visor and bevor (the latter often fitted with gorget plates) all pivoted on the same axis from a point each side of the helmet. The pivots themselves were initially simple rivets, sometimes with decorative heads; later, however, they were sometimes threaded studs or bolts, to permit easy dismantling for cleaning and repair. Like the late fifteenth century German form of armet, the

close-helmet could also be furnished with a turn around the edge of the neck, instead of gorget plates. This engaged with the rim of the gorget proper, enabling it to rotate without a vulnerable crack opening in the neck joints which could admit a lethal thrust from a pointed weapon.

The breastplate was rounded and globose in profile, generally with rather a 'wasp' waist, below which the fauld and tassets then swelled out in a corresponding curve. Full leg harness was worn, the sabatons being the same blunt splay-footed shape current in civilian fashion all over Europe, unlike the long, pointed toes fashionable previously. The gauntlets were still usually of mitten form.

The two main centres of armour manufacture remained Italy and Germany, but to an increasing extent lesser centres managed to establish themselves, either to serve a local or international need, or as the direct result of royal patronage by kings, princes and their courts anxious to emulate their neighbours and impress the world at large. For some monarchs, it was not enough to continue purchasing 'export' armours from the well-established centres abroad, but desirable and prestigious instead to found their own workshops. Such 'lesser' centres often produced armour of sufficiently high quality to be noteworthy. By the beginning of the sixteenth century, the Low Countries had already become a significant manufacturer and exporter of low- to medium-quality 'munition' plate, though good-quality work was also carried out. Unfortunately it is often

Above: Helmet of 'true' close-helmet construction, pivoting open at the sides. It was made in Nuremburg, c1530, and is fitted with a 'parade' visor in the form of an eagle's head.

Above left: A sixteenth century close-helmet of 'armet' construction, made by Wolfgang Grosschedel, c1535-40. This helmet is furnished with a pivoted prop to keep the visor open when required. The etched decoration includes a representation of a spiked dog collar around the neck. It is now preserved in the Wallace Collection, where there is also an 'exchange' visor for it.

Right: A German armour, c1510, possibly made for Wladislas, King of Bohemia and Hungary, who died in 1516. It is now in the Wallace Collecion. See also pages 177-181.

early as 1511 it is known that Italian armourers (almost certainly based at Greenwich) were working in England at the command of the King. Henry had also invited a group of German armourers, and it was these craftsmen who were to form the nucleus of the new 'Greenwich school'. They made armours primarily for the King, but also did work for the nobility, especially during the reigns of his successors. Almost immediately, Greenwich armour started to develop an individual style which did not reach its full potential until the middle and second half of the century. In particular, it saw the development of a characteristic style of decoration, incorporating broad bands of gilt etching arranged in very geometric patterns on an oxidized blued ground.

Italian armours of the period tended to be smooth and plain, except for restrained areas of the etched and gilt decoration that was to become so popular later in the century. This occurred in decorative scenes or mottoes (usually of a religious nature) on the breast, or along the edges of the main plates, which were commonly finished around their borders with a sunken band. The extreme edge ended in a narrow turned ridge frequently decorated with filed lines resembling the twist of a rope (hence the term 'roping', or 'roped' edges). This became almost universal, except on English armour of the Greenwich school, after about 1520. Prior to 1510 the edges of plate armour tended to be turned outwards; after that date the turned edge was usually inward facing. On the poorest quality armours, especially later in the century, the lines of the roping were often roughly put in with a cold chisel, and resembled little more than a series of dashes.

difficult today to distinguish this from armour produced in the well-established centres, largely because of the migration of skilled workers taking with them distinctive national styles and methods of armour manufacture, design and decoration, to reproduce or adapt in their new homeland. It is known that armours were being made in France at this time, also, but there is some controversy as to whether a number of surviving fine quality pieces that do not seem to be either German or Italian, may be Flemish or French.

One workshop about which there is less confusion is that established under the patronage of Henry VIII at Greenwich. As

Right: A war saddle probably made by Jorg Seusenhofer of Innsbruck. It retains its original heavily padded and quilted leather upholstery. The front saddle-steel is dated 1549.

Whereas Italian armour owed much to the form and style of the previous century, the armourers working in Germany or under German influence (in Venice at this time, for example) were a little more adventurous. The fluted and cusped plates of High Gothic armour now evolved into the style of decoration referred to as 'Maximilian', after the Emperor Maximilian I (1493-1519). This was very popular in the first third of the sixteenth century, especially in Germany; although the Germans had readily adopted the full, rounded outlines of Italian armour, this form of decoration seems to have been purely their own. The entire surface of the armour (except for the greaves) was covered with narrow embossed vertical fluting, sometimes delineated with engraved lines and sometimes also interspersed with broader bands of etched decoration or a plain surface. Narrower fluting usually indicates a later date of manufacture.

Simultaneously, in accordance with the new flamboyant spirit of the age, the Germans developed a taste for extravagant embossing, much of which imitated the puffed-and-slashed Landesknecht costume of the period (wherein 'puffs' of rich, brightly coloured material were pulled or showed through 'slashes' in the outer fabric layer). It also took the form of grotesque faces, animals, dolphins, dragon's wings or tails and so forth; much of this form of decoration was applied to 'parade' armour, which was never intended for use either in war or in the tournament. Occasionally, however, either or both styles of embossing were combined (usually in a more restrained form) with functional armour, which was

Left: A 'Maximilian' style fluted armour, c1520, made for Otto Heinrich as a young man. The equestrian harness illustrated on page 175 was made for him some 16 years later.

often decorated in the Maximilian style. The visors of helmets, for example, sometimes took the form of grotesque masks. These armours were frequently richly etched and gilt; in the case of the 'puffed-and-slashed' armour, often to resemble the damask silks and brocades of the corresponding civilian costume. This style of decoration did not survive long outside Germany though; it was at its most flamboyant in about 1520, but gradually became less fashionable in the decade following, and was not much seen after the mid-1530s.

The tradition of embossed decoration lived on, however, in Italy and Germany. It flourished especially in its application to

Left: Parade helmet by Kolman Helmschmid of Augsburg, c1520. The wings and dolphin mask are removable, enabling the helmet to be used for the field or tournament (with the addition of a falling buff to protect the face).

Left: An embossed and gilt north Italian (Milanese) parade casque of burgonet form made in about 1540, now in the Wallace Collection.

'parade' armour, where it was used in conjunction with other decorative techniques, such as mercury gilding and counterfeit damascening in silver and/or gold. To attain the depth of embossing required, the metal worked had to be very thin and malleable; this fact led to many such armours being made of thin, light wrought iron rather than hardened steel. Having lost most of its functional beauty, armour of this sort was, in effect, a form of 'fancy dress'; the deep embossing, far from presenting a glancing surface to the point or edge of a weapon, actually retained and trapped it, thus virtually ensuring its penetration.

Not all parade armour was embossed, of course; much of it was richly etched and gilt overall, the surface remaining relatively smooth and uninterrupted. This enabled field and tournament armour to be decorated in this way also, without impairing its function. At the turn of the century, etching was carried out by applying acid-resistant wax to the surface of the plate requiring decoration, and then scratching the design with a scribing tool through this wax onto the underlying metal. On treating the whole with acid, this design became etched into the surface, the wax-protected ground remaining unaffected. The style of such decoration was very simple, often incorporating bands of uncomplicated scrollwork or foliage on a simple hatched ground. By the second decade of the sixteenth century, however, this had been overtaken in popularity by etched and gilt bands of decoration in which the design was left in relief, the background having been etched away. This was accomplished by painting the design itself onto the surface of the metal, and then etching out the ground. The ground itself was frequently

decorated with small dots. This type of background remained fashionable for the rest of the century, especially on German armours.

Etched decoration on armour was often gilded from the early years of the sixeenth century onward; an amalgam of powdered gold and mercury was spread as a paste over the area to be plated and then heated. The heat burned off the mercury (as highly poisonous fumes), leaving the gold chemically bonded to the surface of the metal. Other

Right: 'Puffed and slashed' armour of Wilhelm von Roggendorf, made by Kolman Helmschmid in Augsburg, c1520.

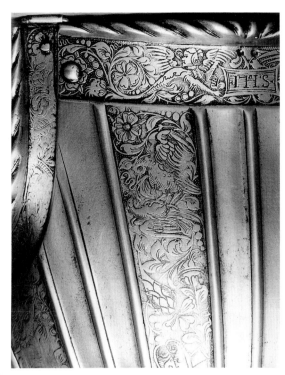

Far left: Cuirass and tassets, dated 1523, by Kolman Helmschmid of Augsburg. The fine quality etched decoration (see detail, left) is probably by Daniel Hopfer.

use on the battlefield, and too heavy and constricting for casual or parade wear, at the very height of its development the truly functional and meaningful armour of the knight was in fact doomed to a slow decline.

As to weaponry, trends established in the previous century continued into the sixteenth, in particular with regard to the development of firearms. The traditional weapons of the knight remained essentially the same, but those of his non-noble adversaries continued to evolve until eventually in the seventeenth century they drove the fully

decorative techniques, such as engraving and the pointillé work used occasionally in the latter part of the previous century, continued to be employed of course, but much more rarely. Some armour, such as the harness made *c* 1515 for Henry VIII in celebration of his marriage to Catherine of Aragon in 1509, was even silvered rather than gilt (although it may have been gilded also), but these were expensive rarities and exceptions to the general fashion. By the 1530s, the appearance of armour had been set for throughout the rest of the century; etched and gilt decoration predominated, either as borders, designs of strapwork, or covering the entire surface.

Such was the opulence of decorative parade armour, however, that its popularity and use escalated while, except for the tournament, the more functional forms were increasingly dispensed with. Impractical for

Left: The breastplate of Henry VIII's silvered and engraved armour, made and decorated in England, c 1515, by Italian or Flemish craftsmen. The complete harness is illustrated overleaf.

145

Top right: A German sword, c1520, with a simple finger guard.

Bottom right: An Italian hilt, c 1540-50, which illustrates the evolution of the 'swept' hilt.

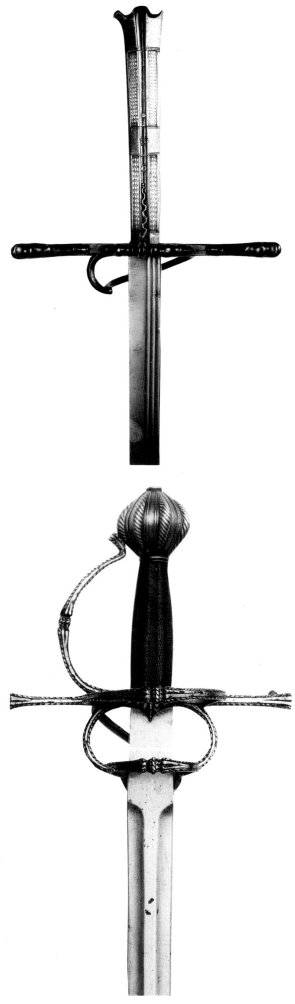

armoured horseman completely from the battlefield. This process was already well under way by the turn of the fifteenth century; the lance had reached the zenith of its development and could evolve no more, save to go backwards and become once again a light, easily-manoeuvrable and versatile spear. The sword of war, too, could go no further; save for the improvement of fitting simple additional guards to afford more protection to the hand during a melee, the forms of sword employed by the knight in the fifteenth century were much the same as he continued to use in the sixteenth. The chief difference lay in the richer decoration of the latter weapons, in accordance with Renaissance taste; it was in the style of fighting and

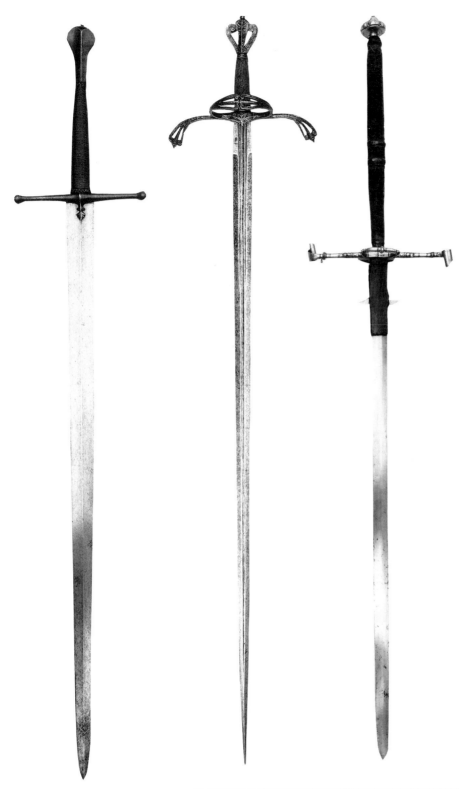

the design of swords used by civilians and infantry that the greatest innovations were to occur.

From as early as the late fourteenth century, simple finger-guards had occasionally been applied to the cross-hilts of swords, and additional guards for the hand (including a knuckle bow) are found on some swords dating from the mid-fifteenth century (especially falchions). In the early 1500s, this trend was continued, until by the middle of the century the almost fully developed 'swept' hilt was in existence. A design book by the Italian master-craftsman Filippo Urso of Mantua, now in the Victoria and Albert Museum, shows this clearly; dated 1554, its sketches nonetheless depict virtually all the basic forms of swept hilt more usually encountered in the later sixteenth century. Much of this development was due not simply to the increasing importance of infantry and modes of fighting on foot, but more significantly to the need to protect the unarmoured hand, a result of the Renaissance predilection for wearing swords with civilian dress, in accordance with fashion, for self-defence and for settling quarrels by duelling. The wealth of the noble classes and the Renaissance taste for rich, intricate styles of decoration led to many of these weapons being extravagantly decorated with gilding, chiselling, piercing, enamelling and silver or gold encrustation rendering them rich in appearance, costly or unusual. The foremost artists of the age were involved in the design of sword hilts – Hans Holbein the Younger, for example, is known to have produced such designs – and famous artist-craftsmen such as Benvenuto Cellini, executed them.

The necessity for fighting with the point of the blade, brought about initially by the wearing of armour, was carried over into a 'new' essentially non-military style of fighting for which the long-bladed rapier (a term

Above: Left to right, a late fifteenth century sword of war; a late sixteenth century 'arming' sword with an English hilt; and a German Landesknecht's two-handed sword, c1540.

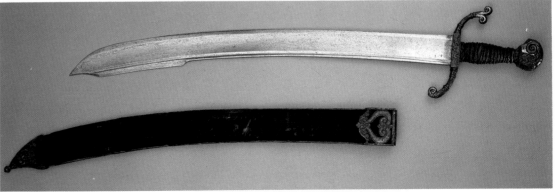

Right: Italian falchion, c1550, decorated in typical Renaissance style.

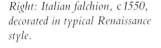

first used to describe any purely 'civilian' sword) was the best weapon. Schools of fence and text books on the subject are known from the fourteenth century; in the fifteenth century fencing 'academies' were established in Venice, Milan and Verona, and no doubt in other centres too. The styles of sword fighting then still included slashing blows as well as the all-important thrust, but by about 1500 two distinct styles of true fence had emerged: the Spanish and the Italian. Fighting with the point of the blade became an art and a science. The blades themselves were long and thin (mid- to late-sixteenth century examples becoming quite flexible) and were often of flattened diamond section, with a short fuller either side at the forte; this was frequently struck with the bladesmith's name, and the ricasso was also stamped with his mark. There was a tremendous export trade in blades from Spain, Italy and Germany; German makers often copied the marks and signatures (frequently misspelt) of well-known foreign bladesmiths such as Caino and Piccinino of Milan, or Sahagun and Hernandez of Spain. From the beginning of the sixteenth century, the wearing of swords became fashionable for 'gentlemen' rather than the exclusive prerogative of the knight, and thus the rapier began its evolution into the most commonly used and

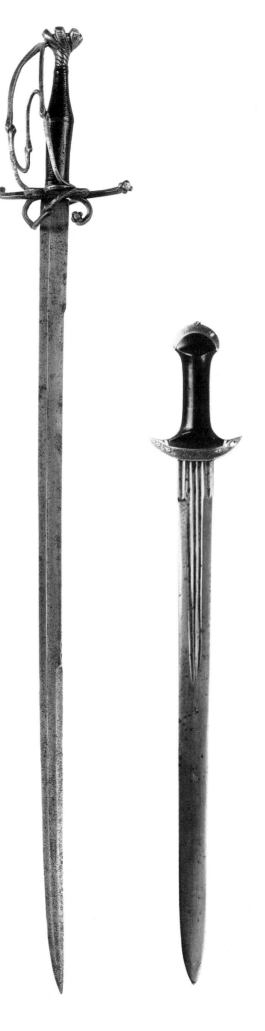

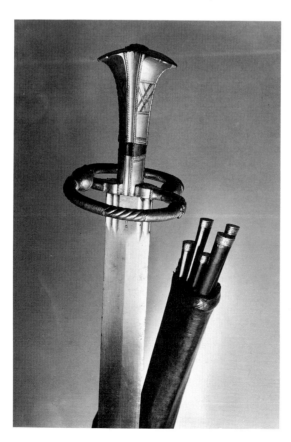

Right: Early sixteenth century German Landesknecht short sword (known as a Katzbalger) *with original scabbard retaining a set of by-knives and prickers.*

Centre right: Swiss sabre, c1530, with a hand-and-a-half grip and a complex guard.

Far right: Swiss or German 'baselard' short sword, c1530. Daggers with the same form of hilt were known by the same name.

recognized sword throughout Europe.

The sword used by the knight in war during the early 1500s remained essentially the same as in the previous century, but certain categories of sword were also developed during this period in response to specific needs and requirements. The two-handed Landesknecht sword was one of these; carried by lightly armoured infantry who often bore no other weapon, it could be wielded with deadly effect to 'soften up' an enemy force before the main attack, for example by lopping off the heads of pikes and generally demoralizing his infantry. The ricasso of the blade was usually covered with leather to enable one's grip to be extended to the maximum possible width when used in this way. The other form of sword carried by the Landesknechts was the shorter 'katzbalger', which had its quillons horizontally recurved into a characteristic 'S' shape. This weapon was used in one hand; such swords were rarely equipped with knuckle-guards, which were mostly found on single-edged swords designed primarily for slashing cuts, hand-and-a-half swords or sabres from Switzerland or Germany. Sabres had long single-edged, slightly curved blades back-edged at the point. More complicated forms of guard incorporating side-rings and knuckle-guards of more than one bar soon developed in both Italy and Germany in the first few decades of the sixteenth century, however.

The dagger, of course, was already well established as a personal sidearm. The most popular type in northern and northwestern Europe was the ballock knife, which by now was tending to replace the rondel dagger of the previous century. The baselard was also popular, especially as a civilian weapon; its hilt had evolved into an elegant 'I' shape with rounded contours, usually set upon a broad double-edged blade of various proportions. In southern Europe more unusual styles evolved, largely through Eastern influence; for example, in Italy, and in Venice especially, an 'eared' dagger hilt became popular, this form also being applied to some swords. As the century progressed, however, the simple quillon dagger became almost universal throughout Europe, popularized by its use with the rapier as a mode of fighting.

The mace continued to be popular, largely due to its effectiveness against armour although by the second half of the century it was becoming increasingly restricted to the tournament rather than regarded as a necessary weapon for the battlefield. By this time, in both Germany and Italy, the standard form of mace was the all-steel flanged variety. The warhammer similarly retained its popularity; both in its shortened form, used from horseback, and as the pollaxe, used on foot. It too was more often seen in the tournament than on the field of battle. Like the hilts and, by the first decades of the sixteenth century, the blades of knightly swords, war hammers became richly decorated with etching and gilding, often attaining (to the modern eye) the status of works of art rather than functional weapons.

Both longbow and crossbow continued to be used in warfare, but the gun rapidly overtook them in importance. At his death in 1547, Henry VIII had 3000 bows in the royal arsenals, together with 13,000 sheaves, each containing 24 arrows; however, the number of hand guns totalled 7700 and as early as 1513

Left: Italian (Ferrarese) short sword, known as a 'cinquedea', c1500. Its sheath is made of cuir bouille, *embossed and tooled, with provision at the back for a by-knife and pricker. Like the baselard in Northern and Western Europe, the cinquedea was especially popular for civilian use and wear, but was rarely seen outside Italy and the Mediterranean.*

*Right: Left to right, top row.
German or Swiss quillon dagger,
with a chiselled iron hilt fitted
with horn grip-plaques, c1530.
French rondel dagger with an iron
hilt and a wooden grip decorated
with brass, c1440-50.
'Ear' dagger with grip-plaques of
green horn. Venetian or Spanish,
c1500.
Left to right, bottom row.
Flemish or north German ballock
dagger. The hilt is maple-wood
mounted with silver, and it
retains its original leather-covered
wooden sheath containing a
matching by-knife and pricker
c1550.
German Landesknecht dagger,
with an inlaid wooden hilt and an
iron sheath damascened in silver
and gold, containing a by-knife
and pricker, c1570.*

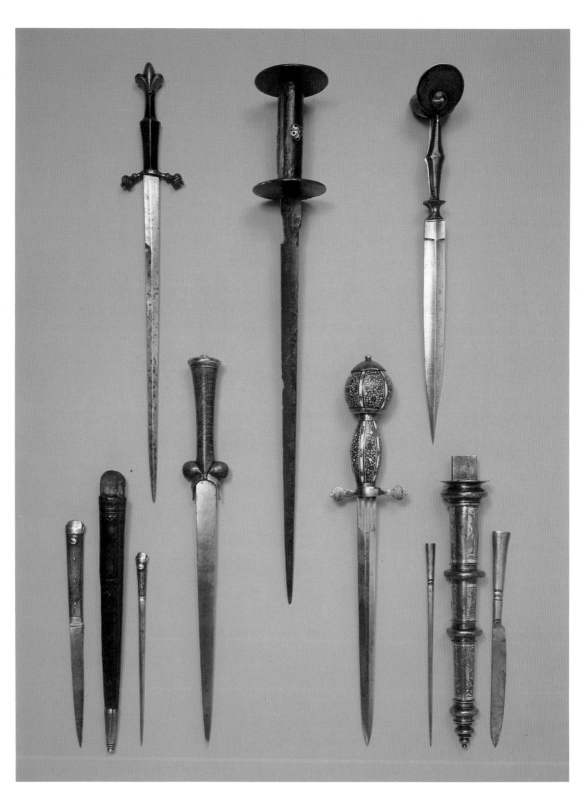

the ambassador of Venice had reported that the king possessed 'cannon enough to conquer hell'. Henry was a keen archer, reputed to be able to out-shoot his own hand-picked bodyguard; he enforced the statutes by which every able-bodied man in the realm between the ages of 16 and 60 was obliged to own a bow and practise with it weekly at the butts. Although becoming less important, the bow remained in use by the forces of the Crown until finally forbidden by an Order of Council in 1595. In common with most of his royal contemporaries, however, Henry VIII was fascinated by the power of the gun; it was significant, therefore, that eventually he was to authorize its use alongside the bow, for practice at the butts.

Crossbows were gradually superceded by firearms in war, but became increasingly popular for sporting use; like hand guns, they could be held or aimed ready to shoot for long periods of time without strain and, un-

Left: Early sixteenth century German sporting crossbow with a composite horn and sinew bow-stave covered in tooled and gilt parchment. The wooden tiller is richly inlaid with ivory.

Below, far left: Late fifteenth or early sixteenth century German crossbow quiver, made of wood covered with boar-skin (retaining some hair). The lid is missing. With it are eight crossbow bolts or 'quarrels' with iron heads and wooden flights; the shafts vary in length from 13 inches (33cm) to 19½ inches (49.5cm).

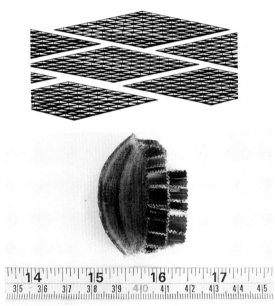

Left: A diagram of the longitudinal section through a typical composite crossbow stave, showing how pieces of horn were shaped. Their surfaces were cross-cut before finally being glued together.

Left: Cross-section (taken at right angles to the drawing) through a late fifteenth century composite bow-stave, showing segments of horn on the right of the photograph (the 'back' of the bow), and layers of sinew glued and fused together into a solid mass on the left (the 'belly' of the bow).

like guns, they were silent in operation. Emperor Maximilian was a keen crossbowman; a contemporary engraving *c* 1515 shows him shooting chamois with a composite sporting bow, and the 'Der Weisskunig' by Hans Burgkmier (*c* 1517) depicts the Emperor on horseback, his bow fully spanned and ready to shoot a quarrel with a broad forked iron head. With one of these he was reputed to be able to cut the jugular vein of a deer at 100 paces. By the middle of the century sporting bows were becoming very ornately decorated, usually with bone and mother-of-pearl inlay, and were also being fitted with complicated lock mechanisms incorporating hair triggers and other such refinements. From the first quarter of the sixteenth century composite bow-staves were replaced almost universally by the more powerful and longer-lasting steel bow. The use of crossbows as sporting weapons was widespread on the continent during this century, espe-

Left: A north Italian war hammer, richly etched and gilt, c1510.

Above: Three sixteenth century staff weapons. Left to right, an Italian partisan, c1550; an infantry spear, c1550; and an Italian trident or 'spetum', 1500-30.

Below: A richly decorated mid-sixteenth century wheel-lock gun, intended for sporting use.

grayned' staff, for example, was probably a variety of 'corséque' (a form of trident with three stright blades stemming from a common base), of which the 'runka' and 'spetum' were derivatives. The 'partisan', a staff weapon bearing a long tapering double-edged blade with two small up-curved flukes on either side of its base, saw widespread use in Italy and southern Europe from the early years of the sixteenth century, its popularity rapidly reaching north subsequently.

As with various other types of arms, there was a brisk trade across Europe in staff weapons, especially from Italy, Germany and the Low Countries. It is known, for instance, that Henry VIII purchased large numbers of Italian bills; it may be that the 'Tudor Rose' emblem etched on the blades of some surviving examples of such weapons may indicate a royal provenance. One of the features of the early sixteenth century was the formation by princes and monarchs of personal bodyguard units, most of whom were equipped with staff weapons, often richly decorated, like the blued, etched and gilt bladed partisans that the Yeoman of the Guard still carry today. Halberds and glaives were the other most popular weapons for this purpose, the large surface area of the heads lending itself to such decoration, which frequently incorporated the coats-of-arms of a royal or noble patron.

Above any other weapon, it was the development of the hand gun that changed the face of warfare in the sixteenth century. Simple matchlocks were quite common; there is documentary evidence, however, that the wheel-lock system of ignition was already in relatively widespread (though select) use within Germany and parts of Italy in the first decade of the sixteenth century, spreading rapidly to the rest of Europe during the next 10 years. An account book dated 1507, for the household of Cardinal Ippolito d'Este, Archbishop of Zagreb (then in Hungary), refers to four florins paid to a servant for the purchase in St Farkas, Germany, of 'a gun of the kind that is fired with a

cially by the noble classes, but despite the temendous power of the military 'windlass' crossbow, its place on the battlefield was increasingly taken by the gun.

The effectiveness of staff weapons against the mounted knight had already been established in the previous century; the use of halberd and pike, in particular, became widespread in Europe following the example set by the Swiss, and the bill and glaive followed close behind in popularity. The English bill and the longbow remained the most common weapons for the ordinary infantry of Henry VIII's army during the first two decades of his reign; they more than proved their worth at Flodden in 1513 against the pike blocks of the Scots, which lacked support from billmen or halberdiers. There was a vast multiplicity of staff weapons in the sixteenth century, many of which are referred to in lists and inventories by names often difficult to relate to surviving weapons. A 'three-

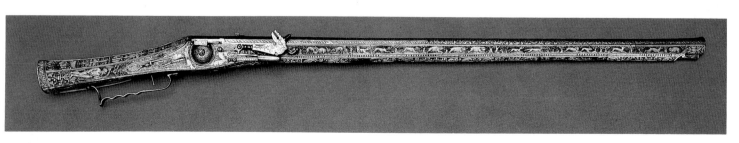

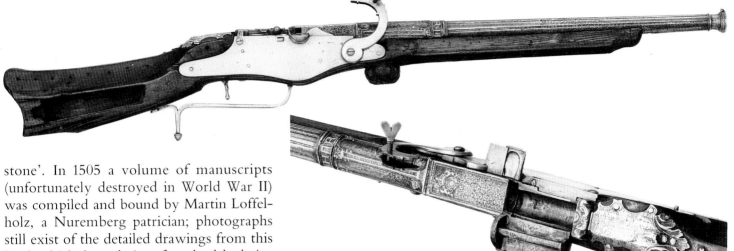

stone'. In 1505 a volume of manuscripts (unfortunately destroyed in World War II) was compiled and bound by Martin Loffelholz, a Nuremberg patrician; photographs still exist of the detailed drawings from this book which show designs for wheel-lock tinderlighters, similar in form to the mechanical 'dead-fire' devices sketched by Leonardo da Vinci in his *Codex Atlanticus*. Leonardo's drawings, now thought to date from the beginning of the sixteenth century, include a design for the workings of a wheel-lock gun mechanism; it is not clear whether this was in fact invented by Leonardo, or simply a sketch of an existing example seen by him, as is obviously the case with many of the other illustrations in the *Codex*. Whatever the case, by the end of the second decade of the sixteenth century, ordinances banning the use of these ideal assassin's weapons proliferated throughout Europe: in 1518 Emperor Maximilian attempted to enforce such a mandate, and in 1522 the Duke of Ferrara mentioned 'stone or dead-fire guns' in an ordinance banning the carrying of certain weapons in the streets of the city. A similar ban enforced in Venice by the Council of Ten in 1532 leaves no doubt as to the reasons behind such legislation: 'a kind of gun has been invented recently that makes fire by itself, and because these are small they are carried under the clothes so that nobody sees them.' Matchlocks, reliant upon a smouldering slow match for ignition, were clearly not practical for such use.

The wheel-lock gun depended for its ignition upon a piece of iron pyrites pressed against the serrated edge of a revolving wheel which was released by pressing the trigger; the resultant shower of sparks ignited gunpowder in the pan on top of the lock, sending a flash of flame through the vent hole to explode the main charge in the breech of the barrel. The powder and ball for this were almost invariably loaded down the muzzle of the gun, thrust home with a ramrod or

'skouring sticke'. Breech-loading hand guns with reloadable iron cartridges made on the same principle as that used in contemporary artillery were expensive prestige pieces; two breech-loading matchlock arquebuses known to have belonged to Henry VIII are in the Royal Armouries at the Tower of London, and by the third decade of the century richly decorated wheel-lock examples of such guns were being made, largely for sporting use. By the mid-1530s, short wheel-lock firearms (initially known as 'dags', and only later called pistols) were being used by light cavalry from holsters slung either side of the saddle, and longer wheel-locks were being carried by mounted arquebusiers. Gunpowder at this date was of poor quality, slow to burn, and caused considerable fouling after ignition. Long barrels giving maximum compression to achieve both power and an effective range in battle (usually 100 yards/90m) were fitted to infantry firearms, but for the short wheel-locks used from horse-back only point-blank range was really effective. Rifled barrels improved accuracy but were rare except on sporting wheel-locks. In war, however, the matchlock was to remain king of the battlefield until the end of the seventeenth century, due to its cheapness, ruggedness and ease of use; the wheel-lock failed on all three counts, and as a result was employed chiefly by cavalry and the nobility. Artillery became steadily more mobile as the century progressed, and the use of firearms by mounted troops as well as by infantry ensured that the military role of the heavily armoured knight was finally at an end.

Above: Henry VIII's match-lock breech-loading hand gun, early sixteenth century. The lock mechanism is a restoration, but the breech-loading barrel (see detail) is entirely original, as is the wooden stock. The butt is hollowed out with a 'patch-box', the lid of which is missing. Such a gun would fire iron cartridges preloaded with gunpowder and a lead ball or balls.

CHAPTER SEVEN
Tournaments
The Sport of Princes

Far right: Thirteenth century illuminated manuscript showing a jousting knight being killed before an audience of ladies.

Below: Emperor Ferdinand I's close-helmet for the foot tournament, by Conrad Richter (1555), representing the height of the armourer's achievement.

Since men first began fighting wars, mock combats have been used both as a form of sport and also as a means of practising one's skill at arms. Tournaments existed in Europe before 1100, using the armour and weapons commonly employed in war; they generally consisted of wide-ranging and often destructive battles between rival groups of knights, lasting all day and often resulting in no clear 'winner'. There were virtually no rules, and injury or death was common. The justifica-

tion for these activities was ably argued by Roger de Hoveden, writing in the twelfth century: 'A youth must have seen his blood flow and felt his teeth crack under the blow of his adversary, and have been thrown to the ground twenty times' before he is truly capable of facing 'real war with hope of victory'. Nevertheless, the Church castigated these sinful 'sports', and Pope Innocent II banned them in 1130 at the Council of Clermont. Until 1316, when Pope John XXII finally lifted the ban, successive injunctions were issued against tournaments, and those killed while fighting in them were often denied Christian burial, although they were allowed extreme unction and the sacrament. Such measures had little lasting effect, however, and the tournaments continued.

Gradually the prowess of the individual began to be of greater importance than the result of a general melee, and knights found profit as well as honour and renown by capturing and ransoming their opponents rather than killing them. William le Marechal, companion-at-arms of Henry III of England, is said to have captured a total of 103 knights, together with their horses and equipment, between the feasts of Pentecost and Lent (a period of about nine months); he presumably profited greatly from their ransoms. The joust, used in its early sense as a duel between single opponents, is first mentioned in England by William of Malmesbury in 1141 and rapidly became a vehicle for personal glory, profit and exercise of arms. It was also an ideal opportunity to meet with, and show off to, knightly equals.

In 1194 Richard I of England legalized tournaments in his own realm, having been a very enthusiastic combatant himself while still Count of Poitou. As a result, the tournament received its first real control. Previously, other than choosing areas of neutral

Right: A pair of knights jousting with couched lances. They form part of the decoration on the chandelier (c1140) formerly in the Abbey Church of Gross-Comburg. Their armour is that of the Norman knights in the Bayeux Tapestry.

ground to harbour the wounded, there were no regulations as to the form or conduct of the illegal but very popular sport. Now, however, they could only be held with the permission of a king's officer, an oath had to be sworn that there would be no private feuds, and a tax was levied on those taking part. This somewhat reduced the frequency of armed bands of knights rampaging through the countryside. The popularity of the joust also contributed to this process, it being easier both to regulate and to judge.

Judges and heralds began to make an appearance by the end of the twelfth century, to keep the scores and also to keep order.

The science and art of heraldry developed during this period, probably initially as a result of the Crusades, in which for the first time tens of thousands of men from different parts of Europe, often speaking different languages and owing different feudal allegiances, were gathered together for a single purpose. The confusion this caused could only be overcome by common recognition

Right: Fourteenth century misericord in Worcester Cathedral, depicting jousting knights. Note the shield 'bouched' on its right side for the lance.

signs, which began to be well-established throughout Europe from the fourth decade of the twelfth century. The first Crusaders had carried and used the sign of the Cross to signify their devotion and calling; the first of the religious Orders of Knighthood also wore the Cross, in conjunction with distinctive colours of mantle or surcoat. On 13 January 1188, at the town of Gisors in north-eastern France, just prior to the Third Crusade, Henry II of England, Philip II of France and Count Philip of Flanders agreed upon a systematic recognition code for the Crusaders under their command; the English were to wear crosses of white, the French red and the Flemish green.

Coats of arms significant to their owners appeared in the last quarter of the twelfth century, but did not become widespread until the thirteenth. The use of a helmet which covered the face necessitated some form of identifying feature so as to make the knight recognizable; this was even more necessary in tournament than in battle as the knights travelled long distances and the numbers of strangers made identification of the combatants very difficult. Heralds helped to overcome this problem, and brought order to the proceedings. Crests on helms and coats of arms on the shield and surcoat of the knight and, by the thirteenth century, on the trappings of his horse also, similarly helped with identification.

In the thirteenth century increasing importance was attached to safety, in an effort to reduce the drain on the nation's reserves of trained warriors caused by their death or injury during tournaments. Rebated lances (that is, lances with blunted heads) first appeared in the early years of the century, and from about 1250 onwards distinctions were drawn between the jousts of peace (*joust à plaisance*) and those of war (*joust à outrance*). The former type did not employ the weapons commonly used for war, but instead specific forms of tournament equipment were devised. For example, the financial accounts for the royal tournament at Windsor which took place on 9 July 1278 indicates that the armour was of leather (presumably hardened, possibly cuir-bouilli) and the blades of the swords were made of whalebone. The ground prepared for the tournament was henceforth generally referred to as the 'lists'.

The first item of plate armour to be speci-

fically designed for the joust was the characteristic 'frog-mouthed' helm, which appeared towards the end of the fourteenth century and remained, with modifications, the most common form of headpiece for the joust until the third decade of the sixteenth century. It was fastened to the front and rear of the cuirass by 'charnels' (basically a simple form of hasp and staple), and was heavier than the war helmet of the time. The vision slit was adequate for the more limited sight and mobility required for jousting. Raising the head a split second before impact ensured that no opening was available for an opponent to insert his lance. Under ordinary circumstances, the knight would ride leaning slightly forward in the saddle, so as to be able to see where he was going. These helms were pierced with holes for the attachment inside (usually by pairs of points) of a padded lining, which was often in the form of a

Above: Scene from a thirteenth century manuscript illustrating a tourney with swords. The two defeated knights have lost their helmets in the melee (one can be seen on the ground at their feet). They are wearing coifs of mail under their helms.

Above: A later manuscript illumination of the tournament at St Anglevert in 1390, described in Froissart's Chronicles. *The fifteenth century illuminator has included a tilt barrier, although in fact fourteenth century jousts were run without them.*

Far right: Knights tilting, from The Ordinance of Chivalry, *a fifteenth century English illuminated manuscript by Sir John Astley. This scene depicts the splintering of lances; the coronel heads are clearly visible.*

hood; in fifteenth century examples of this form of helm, ventilation holes or breaths (similar to those found on warhelms of the second half of the thirteenth century) were sometimes pierced in the front, both to make breathing easier and to give a degree of vision towards the ground. The left side (that confronting an opponent's lance) was frequently left smooth and uninterrupted, however. On some jousting helms dating from as early as the mid to late fourteenth century the front left-hand side is protected by a reinforcing plate; the funerary helm of Henry V (*c* 1400) in Westminster Abbey, London, is of this type.

For safety reasons, from about 1420 in Italy a barrier was introduced to separate the contestants in the lists. This was called a 'tilt barrier', and any joust which made use of it was called a 'tilt'. At first the barrier was of cloth hung over a rope, but later it became a stout wooden fence between 5 to 6 feet (1.5 to 1.8m) high, capable of withstanding at least a glancing collision from a charging horse.

Starting at opposite ends of the lists and on opposing sides of the tilt barrier, the knights charged towards each other with the barrier on their left side, each carrying his lance raised initially, lowering it at the last moment to carry it couched under the right arm with its head pointing diagonally across the neck of the horse, towards his opponent. At this angle (about 20-30 degrees) the impact of a lance striking the knight would exert the least force; in addition, since the combatants were kept apart there was much less risk of a serious collision. Even in courses run 'at random' or 'in the field' it was primarily the left side that bore the brunt of the blows. This was invariably the case with the tilt, however, so high-quality tilt armour was made thicker and heavier on that side, and also made stronger by the addition of reinforces. Henceforth, on helmets for the tilt, breaths were generally pierced only on the right side. Broad glancing surfaces were designed to carry an opponent's lance head away from the line of the body; deflection was considered as

Right: An illustration from the fifteenth century Beauchamp Chronicles, *showing a tourney with blunted swords. The Earls of Warwick were drawn from the Beauchamp family, and the Warwick badge (a 'bear and ragged staff') can be seen as a crest on the helmet of one of the combatants.*

important as preventing penetration.

These factors tended to reduce fatalities, but a strong element of risk remained. In the joust of war, on the other hand, sharpened weapons were commonly used, the aim sometimes being to actually disable or kill one's adversary, and throughout its history the tournament remained associated with the medieval concept of 'trial by combat'. More usually, the lance for the joust of peace was fitted with a crown-shaped iron head called a 'coronel', designed not to pierce armour but to spread the force of impact, either to unhorse the knight or to break the lance. Even 'sharpened' lances often only came to a blunt point.

Points were awarded for the shattering of lances; contemporary literature made great play of lances splintering in battle, and this idea was eagerly adopted in the tournament for visual effect. Hollow or jointed lances were developed to facilitate the impressive spectacle of them shattering on impact. More points were awarded for a strike against the head than the torso, and points were deducted for fouls (accidental blows hitting the horse or legs of the rider). Weapons 'of courtesy' became increasingly common in tournaments, without detracting much from the danger and excitement of the sport.

By the end of the fourteenth century courtly grace and skill were being admired and pursued as much as brute force and endurance, and the tournament increasingly became a social occasion. From the end of the fourteenth century until the seventeenth, it developed into the most popular of spectator sports, incorporating pageantry, music, dance and parade. Costumes and disguises (including knights dressed as Cardinals, Romans, monks or even women) became ever more fashionable. The influence of courtly Romantic literature also made itself felt, with much Arthurian legend and naming being incorporated into the contests and pageantry, even to the extent of re-creating 'round tables' of knights, glorifying a supposed by-gone age of chivalry. Prizes were awarded by ladies, who commonly gave kisses or rings (symbolic of sexual and eternal love); 'favours' were also often granted to the knights, these being carried during the combats, with victory dedicated to the lady concerned. Women generally became more highly regarded during the later Middle Ages, this feeling being reinforced by such phenomena as the 'Cult of the Blessed Virgin Mary', in which the biblical 'patroness' of womankind was no longer sinful Eve, but the Holy Virgin. One of the reasons for the Church's disapproval of tournaments, in fact, was the eroticism which it believed that they evinced. Nonetheless, a religious element was usually present, the knights regarding themselves as serving God and the cause of Christian justice, honour and truth.

Besides the tilt, tournaments also included foot combat duels, in which the knights initially wore field harness (armour for war) and used their ordinary weapons – swords, axes, maces or clubs and also staff-weapons, of which the pollaxe was the favourite. These duels were either fought in an enclosure (called in France the 'champ clos') or, like the tilt, over a barrier separating the contestants. In the latter case, of course, it was often not necessary for the legs to be armoured at all. A general melee in which groups of knights fought each other as in a battle was a popular way of ending the tournament. By the fifteenth century there was a multiplicity of rules and different forms of combat that could be employed.

Specialized armours were now commonly assembled for the joust. A French manuscript of 1446 lists the following: a cuirass (or sometimes a brigandine) furnished with a lance-rest; a helm (secured to the cuirass with straps and buckles); a large gauntlet (called a *main de fer* or 'manifer') for the entire left lower arm and hand; a small one-piece pauldron for the left shoulder; a small laminated pauldron and a large besagew for the right shoulder; and a large *épaulle de mouton* ('polder-mitten') for

the right arm, consisting of a lower cannon to which a large shell-like plate was attached, flaring out over the elbow and protecting the lower part of the upper arm. In addition a light gauntlet, probably made of leather, was additionally worn on the right hand. A small rectangular wooden shield, apparently in this case faced with square plates of horn (although surviving examples are more commonly painted) was hung from a cord over the left side of the cuirass; a wood or leather pear-shaped 'poire' was worn on the left side of the chest to act as a buffer between it and the shield. According to this manuscript, the French knights also commonly wore leg harness (implying, perhaps, that elsewhere the use of the tilt and specialized forms of joust saddle had made such harness redundant). This type of armour, modified slightly

Above: Roger van der Weyden's portrait (1464) of Antoine, 'Grand Batard de Bourgogne'. Antoine was a Marshal of the Lists, and is therefore shown holding a white arrow; at tournaments, throwing this down before the combatants was the signal for them to cease fighting.

Above: A late fifteenth century
painted tournament shield
portraying the medieval ideal of
courtly love: 'Vous ou la Morte'
(You or Death).

throughout Europe, continued in general use alongside field armour until the early sixteenth century. Field armour was also occasionally employed for the joust, usually with the addition of plate reinforces. Harness designed for the joust, of course, was never ever seen on the battlefield.

The tilt barrier does not seem to have been introduced into Germany from Italy until the early sixteenth century. Jousting, however, was very popular in Germany and the lands of the Holy Roman Empire; it attained considerable complexity both in the types of armour worn and the categories of 'course' run. The most common course was the 'Gestech', the armour for which was called 'Stechzeug'. Dating from about 1400, its object was to splinter lances and unhorse one's opponent; obviously, variations were practised which favoured one or other of these aims (or indeed, both of them simultaneously). An ordinary saddle was generally used, but without the high cantle which in war supported the knight in combat. In the third quarter of the fifteenth century it was supplemented by a specialized form of joust defence known as a 'stechsack', a heavily-padded buffer carried by the horse around its

neck and chest so as to protect both it and the legs of the rider from accidental lance blows.

By the late fifteenth century tournament armour had become much heavier than that designed for war; it weighed approximately 100 pounds (45kg), as opposed to 60 pounds (27kg) for the latter. The helm, or 'stechhelm', was still of the frog-mouthed variety; by now, however, it was usually screwed down on to the breastplate, which was of great weight and thickness.

A strong iron bar or 'queue' was bolted to the breastplate, which was of boxed form flattened on the right side to receive it; the end of the queue, which projected backwards behind the knight, bore a simple hook which was designed to retain the butt of the heavy jousting lance. A stout lance rest, also bolted on to the right side of the breastplate, ensured that the lance was supported during the joust, enabling the rider to concentrate on his aim. The backplate, which was not needed for any other purpose than to support the breast and helm, was usually light and often consisted of no more than a simple iron 'X' frame secured to the sides of the breastplate by hinged hasp-and-staple fittings. The arm harness remained of similar form to that described in

Right: A foot combat with
pollaxes, in an enclosure called
the champ clos. This
illumination is taken from a
French manuscript ordinance of
Philip IV, c1475.

Left: A German illuminated manuscript of the joust showing a course of the Gestech being run in the field, without a tilt barrier. All the features of Stechzeug armour for horse and man are clearly visible.

the French fifteenth century manuscript referred to earlier, although it was probably heavier. The pauldrons were laminated, the right one carrying a large besagew; alternatively, both armpits could be protectd by besagews. A short peg was sometimes fitted to the point of the right shoulder, to support the lance when carrying it upright and ensure that it did not slip off the smooth surface of the pauldron. Small tassets were commonly worn but leg harness was not. The small wooden shield (termed a 'stechtartsche') was worn as before. The lance was now supplemented by a large circular vamplate of steel for the protection of the hand, and was usually fitted with a three-pronged coronel lance head. The horses wore shaffrons of plate armour to protect their heads; in these forms of joust it was common for 'blind' shaffrons to be fitted, to prevent the animals from taking fright and shying at the moment of impact.

Many variations of the Gestech were devised, incorporating different rules and various alterations to the forms of armour worn; the most significant of these variations was the so-called 'Hohenzeuggestech', which first appeared at the end of the fourteenth century. In its early form, it was probably fought in a joust helm and field armour without any leg harness. The objective was still to splinter one's lance but the form of the saddle was radically different to that com-

monly employed for war and the simpler types of joust. It was constructed so that the rider was raised 10 inches above the horse's back into a standing position, and his thighs were supported by two high, curved

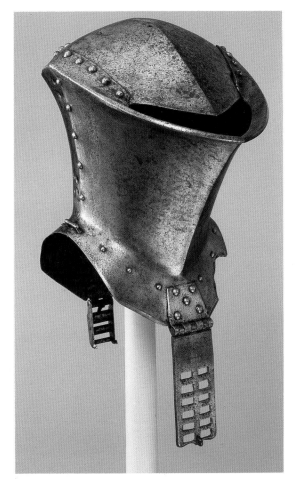

A 'frog-mouthed' jousting helm, now in the Royal Armouries. It is south German, c1480, and weighs 22 pounds 8 ounces (over 10kg).

163

Right: Another scene from the fifteenth century Beauchamp Chronicles. *A splintered lance from the previous joust lies at the foot of the tilt barrier. In Germany this joust of peace with coronel-headed lances would have been termed a 'Gestech' course.*

wooden bars at the rear. The front of the saddle consisted of a broad wooden 'fork' resting over the withers of the horse, completely protecting the rider's legs from his feet upwards, and extending to just above his waist. Specialized armour for this course was probably developed later, since this is referred to in an inventory (dating from 1436) of armour owned by the Archduke Friedrich of Tyrol. It was certainly in existence by the end of the fifteenth century and in the early years of the sixteenth, when its popularity, which had been declining for the past 50 years, was revived by Maximilian I, whose passion for the joust knew virtually no bounds.

Besides the Gestech the other most popular form of joust was the 'Rennen' or 'Scharfrennen'. This involved the use of a pointed lance as opposed to the coronel lance of the jousts of peace, and so was generally known as a joust of war. Its object was primarily to unhorse the opponent, but in some tournaments points could also be awarded for shattering lances. The first reference to it by name is found in the Archduke Friedrich's inventory, but it was probably in use from the beginning of the century. At this point, relatively early in its development, the Rennen seems to have been a comparatively light course; it was apparently run wearing a light half-armour, or even a brigandine, together

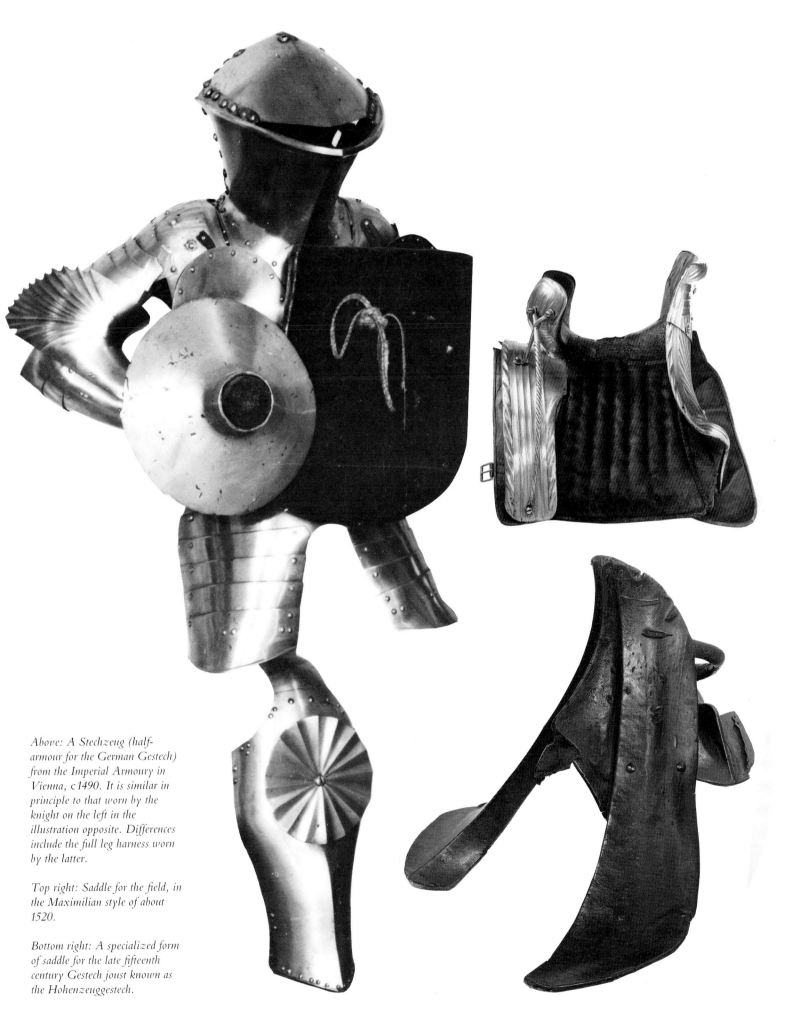

Above: A Stechzeug (half-armour for the German Gestech) from the Imperial Armoury in Vienna, c1490. It is similar in principle to that worn by the knight on the left in the illustration opposite. Differences include the full leg harness worn by the latter.

Top right: Saddle for the field, in the Maximilian style of about 1520.

Bottom right: A specialized form of saddle for the late fifteenth century Gestech joust known as the Hohenzeuggestech.

Right: A pair of bronze 'toy' jousting knights, drawn together by strings; each rider pivots backwards if hit by the other's lance. It dates to c1500.

Far right: Rennzeug; armour for the Rennen, the joust of war. Made in about 1500 for the court of Maximilian I.

Below: A painted and gilt Renntartsch (jousting shield for the Rennen) made in about 1480. It may have been made for the future Emperor Maximilian I.

with a sallet and bevor to protect the head and face, and a rectangular wooden shield on the left side of the body.

By the third quarter of the fifteenth century more specialized forms of armour were developed, several of which have survived. The main collection is in the Imperial Armoury in Vienna. The Rennen armour *c* 1480-1500 consisted of a deep one-piece sallet or 'Rennhut' furnished with a slit for vision; the brow of this helmet was reinforced with a plate divided into two halves which flew off when struck by an opponent's lance. The breastplate was similar to that used for the Gestech, but the plackart, fauld and tassets were generally heavier. The tassets usually extended virtually to the knees, and were supplemented with reinforce pieces known as 'tilting cuisses'. A deep, full bevor was screwed to the front of the breastplate but no pauldrons or arm harness were worn. Their place was taken by the vamplate of the lance, extended to cover the entire right side of the upper torso, and a large leather-covered curved wooden shield. Called a 'Renntartsch', this shield was permanently bolted to the bevor and breastplate and protected the entire left side including the bridle-hand. Leg harness tended not to be worn, and heavy leather boots extending to the knee completed the harness. Rennen armours continued to be made in this general form until the third decade of the sixteenth century, although Maximilian devised or introduced many variations of his own. One such was the 'Mechanisches Rennen', in which the breastplate incorporated a spring-loaded mechanism designed to hurl fragments of the shield (in this case of metal, constructed in segments for this specific purpose) high into the air on being struck with an opponent's lance. These oddities were rarely, if ever, used outside Germany, however.

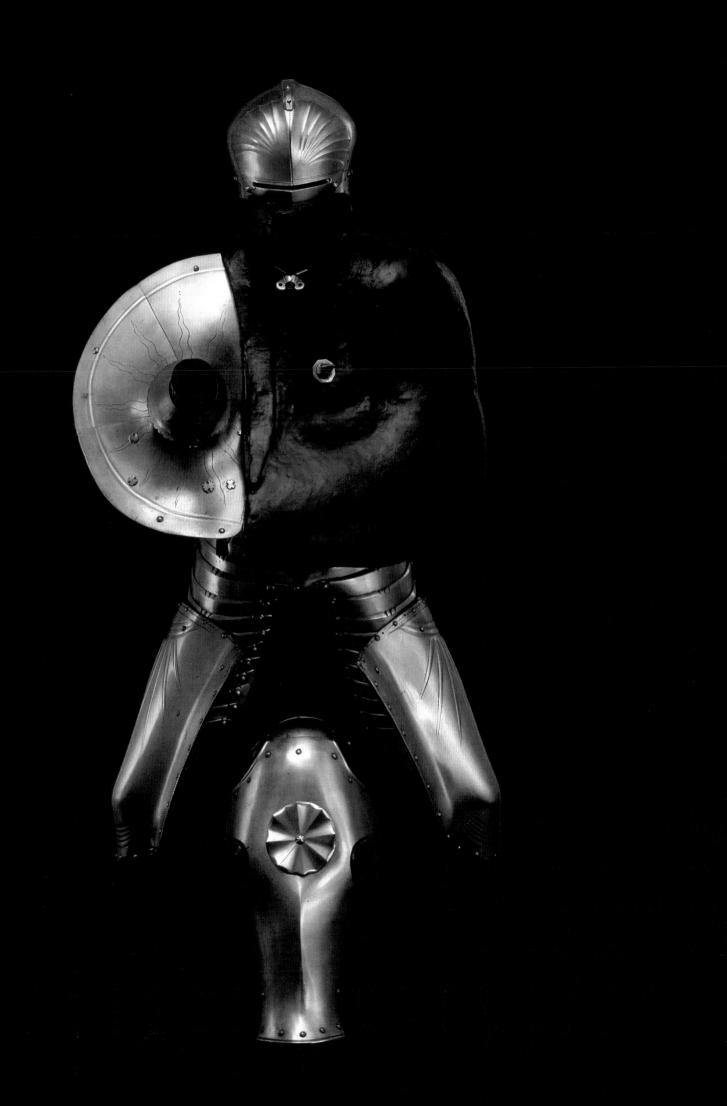

For the tourney ordinary field armour seems to have been worn throughout most of Europe. Depending upon the circumstances, this could be supplemented by the addition of reinforces, some of which could then be voided deliberately during combat, once they were no longer required. The tourney was a form of 'melee' in which groups of knights fought each other and in which other weapons than the lance could be employed, often after an initial joust or series of jousts and the shattering of lances. As with the other forms of tournament combat, many varieties of tourney existed, and the word itself was used loosely; in fact, during the sixteenth century it came to signify combat between a single pair of knights only, and was the second event in English tournaments, following the jousting. A fifteenth century form, called the 'Kolbenturnier' in Germany, was fought with cudgel-like clubs or maces; a special type of large, globose helmet was designed for this, with a multi-barred face-guard giving full protection but also a good degree of vision. The helmet for combat with clubs was often made of leather reinforced with metal. Rebated (blunted) swords were also popular tourney weapons. For foot combat, the great basinet or one of its derivatives was usually worn, strapped (and later screwed) to the breastplate. Until the end of

Above: A breastplate for the Mechanisches Rennen devised by Maximilian I. The visible mechanism was originally covered by a segmented metal plate which burst apart when hit by the lance.

Right: Woodcut by Lucas Cranach, 1509, depicting a tourney. On the bottom right one of the knights has discarded a reinforce piece.

Far right: Rear view of Henry VIII's foot combat armour made for the Field of the Cloth of Gold in 1520, but probably never used.

the fifteenth century the most popular form of visor was the hounskull variety, sometimes exaggeratedly globose in form, and pierced with many breaths, through which the wearer was also able to achieve reasonable vision. The bellows visor, introduced at the end of the fifteenth century, became increasingly popular and remained so until the middle of the sixteenth century.

In 1500 another type of foot combat armour became popular in Germany, and spread rapidly to the rest of northwestern Europe. It retained the great basinet, and was equipped with symmetrical pauldrons and cuisses, the latter often completely enclosing the upper legs. Following the contemporary fashion in civilian dress, it bore a wide, flaring knee-length skirt, called a 'tonlet'. This form of armour remained in use, especially in Germany, until the middle of the century. A tonlet armour for Henry VIII was hastily assembled at Greenwich for the 'interview' with Francis I in 1520. The title of this glorious occasion was later romanticized into The Field of the Cloth of Gold. It incorporated a tournament as an integral and significant part of the celebrations; only two months before it was due to take place, however, the French king altered the rules under which the foot combat was to be fought. This diplomatic meeting was to take place on French soil, so Francis did have this right. Henry could hardly argue with his host, and so the armour that had already been made for him was laid aside in favour of the tonlet harness. The form of the previous armour was of a type only made between about 1515 and 1530, although in fact it was aesthetically more satisfying and structurally required more skill in its manufacture. It did not have a fauld with tassets, or a tonlet; instead the entire body, including the legs and trunk, was completely encased from head to toe in steel, fully articulated where necessary. This particular armour has survived to the present day, and is in the Royal Armouries at the Tower of London. It is said that when scientists working for NASA were asked to design a rigid yet flexible spacesuit for their astronauts, it was the foot combat armour of Henry VIII that they examined and took as their model (without however, incorporating a codpiece). The 'codpiece', by then prominent in civilian fashion, was equally prominent in the design of early sixteenth century armours.

Below: Front view of Henry VIII's foot combat armour in the Royal Armouries. It is shown with a contemporary pollaxe. (See page 169 for the rear view.)

Below: Henry VIII's tonlet armour, hurriedly made for the Field of the Cloth of Gold in 1520, and worn in place of the harness on the left.

Far left: A parade sallet of steel, encased in gilt to resemble the head of a lion. Italian (Venetian), c1460.

Left: German tilt armour c1590, from the workshop of Anton Peffenhauser. This was the last form that armour took before the sport of jousting fell into a decline in the seventeenth century. Note the steel shield (targetta) bolted permanently to the breastplate.

Below: The commencement of a tourney from a mid-fifteenth century illuminated manuscript by Rene d'Anjou. A variety of armour and weapons can be seen, including those for combat with clubs and maces.

Right: Parade armour with a tonlet, made for Margrave Albrecht von Brandenburg in about 1525. Sections of the tonlet can be removed by releasing sneck hooks, enabling the wearer to ride a horse.

It is known that as early as 1510 interchangeable alternative pieces (called 'exchange pieces') were being made for field armours to convert them for the tournament. The harness of Andreas von Sonnenburg, in Vienna, is one of these; it was furnished with an alternative helmet, and reinforcing pieces for the bevor, breastplate, left couter and left gauntlet. These converted it from a field armour into one for the tourney. Between 1520 and 1530 the idea of the 'garniture' had spread to most of Europe; rather than purchase separate armours for field, joust, tilt, and tourney, it was far more sensible and economical to make up the form of armour desired by using some pieces in common, adding others as required. A Greenwich field harness, for example, could be converted into a tilt armour by substituting for the field helmet a heavy tilting helm (or a heavier visor for the field helmet), and then adding a 'grandguard' (reinforce for the left and part of the right side of the breastplate), a 'pasguard' (reinforce for the elbow) and a manifer (reinforce in the shape of a large 'mitten', worn over the left gauntlet). By the middle of the sixteenth century, garnitures were already attaining tremendous size and complexity, reaching the peak of their development at the end of the century.

Tournaments remained popular throughout the sixteenth century, and a 'debased' form of joust (the 'carousel') continued into the seventeenth. They were never just social or sporting occasions, however, but constituted a visible manifestation of the social and

Above: An English great basinet of about 1515, worn for the foot combat or the tourney.

Above left: Tourney helm for combat with mace or sword, similar to those visible in the illuminated manuscript on page 171.

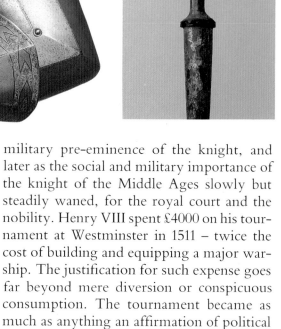

Right: Pieces of exchange for a mid-sixteenth century south German field harness in the Royal Armouries. It was reinforced, especially on the left side, for jousting 'in the Italian fashion' (that is, using a tilt barrier). Wallace Collection.

Far right: Jousting lance, perhaps once belonging to Henry VIII.

Opposite page: Equestrian harness (part of a very large garniture and similar armours assembled over several years) for Otto Heinrich, Count Palatine of the Rhine. Pieces are dated 1532 and 1536.

Below: Henry VIII jousting in the tilt-yard at Westminster during the 1511 tournament, watched by Catherine of Aragon and her ladies. It was a dangerous sport; the king was nearly killed during a tilt in March 1524.

military pre-eminence of the knight, and later as the social and military importance of the knight of the Middle Ages slowly but steadily waned, for the royal court and the nobility. Henry VIII spent £4000 on his tournament at Westminster in 1511 – twice the cost of building and equipping a major warship. The justification for such expense goes far beyond mere diversion or conspicuous consumption. The tournament became as much as anything an affirmation of political power, status, wealth and glory.

The Construction of Mail

Right: A theoretical sequence (since no original tools survive) of medieval mail manufacture. Drawn soft iron wire wrapped around an iron mandrel is cut into links with a cold chisel. A simple punch and former (bottom right) may have been used to form the rings. Another tool (top right) simultaneously flattens and shapes the end of each link, and a third (bottom left) pierced each with a slot. Wedge-shaped rivets were probably cut from a flat metal strip, and the mail assembled (four links through every one). The raised rivet heads faced out. The mail was case-hardened (or if mild steel, quench-hardened).

Below: Left to right, a recent (Eastern) butt-jointed mail ring, a sixteenth century European riveted iron ring (the rivet removed), a similar ring (the rivet in place), and a third fully closed.

Bottom: Detail of the German fifteenth century riveted mail shirt illustrated on page 130, showing the brass ring stamped BERNART COUWEIN. *The diameter of each link is 0.4 inches (1cm), and the shirt weighs approx 20 pounds (9kg).*

Below right: A fifteenth century mailmaker. Over 30,000 links were needed to make one mail shirt.

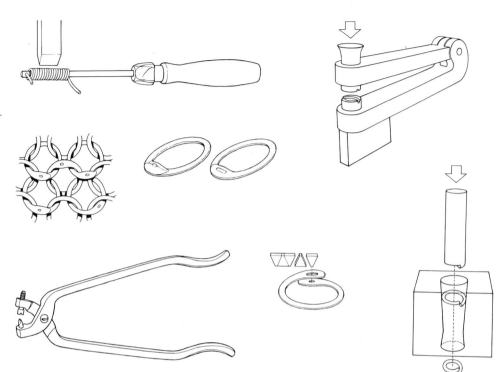

Armour: Construction

Hinge for the cheek-piece on an Italian (Milanese) archer's sallet (barbuta) c1470.

Side view of the same hinge. It is 1.5 inches (3.8cm) long and is made of iron; the iron rivet heads are original.

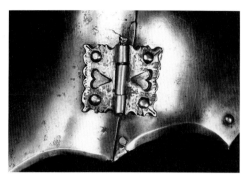

Hinge of pierced and engraved latten measuring 2 inches (5cm) square, on the peytral of the c1480 'Gothic' equestrian harness on page 127.

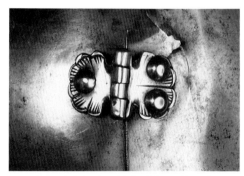

Brass hinge 1.25 inches (3.1cm) long, from the greave of the armour on page 127. Engraved lines form the decoration. The rivet heads are modern.

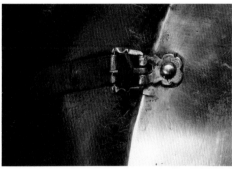

Tinned latten buckle 1.5 inches (3.8cm) long on the shaffron of the 'Gothic' harness on page 127. The sides were probably filed.

Detached brass buckle 1.5 inches (3.8cm) long from an early sixteenth century 'Maximilian' armour. The decoration is stamped and filed.

Vambrace from the armour of King Wladislas, probably made in 1510, illustrated on page 142; it is closed with a stud and hole fixing.

The vambrace of the Wladislas armour (closed in previous photo) now open; the springiness of the metal is sufficient to keep it shut.

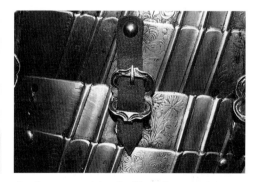

Leather strap and iron buckle with stamped decoration, joining the cuirass and tassets made by Kolman Helmschmid in 1523 (see page 145).

Steel hinge 1.9 inches (4.8cm) long, instead of the more usual strap and buckle attaching the tasset to the fauld on a 'Maximilian' armour, c1530.

Stamped sheet-brass plume-holder on a German demi-shaffron dating from 1550. The tube is 2.5 inches (6.3cm) high.

A shaped 'wing nut' on threaded studding riveted to the side of the peytral (perhaps to carry a flanchard) on the same harness as on page 127.

Gauntlets: Construction

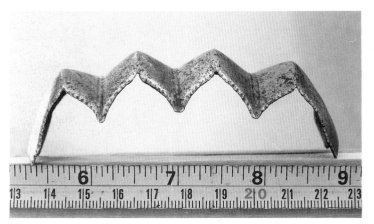

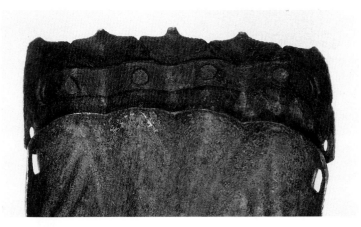

Top: 'Gothic' German gauntlet, c1480, in the Wallace Collection. Total length is 12 inches (30.5cm) and it is 2.5 inches (6.4cm) wide at the narrowest part of the wrist. The fingers and thumbs are missing, but the gadlings (detail below) survive. Even allowing for corrosion, the metal was not more than about 0.02 inches (0.5-0.8mm) thick. The gauntlet weighs 10.5 ounces (0.3kg).
Above: profile view from the front of the knuckles (gadlings) detached from the gauntlet above. This plate carried the fingers, and, to give flexibility, was attached by a sliding rivet to each side of the main plate covering the hand.
Above right: Interior view of the main plate for the hand on the gauntlet above, with the gadlings in place but not secured. The slots for the sliding rivets can be seen each side of the main plate. Note the metal strip riveted to each side of the knuckles; to this were riveted the leathers carrying overlapped metal plates to protect the fingers.
Right: Interior view of a mitten gauntlet of the Wladislas armour, c1510. The rivets for a leather lining strap (missing) are visible along the outer edge of the last plate, covering the finger-tips. To this and another such strap at the cuff would have been sewn a leather glove. When dirty or damaged this was removable by cutting the stitches.

Armet and Gorget: Construction

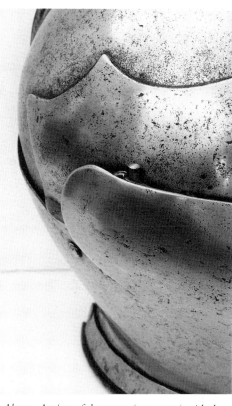

Above: Detail of a similar Wallace Collection armet showing the hidden pivot for the visor; a fitting on the latter still holds the retaining pin.

Above: To release the Wladislas armet's visor a press-stud operates a spring-loaded notched peg protruding from inside the helmet.

Above: A view of the armet (top centre) with the pivot-pin for the visor in place, driven through slightly from underneath so that it becomes visible.

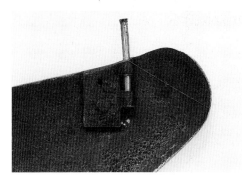

Above: Inside of the cheek-piece on the Wladislas armet, to which is riveted a spring-metal strip carrying the press-stud and visor locking peg.

Above: Wladislas armet and gorget. Each shoulder of the gorget shows the retaining pegs which have a spring-loaded pivoted flange to secure the pauldron.

Above: View of the interior of the visor from the armet (top centre), showing the concealed pivot fitting with its protruding retaining-pin.

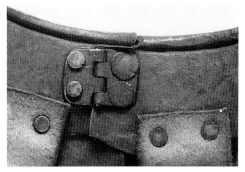

Above: Front of the Wladislas armet demonstrating how the hinged cheek-pieces overlap at the chin and are secured there by a slotted keyhole stud.

Above: Gorget from the Wladislas armour; the rim around the neck engages with the turn around the base of the armet to permit movement.

Above: Interior view of the gorget on the left, showing the turned rim and the hinge. The pair of rivets on the right are original, the others modern.

Wladislas Armour: Construction

Above: Interior view of the gorget, showing how the overlapping lames of the neck are riveted to 'leathers' (straps), to permit a degree of flexibility. All the rivets bar the bottom pair are concealed by the overlap of the plates.
Right: Side view of the cuirass and tassets shows the usual profile of armour at this period. The three-hole fastening at the waist allows for expansion of girth or wearing of a thicker arming doublet. The shoulder straps are steel.
Below: Interior of the fauld and tassets. The lames are secured on two buff leathers and a single line of 'sliding' rivets, held by washers and operating within slots, to prevent the plates opening up during flexing.

Above: Interior view of the arm harness showing the lames of the pauldron held together by two leathers and a line of sliding rivets (on the right). It was attached by a strap and buckle to the upper vambrace. This was usually laced to the arming doublet (note thongs) to help distribute the weight. Below: A leg harness. The cuisse is secured to the thigh with a strap and buckle, the poleyn to the greave by a slotted keyhole stud and a strap and buckle (missing but note the slot for the strap end).

Above: The cuirass and tassets; note the curvature of the latter. The hole for the peg to carry the codpiece has been (incorrectly) filled. The lance rest (detached) was bolted to the breastplate; the two holes for it in the breast are clearly visible.

Left: The slotted keyhole stud by which the fauld attaches to the lower edge of the breastplate. The breastplate weighs 5 pounds 14 ounces (2.7kg); the backplate 5 pounds 1 ounce (2.3kg).
Below: An early sixteenth century codpiece. The hole in the top would originally have held the peg by which it was secured to the lower plate of the fauld. This peg incorporated a spring clip to retain it, like those on the gorget to carry the pauldrons.

Helmets and Helmet Linings

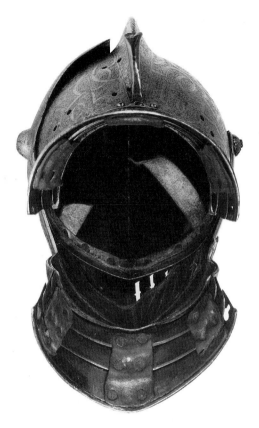

Above: Interior of Ferdinand I's gilt close-helmet (page 154), showing remnants of the leather cross-straps and a lining strap to sew the lining to.

Above: A heavily padded and quilted arming cap for a German jousting helm c1484. The leather laces were tied through pairs of holes in the helmet.

Above: Quilted lining stuffed with dried grass and horse-hair. This was once sewn to a lining strap riveted inside a sixteenth century close-helmet.

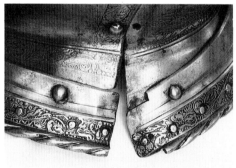

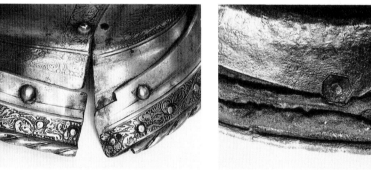

Above: Detail of a sneck hook closing the side of the sixteenth century eagle-visored close-helmet illustrated on page 141. A pair of lacing holes to attach the padded lining are visible on the left.
Above centre: Gorget plates at the base of the partly opened eagle-visored helmet. The front (left) overlaps the back (right), edged by a line of rivets for the leather lining strap inside.
Above right: Interior view of one of the gorget plates illustrated on the left, showing the leather lining strap for the lining (not present, only the skull lining, right, survives on this helmet).
Right: Quilted skull lining padded with tow, from the same helmet as above. It is still sewn to fragments of the lining strap once riveted inside.

Glossary

Action *see* aketon

Ahlespiess Fifteenth century staff weapon epecially popular with Swiss infantry. It had a long, spike-like head of square section with a rondel at its base to protect the user's hand, and was designed specifically for thrusting.

Ailette A flat plate of leather or parchment (square, round or diamond-shaped) which tied to the point of the shoulder. Worn between 1250-1350 to display the owner's coat-of-arms.

Almain Rivet A light munition half-armour or corslet, imported from Germany in the early sixteenth century.

Aketon A padded and quilted garment, usually of linen, worn under or instead of plate or mail.

Anime Also called anima. A 'splinted' cuirass or breast-and-back, composed of horizontal overlapping lames.

Arbalest Also called arbolest. Crossbow with a steel bow spanned by mechanical means.

Arçons Also called arsons. Bow and cantle of a medieval saddle.

Armet Fifteenth century helmet of Italian origin consisting of a skull, two hinged cheek pieces which lock at the front, and a visor.

Armiger A squire.

Arming doublet Quilted garment worn under armour from the early fifteenth century, equipped with points to attach mail gussets and pieces of armour.

Arming points Ties (usually of flax or twine) by which armour was secured in place.

Arming sword Cut and thrust fighting sword; part of the knight's equipment for war.

Arquebus Also called Harquebus, Hackbut or Hagbush. A short gun used by infantry throughout the sixteenth and early seventeenth centuries; the butt was sometimes curved so that when levelled it rested against the chest instead of the shoulder.

Arrière-ban Medieval militia of France.

Aventail A curtain of mail attached by means of staples (vervelles) around the base of a helmet (especially the *basinet*), and cover-ing the shoulders. Also called camail (a French term).

Backplate Plate armour defence for the back.

Back Sword A sword with a single cutting edge, the other side of the blade (the 'back') being blunt except for a few inches at the tip, where it is double-edged.

Ballock Knife Contemporary name for a dagger having a pair of rounded lobes at the base of the grip (usually carved in one). Also called a ballock dagger and a kidney dagger (the latter a Victorian nicety).

Barbote A high bevor with a falling lame containing eyeslits; used in Spain.

Barbut Also called barbute, barbuta. An open-faced shoulder-length Italian helmet, made in one piece, with a T-shaped face opening. Barbuta is the Italian term.

Bard A full horse armour, which could include a shaffron, crinet, peytral, crupper and flanchards.

Bardiche Also called berdiche. A pollaxe with a long, slightly curved blade, principally used in north-eastern Europe.

Barrier A fence-like structure over which foot combats were fought from the late fifteenth century onwards. *See also* Tilt.

Baselard A civilian dagger or short sword with an H-shaped hilt. Particularly common in the fourteenth and fifteenth centuries in north and northwest Europe. Also called a hauswehr.

Bases Cloth skirts worn over armour in the sixteenth century. *See also* tonlet.

Basinet Also called bascinet, basnet. An open-faced helmet with a globular or conical skull enclosing the sides of the face and neck. Usually worn with an aventail, and occasionally a visor.

Bastard sword A contemporary term, now used to describe a sword wielded by one or both hands. Also called a hand-and-a-half sword.

Bec-de-faucon Axe or hammer with a fluke curved to a sharp point in the form of a falcon's beak.

Bellows Visor A modern term for a visor with horizontal ridges, such as on 'Maximilian' German fluted armours of the early sixteenth century.

Besagew Defensive circular plate suspended over the wearer's armpit.

Bevor Also called bavier or buffe. A chin-shaped defense for the lower face, incorporating a gorget plate. The buffe was an early sixteenth century variant, worn strapped to an open-faced helmet such as the burgonet. *See also* falling buffe or buff.

Bill A staff weapon (dating from the thirteenth century) based upon the agricultural hedging bill; its curved blade is fitted with a top and rear spike.

Birnie Also called byrnie. A mail shirt. *See also* hauberk.

Bishop's Mantle Modern term for the cape of mail worn (largely in Germany) in the early sixteenth century.

Blueing An oxidized blue surface on plate armour, produced through heat treatment.

Bombard A wrought-iron cannon of large calibre used in sieges.

Bouche The notch cut in the top (dexter) corner of a shield, to rest the lance when jousting.

Bow *see* arbalest, crossbow and longbow

Bow Also called saddle-bow. The front of the saddle, resting across the horse's withers. The medieval bow was usually high, and was fitted with steel plates in the fifteenth and sixteenth centuries for the protection of the rider. *See also* arçon.

Bracer Early fourteenth century form of defence for the lower arm; also a term for an archer's arm guard to protect the forearm from the bowstring.

Breastplate Plate armour protection for the front of the torso, to the waist. *See also* plackart.

Breaths Holes or slits in the visor of a helmet or the lames of a falling buff or bevor, for ventilation; also usually permitting a degree of extra vision.

Breech The rear end of a cannon or gun barrel; usually the point of ignition.

Brigandine A flexible body defence consisting of a large number of metal plates riveted inside a cloth covering.

Buckler A small round shield carried by infantry.

Buffe *see* bevor and falling buffe

Burgonet A light, open-faced helmet popular in the sixteenth century as an alternative to the close-helmet for light cavalry. It was usually furnished with a peak over the brow, a combed skull, and hinged ear-pieces. The face opening could be closed by the addition of a falling buffe.

Butts Area of ground prepared for archery practice.

Byrnie *see* birnie

Cabacete A type of Spanish war hat (popular throughout fifteenth century Europe) with a turned-down brim and an almond-shaped skull ending in a stalk. *See also* morion.

Cabasset *see* morion

Caliver A light hand gun of the late fifteenth and sixteenth centuries, usually fitted with a match-lock ignition mechanism. Shorter barrelled than the standard infantry musket or arquebus, it nonetheless still had a large musket-size bore.

Camail *see* aventail

Cannon The first European artillery pieces appeared in the early fourteenth century, used against fortifications rather than as tactical battlefield weapons. By the end of the sixteenth century, the following cannon sizes and types were in common use: the cannon royal was largest, then cannon, culverin, demi-culverin, saker, minion, falcon, falconet and serpentine.

Cannon Individual plate armour defence, of tubular form, for the upper and lower arm. *See also* vambrace and rerebrace.

Cantle The rear part of the saddle comprising the back of the seat, usually quite strong and high so as to support the rider. *See also* arçon and bow.

Cap-à-Pied Term derived from the French meaning 'from head to foot'.

Case-hardening A method (described in the twelfth century treatise 'De Diversis Artibus', by Theophilus the Monk) for surface hardening wrought iron (or low-carbon steel) by packing it in charcoal or other organic material and heating it for hours above 900°C.

Casque, casquetal A light, open helmet; usually late fifteenth to mid-sixteenth century helmets of 'antique' form, such as Italian parade 'casques' of the mid-sixteenth century, embossed with grotesques or fashioned in the classical style. These were often similar in shape to the burgonet.

Celata Open-faced Italian sallet, common in the fifteenth century.

Cervellière Steel skull cap.

Champ-Clos A ring, usually surrounded by a wooden barrier, in which two or more equally matched armed combatants fought during a tournament.

Chanfron *see* shaffron

Chape A metal terminal, often decorated, for the bottom of a sword, knife or dagger scabbard to protect it against wear or damage. Also metal strap-ends on belts, horse harness etc. *See also* locket.

Chapel de Fer Also called kettle hat. A simple open-faced helmet with a wide brim.

Charnel The hinged staple or bolt that secured the fourteenth century helm or great basinet to the breast- and backplate.

Chasing Decorative work carried out with chasing tools on metallic or other hard surfaces; the opposite of embossing, which uses a similar technique but from the underside of the metal being worked, to create a decorative scheme worked in relief. Embossed surfaces are frequently chased to render the design crisp.

Chausses Mail protection for the legs, either in the form of mail hose or strips of mail laced round the front of the leg.

Cheeks Contemporary term for 'langets'; long strips of metal riveted to the shaft of a weapon to attach, strengthen or protect the head.

Cinquedea A large civilian dagger or short sword with a broad triangular blade, popular in Italy in the late fifteenth and early sixteenth centuries.

Close-helmet Helmet which, with a full visor and bevor, completely encloses the head and face; modern use of the term tends to refer not to helmets with hinged cheek-pieces opening at the front (the armet) but visored helmets pivoting open on bolts or rivets each side of the skull. Contempor-

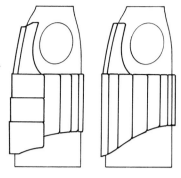
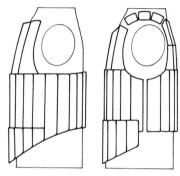

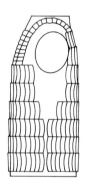

Above: A series of alternative constructions for the fourteenth century 'coat of plates', based upon examples excavated from the mass graves on the site of the Battle of Wisby (1361) in Gotland, Sweden. It is likely that some if not most of these were already old when they were hastily pressed into service against the invading Danes. In particular, the bottom two could well be lamellar armour, later converted.

ary usage, however, makes no such distinction.

Cnicht Anglo-Saxon word meaning a retainer.

Coat armour A quilted garment worn over armour in the fourteenth century.

Coat of fence Also called fence, jack or brigandine. A doublet or tunic lined with small metal plates or, more rarely, just padded with a stuffing of tow. *See also* brigandine and jack.

Coat of plates Also called a pair of plates or simply plates. A cloth garment with a number of large plates riveted inside, worn in the fourteenth century.

Cod-piece Fabric covering for the groin, latterly padded. Its counterpart in armour could be either of mail or, more usually, of plate.

Coif A hood, usually of mail; by the twelfth century it often incorporated a Ventail.

Collar *see* gorget

Comb The keel-shaped ridge, often very pronounced, that passes from front to back of a helmet over the top of the skull, conferring extra strength and rigidity and contributing to its glancing surfaces. In the mid-sixteenth century, the combs of morion helmets were raised and enlarged to an excessive height for 'fashionable' reasons.

Comb morion *see* morion

Coronel A type of rebated lance-head having a blunt 'crown' or three or four blunt prongs instead of a single sharp point. Used in jousts of peace, to shatter lances or unhorse an opponent rather than to inflict injury.

Corslet Also spelt corselet. A light half-armour popular in the sixteenth century for general military use (for example, for town guards). It consisted of a gorget, breast, back and tassets, full arms and gauntlets; the term can also be applied to the cuirass only.

Corsèque *see* runka

Counterfeit Damascening Decorative overlay (rather than 'true' damascening or inlay), usually of softer non-ferrous metals such as silver or gold onto an iron or steel surface.

Couter Also spelt cowter. Plate defence for the elbow.

Crinet Defence for a horse's neck. *See also* bard.

Crupper Defence for a horse's rump. *See also* bard.

Cranequin *see* rack

Crest A heraldic recognitive device fixed to the top of the great helm, introduced in the second half of the thirteenth and in wide use by the fourteenth century.

Crossbow A horizontal bow set at 90 degrees to the tiller and spanned by mechanical means. Originally made of horn, wood, and sinew, the bowstave was later made of steel.

Cuirass Also called pair of curates. A backplate and breastplate designed to be worn together.

Cuir bouilli Leather hardened by super saturating in water or boiled in molten wax, and then dried over a former. Popular as a medium for embossing and tooling.

Cuirie A thirteenth century form of rigid body defence, originally made of leather.

Cuisses Also called cuishes. Defences for the thighs.

Culet Hooped plate defence for the rump, made of horizontal laminations.

Culverin *see* cannon

Dag A small, short wheel-lock pistol, easily concealed and therefore banned when it first appeared at the beginning of the sixteenth century.

Dagger A diminutive form of sword, usually worn on the right hip, with a short single or double-edged blade and a variety of hilt forms. Known in fourteenth century England as a misericorde.

Damascening Also called inlay. A process used for the decoration of metal surfaces; usually silver or gold onto iron or steel. 'True' damascening is a form of inlay wherein grooves or channels are cut in the surface to be decorated and the softer metal forming such decoration is hammered into them, usually as a wire. *See also* counterfeit damascening.

Damascus steel *see* watered steel

Demi-shaffron *see* shaffron

Destrier The war-horse of a knight.

Double-pieces *see* exchange pieces

Ear dagger A dagger with an 'eared' hilt, probably Eastern in origin; popular in Spain, Venice and Italy in the fifteenth and early sixteenth centuries.

Embossing *see* chasing

Elbow gauntlet The cuff of this gauntlet reaches the elbow, replacing both the lower cannon of the vambrace and the couter.

Enarmes Suspension loops or straps attached to the inside of the shield, through which the knight passed his arm in order to carry it.

Espalier An early English name for a light, usually laminated, shoulder defence. It first appeared at the end of the thirteenth century.

Estoc Also called a foining sword or, in English, tuck. A thrusting sword with a long, stiff blade designed purely for fighting with the point.

Etching A decorative process frequently applied to the surface of metals especially in Europe from about 1500 onwards; frequently used in conjunction with blueing and gilding.

Exchange pieces Also called double pieces and pieces of exchange. Supplementary pieces of armour which could be added to, or exchanged with, those comprising a harness, in order to alter its purpose, for instance, from field to joust, or for different types of joust. *See also* garniture.

Falchion A short, single-edged sword with a cleaver-like curved blade, very popular from the thirteenth century onwards with all classes of soldier.

Falcon *see* cannon

Falconet *see* cannon.

Fall A peak over the brow of a helmet. It was sometimes pivotted at the sides.

Falling buffe Sixteenth century plate armour for the chin and lower face, similar to the bevor but made of several lames (usually articulated by means of sliding rivets) held in place by a spring catch or stud which, when released, allowed the buff to fall, thereby exposing the face to permit better breathing and vision. It could replace the visor on an open-faced helmet of burgonet form, and was often made as an exchange piece. *See also* bevor.

Fauchard *see* glaive

Fauld Armour (usually composed of horizontal lames) attached to the bottom edge of a breastplate to protect the abdomen.

Fealty Allegiance and military service due by a vassal to his feudal superior; hence 'oath of fealty'.

Fence or **fencing** The art of sword-fighting.

Fence, coat of *see* coat of fence, jack and brigandine

Field armour Armour for war, that is, 'for the field'. Also called hosting armour.

Fire-lock Term denoting a mechanical ignition system for a gun, or the gun itself; any ignition mechanism involving the making or 'carrying' of fire, for example matchlock, wheel-lock, snaphance or flintlock. *See* dead-fire.

Flanchard An oblong plate attached to the base of the saddle, protecting the flanks of a horse. It closed the gap between the crupper and the peytral. *See also* bard.

Foible Also called faible. The part of the blade nearest to the point.

Foining sword A contemporary term probably denoting an estoc.

Forte The strongest part of the blade, nearest the hilt.

Free-lance A medieval mercenary; literally, a knight owing no allegiance to any feudal overlord.

Furniture The mounts of a weapon, usually metal. The term is most frequently used in connection with guns.

Fustibal A staff-sling capable of throwing heavier shot than a handsling, often used in sieges to launch incendiaries.

Gadlings Protruding studs or bosses (sometimes zoomorphic) on the finger and knuckle joints of a gauntlet.

Gambeson A quilted, skirted doublet of cloth, often made of linen, stuffed with tow, wool or grass. Worn by all classes either underneath a mail shirt, on top of it, or as a separate defence on its own.

Gamboised cuisses Padded and quilted thigh defences worn in the thirteenth and fourteenth century.

Gardbrace A reinforcing plate closely shaped to the pauldron, first appearing in the fifteenth century on Italian armours. It covered the lower three-quarters of the front of the pauldron and was attached to it by a staple and pin.

Gard-cuish, Gard-cuisse *see* tilting socket

Garde-rein Defence for a man's rump.

Garniture An armour complete in itself but also with up to 20 or 30 related interchangeable exchange-pieces or additional parts. An innovation introduced in the sixteenth century.

Gauntlet Defence for the hand, in the form of a glove. It could be of mitten type or individually fingered; initially of mail (see muffler), then of plate. See also mitten gauntlet, elbow gauntlet, and locking gauntlet.

Gestech A form of joust fought with rebated lances, in order to score points by hitting one's opponent or shattering lances (the 'joust of peace').

Gilding Plating with a thin layer of gold. *See also* mercury gilding.

Gipon *see* jupon

Gisarme Also called guisarme. A staff weapon. The head is a cres-cent-shaped axe, the lowest point of which is joined to the staff.

Glaive An infantry staff weapon which first appeared in the fourteenth century and was favoured by the French. It had a long, cleaver-like blade shaped like an enlarged bread-knife, sometimes with a false upper edge, usually attached by langets (cheeks) to the shaft, which had a rondel of steel to protect the hand.

Goat's-foot lever A device for spanning crossbows.

Godendag Primarily Flemish staff weapon similar to a bill; the blade was probably based on the shape of a ploughshare. Popular with the common soldiery in Flanders from the late thirteenth to the fifteenth century.

Gorget Also called a collar. Plate defence for the neck and extreme top of the chest and shoulders. Generally made in two parts joined by a hinge or pivoting rivet on the left and a 'keyhole' and stud to secure it on the right. Sixteenth century examples usually have a high, laminated neck and fittings to carry the pauldrons.

Gothic With regard to armour the term refers in particular to late fifteenth century German armour, characterized by cusped attenuated lines and fluting, often incorporated into fan-shaped designs.

Grand guard A large reinforcing plate designed for the tilt, attached to the left side of the breastplate to cover the left shoulder, the upper arm and breastplate and the left side of the visor.

Graper A stop behind the grip of a lance.

Great helm *see* helm

Greave Also called schynbald or jamber. Plate defence for the leg from knee to ankle, initially protecting only the front, but later the whole lower leg. Constructed of two plates hinged together and shaped to the contours of the muscle. Schynbald and jamber are used in connection with the earlier type.

Greenwich armour English armour made in Greenwich at the armourers' workshops set up by Henry VIII at the beginning of the sixteenth century.

Grip The handle of a sword or dagger, excluding pommel and guard.

Guard chains Chains which linked the breastplate with the sword, dagger and great helm to stop them being lost in action. Popular in the fourteenth century.

Guige Strap attached to the inside of the shield by which it could be slung round the neck of the bearer.

Guisarme *see* gisarme

Gusset In the fifteenth century, shaped pieces of mail sewn to the arming doublet to cover the armpits and portions of the arm left exposed by the plate defences. In the early sixteenth century gusset also referred to laminations at the armpit of the breastplate.

Habergeon, Haubergeon A short type of hauberk. The terms are often used indiscriminately.

Hackbut *see* arquebus

Hagbush *see* arquebus

Halberd An infantry staff weapon especially popular with the Swiss. Its head consisted of a cleaver-like axe blade balanced at the rear by a fluke (hook) or lug, and surmounted by a spike, usually of quadrangular section. From the fourteenth century the head was attached to the staff with cheeks (langets) of steel.

Hand-and-a-half sword *see* bastard sword

Hand gun A gun (either a pistol or shoulder-arm) held in the hand or hands, in contrast to an artillery piece reliant upon a free-standing carriage.

Haqueton *see* aketon

Harness A term used in preference to 'suit' when talking of a complete armour.

Harquebus *see* arquebus

Hauberk A mail shirt reaching to somewhere between the knee and hip and invariably with sleeves. Hauberks could be made of other materials, such as scale.

Hauswehr *see* baselard

Haute-piece Upstanding neck guard attached to the pauldrons.

Heater shield A form of knightly shield which appeared around 1270. Shaped much like the base of a flat iron.

Heaume *see* helm

Heerban Medieval militia of the German States.

Helm, Great Helm An all-enveloping helmet which enclosed the entire head and face, reaching almost to the shoulders. Originally cylindrical in form. Restricted to the joust from the mid-fourteenth century.

Heriot The tribute due to a feudal overlord (usually the king) on the death of a vassal or tenant.

Originally the return of lent military equipment, by the later Middle Ages it constituted a payment in money or in kind.

Hollow ground blade A blade in which the cross-section incorporates concave facets, requiring very skilled forging and grinding.

Hose A cloth leg covering. In Norman times, very loose; by the fifteenth century they fitted closely, the legs being joined..

Hosting armour *see* field armour

Housing *see* trapper

Hunskull An English corruption of the German *hundsgugel* (dog head), a nickname for the pointed visors found on basinets of the late fourteenth and early fifteenth centuries.

Inlay *see* damascening

Jack A jacket or doublet of fence either of linen stuffed with tow or lined with small metal plates.

Jamb Also called jamber, jambart or jambière. An early medieval term for leg armour (schynbald). *See also* greave.

Javelin A spear designed to be thrown rather than used as a thrusting weapon.

Joust Mock combat between mounted knights, who charged each other with couched lances. Jousts often took place within tournaments. Special armour, weapons and equipment for the joust began to be introduced in the fourteenth and fifteenth centuries.

Jupon A tight-fitting garment, usually padded, and worn over armour from *c*1350-1410. Often used to display the wearer's arms.

Kastenbrust A modern term used to describe a particular type of angular breastplate common in Germany between 1420 and 1450.

Kettle hat An open-faced helmet consisting of a bowl with a broad brim, resembling the 'tin hat' of the British Army 1914-48.

Kidney dagger *see* ballock dagger

Kite-shaped shield A large, elongated triangular shield with a rounded top used throughout Europe from the tenth to the thirteenth century, commonly associated with the Normans.

Klappvisier A modern term for a globular visor worn in Germany in the fourteenth century to accompany the basinet; it only covered the area of the face left exposed by the aventail.

Knuckle-guard or **-bow** The curved guard of a sword hilt,

designed to afford some protection to the hand; a metal bar curving outwards from the quillon block towards the pommel.

Lame A narrow strip or plate of steel, sometimes used in armour to provide articulation.

Lamellar armour Armour consisting of small plates laced together to give a rigid defence. Of Near Eastern origin, used throughout the Middle Ages in Eastern Europe, but not common in the West.

Lance A horseman's spear approximately 14 feet (4.27m) long and usually made of ash, with a small steel head. After the fourteenth century it swells in front of and behind the grip, tapering at either end and was equipped with a vamplate to protect the hand.

Lance rest A support for the lance when couched; this was bolted to the right side of the breastplate and was often hinged.

Landesknecht A type of lightly armoured German soldier (early sixteenth century), usually of lesser-knightly rank.

Langets *see* cheeks

Latten also called latoun. Copper alloy closely resembling brass, widely used in the Middle Ages.

Lists An enclosure prepared for a tournament.

Livery Among other things this term applies to the robes worn by the adherents or servants of a lord, bearing his badge and in the tincture of his coat of arms. This indicated the partisanship of an individual to a superior, and could be worn by people of any rank.

Lock The ignition mechanism for a gun (usually hand and shoulder arms).

Locket The top mount, usually made of metal, on a sword, knife or dagger scabbard or sheath, designed to protect its mouth and also occasionally as a point of suspension or fastening to a belt. *See also* chape.

Longbow The traditionally English 'self' bow of the thirteenth and fourteenth centuries, in use until the sixteenth.

Lucerne hammer A staff weapon with a hammer-head balanced by a fluke, popular with Swiss infantry in both the fifteenth and sixteenth centuries.

Mace A short club-like weapon, latterly with a flanged head, usually made of steel.

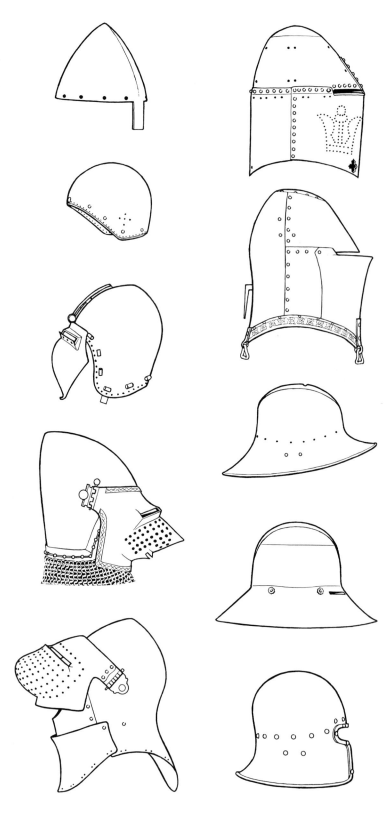

1 'Norman' style conical helmet, *tenth to the thirteenth century.*

2 *Cervellière (early form of basinet). Probably German, c 1330.*

3 *German basinet with klappvisier, c 1370.*

4 *Basinet (hounskull) with aventail. North Italian (Milanese), c 1390.*

5 *Great basinet from Pamplona Cathedral. Spanish, c 1425.*

6 *The Black Prince's helm. Probably English, c 1370.*

7 *Henry V's funerary helm (Westminster). Probably English, c 1400.*

8 *Kettle-hat (usually worn with a bevor). Probably Italian, c 1475.*

9 *Kettle-hat furnished with sights. German (Innsbruck), c 1460.*

10 *Barbut with a T-shaped face opening, c 1450-60.*

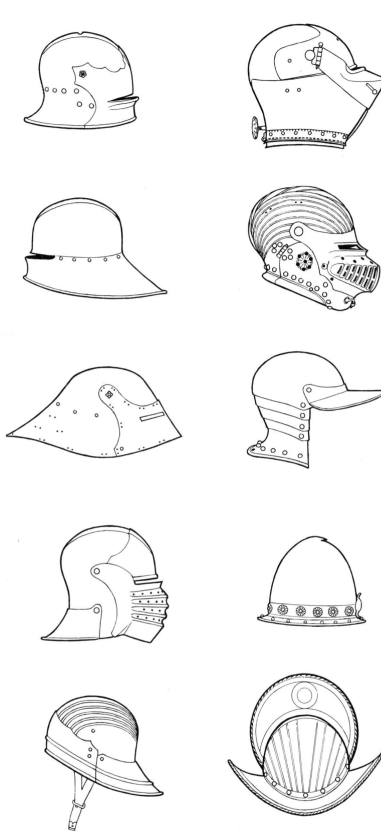

11 *Sallet made for the export trade. North Italian (Milanese), c 1450.*

12 *Sallet of 'Gothic' form. German (Landshut), c 1470-80.*

13 *South German 'black' sallet, rough from the hammer, c 1490.*

14 *Sallet with 'bellows' visor. North Italian (Milanese), c 1490.*

15 *Sallet with brow reinforce. North Italian (Milanese) c 1500.*

16 *Armet (an early form of*

close-helmet). Milanese, c 1450.

17 *Armet in the 'Maximilian' style. German (Innsbruck), c 1510.*

18 *Burgonet, called a 'casquetel'. North Italian (Milanese), c 1510.*

19 *Spanish morion, sometimes called a 'pot'. North Italian, late sixteenth century.*

20 *Comb morion (often etched and gilt). North Italian, late sixteenth century.*

Mail A flexible defence constructed of interlinked and riveted rings of metal, the origin of which seems to be Celtic. Each link passes through four others and the garment is shaped by the addition or subtraction of rings in appropriate places.

Manifer A plate defence for the lower part of the left hand and arm, usually constructed in one piece and designed for the joust.

Martel *see* war hammer

Match *see* slow match

Matchlock A simple ignition for early firearms, first appearing in the fifteenth century. A pivoted arm is activated by a lever or trigger to lower a smouldering piece of *slow match* into a gunpowder-filled pan at the side of the gun barrel, connecting via the touch-hole with the main charge loaded in the breech.

'Maximilian' armour A modern term applied to the style of early sixteenth century armour characterized by narrow, parallel fluting, popular during the reign of the Emperor Maximilian I (1494-1519) and thereafter until the middle of the century.

Melee Combat between two groups of knights as opposed to single combat between two individuals. *See also* tourney, which usually took the form of a melee.

Mercury gilding A method of gilding known since classical antiquity. Powdered gold is mixed with mercury to form an amalgam. This is applied as a paste to the areas to be decorated, and then the whole is heated overall to burn off the mercury, leaving the gold bonded to the underlying metal. This was a popular decorative technique applied to armour from the turn of the fifteenth century.

Minion *see* cannon

Misericorde A term used to describe a small seat in a church. *see also* dagger

Mitten gauntlet A gauntlet with articulated transverse lames covering the fingers, rather than the fingers each being separately protected by a series of articulated plates. *See also* gauntlet.

Morgenstern *see* morning star

Morion A sixteenth century development of the kettle hat, widely used by infantry, consisting of a skull with a broad brim, flat or turned down at the sides, but sweeping upwards into a peak at

front and rear. There are two main types: the so-called Spanish morion (cabasset) which has an almond-shaped skull ending with a stalk-like projection, clearly derived from the *cabacete*; and the comb morion which has a high central comb along the apex of the skull.

Morning star Also called morgenstern. A form of spiked club, popular in the early sixteenth century.

Muffler A mitten-like extension to the sleeve of a hauberk with a hole at the wrist so that the wearer could remove his hand.

'Munition armour' Mass-produced, cheaply made armour for the common soldiery, produced in very large quantities at the beginning of the sixteenth century. *See also* almain rivet.

Munnions Articulated lames (often attached to the gorget) protecting the shoulders and upper arms.

Musket Sixteenth and seventeenth century long-barrelled hand gun fired from the shoulder. It was heavier than the arquebus and so generally was used with a musket-rest to take some of the weight of the barrel. In Europe, most muskets were fitted with matchlocks until the end of the seventeenth century.

Nasal Plate defence on early medieval helmets, often riveted to the bottom of the skull to cover the nose and middle of the face.

Niello A decorative black inlay used to best effect on a surface of silver or gold. A compound of sulphur combined with silver, lead and a small quantity of copper, it is fixed in place by heat.

Nut Round pivoted component retained within the stock (tiller) of a crossbow to take the string. It is usually made of solid ivory or stag-horn, and retains the crossbow string under tension once the latter is drawn back ready to use. When the nut is released by the trigger or trigger-lever, the string is then freed, shooting the bow.

Outremer Term meaning 'overseas', but used specifically in the Middle Ages to denote the Holy Land.

Pair of curates *see* cuirass

Pair of plates *see* coat of plates

Pan Part of the ignition mechanism of an early firearm, adjacent to the touch-hole at the breech of the barrel; on igniting gunpowder in the pan a jet of flame is sent through the touch-hole to fire the main charge.

Panoply The complete equipment of a soldier.

Partizan A staff weapon, first appearing in the early sixteenth century, consisting of a long, tapering, two-edged, triangular-shaped blade with two projecting flukes at its base.

Pasguard A plate reinforcement for the left elbow of tilt armour.

Pattern-welded blades A method of blade manufacture involving the forging and hammer welding of both iron and steel together to form a specifically patterned homogenous metal.

Pauldron A laminated plate defence for the shoulder, extending at the front and rear to protect the armpit.

Pavise Large, usually rectangular shield carried by infantrymen and frequently used in siege operations to protect archers. The largest pavises were equipped with a prop to support them.

Peytral Horse armour designed to protect the horse's chest. *See* bard.

Pieces of exchange *see* exchange pieces

Pike Long spear with a small steel head, carried by infantrymen. Metal strips (cheeks) were riveted down the shaft from the point, to reinforce it. Pikes were used by the Flemings, Scots and Swiss, becoming as long as 22 feet (6.7 m) from the sixteenth century.

Pistol Small, short-barrelled firearm used in one hand. See dag.

Plackart A plate reinforcement attached to the breastplate, which at first only covered the lower half but latterly, especially on Italian armours, covered nearly the entire breastplate.

Plates *see* coat of plates

Pointillé Decoration popular in the fourteenth and fifteenth century, consisting of designs picked out on a surface (for instance on plate armour) formed of a series of dots.

Points *see* arming-points

Poldermitton Reinforcement for the right arm on a joust armour.

Pollaxe (The preferred spelling to polaxe or poleaxe). A knightly staff weapon, its head being an axehead, usually balanced by a fluke or hammerhead, and surmounted by a steel spike. The shaft

was protected by steel cheeks and the hand by a steel rondel. Used from the fifteenth century for foot combats and for war. The component 'pole' in the name refers not to the staff, but the Old English word 'poll' (head).

Poleyn A cup-shaped plate defence for the knee, usually equipped with a side wing of heart shape.

Pomme A spherial decoration for a helmet, often gilded and worn instead of a crest in the later fifteenth century.

Pommel Also called pummel. A variously shaped counterweight to the sword blade, riveted to the end of the sword tang above the grip.

Pommel On a saddle, the front upper 'curl' of the saddle bow. *See also* bow.

Pot General term for a simple ordinary soldier's helmet (usually of morion form, such as a 'pikeman's pot').

Pricker An awl or pricking device (sometimes used as a single-tined fork) frequently found as an accessory in sword or knife scabbards.

Prick-spurs *see* spurs

Prodd *see* crossbow

Proof Armour 'of proof' is made sufficiently thick or hard to resist a shot from bow or musket. The term first occurs in the texts of early medieval romances.

'Puffed and slashed' armour Embossed armour, often etched and gilt, resembling a style of dress popular in the early sixteenth century, especially in Germany; where 'puffs' of coloured material were pulled through 'slashes' in the sleeves or body.

Quarrel *see* bolt

Queue A shaped iron bar bolted to early sixteenth century joust armours to hold down and steady the rear of the lance, enabling it to be levelled and aimed more easily

Quillon block The central part of the guard of a sword, from which the quillons spring; on early cross-hilted swords, the quillons and quillon-block were made in one.

Quillons The arms of the cross-bar on a sword guard. Term first used in the sixteenth century.

Quintain A pivoted gibbet-like structure with a shield suspended from one arm and a bag of sand from the other. Used in practice for jousting.

Rack Also called cranequin. Contemporary English term for a

device incorporating a ratchet and winding handle, used in the fifteenth and sixteenth centuries for spanning crossbows.

Ramrod The loading rod of a muzzle-loaded gun, used to ram the charge of powder and the projectile down the barrel.

Rapier A form of light, long-bladed sword, often with a complicated guard of thin metal bars, developed in the sixteenth century for the type of 'fencing' reliant largely upon the point rather than the edge, although early forms were used for both cut and thrust.

Rennen A form of joust where the main object was to unhorse one's opponent, although points were also scored for the splintering of lances. It was fought with pointed headed lances(the 'joust of war').

Rennhut A deep, one-piece sallet with a vision slit cut into it, specifically designed for the rennen; sometimes equipped with a fluted brow reinforce and a roller on its lower front edge.

Renntartsche A large shield made of wood and leather reinforced with metal which covered the whole of the wearer's body and his bevor; it was attached to the breastplate by a central screw and to the bevor by a bolt and wing-nut. Designed specifically for the rennen.

Rennzeug Armour designed specifically for the rennen.

Rerebrace Plate armour for the upper arm.

Ricasso The part of the sword-blade nearest the hilt. It is usually thickened and blunted to an oblong or rectangular section, allowing the finger to be curled around it for a more secure grip.

Rondache *see* buckler

Rondel A disc of metal fitted to daggers or staff weapons to protect the user's hand, and to the rear of armets to protect the strap supporting the wrapper.

Rump guard A term used by modern authorities to describe the single oblong plate hung from the lower edge of the culet on fifteenth century armours.

Runka Also called a rawcon or a corsèque. An early sixteenth century staff weapon with a head having a long, straight central blade with two smaller ones at its base projecting out from it at approximately 45 degrees from the horizontal.

Sabaton Sometimes called solleret by the French. A plate defence for the foot consisting of a number of laminations across the foot, ending in a toecap.

Sabre A sword with a curved, single-edged blade (probably originally derived from Eastern scimitars).

Saddle bow *see* bow and arçon

Saddle steel Protective steel plates for the front (bow) and back (cantle) of a war or joust saddle.

Saker *see* cannon

Sallet A light helmet either fitted with a visor or open-faced, varying in form, having a tail to protect the neck. In Germany it took a form somewhat like a sou'wester, and in Italy that of a basinet. In England known as a salade.

Scabbard Also called a sheath. The protective outer case for an edged weapon, particularly swords and daggers. The term scabbard is generally used for swords, and sheath for smaller blades such as knives or daggers.

Scale armour Armour made of small, overlapping scales or plates sewn or laced to a cloth garment.

Schynbalds A plate defence for the lower leg which protected only the shin and was strapped over the chausses. *See also* greave.

Scutage A payment made by a feudal vassal to his overlord in lieu of military service. Often employed when the vassal was a minor, aged, infirm or a woman.

Serpentine The holder for the slow match on the ignition lock of a matchlock firearm. *See also* cannon.

Shaffron Also called shaffrein, chaffron, chanfron. Defence for a horse's head (*see* bard). Forms covering only the upper part of the head became popular in the mid-sixteenth century (demi-shaffron).

Side-ring A modern term to describe the ring-shaped guard springing from the quillon-block at right angles to the quillons on swords of the late fifteenth and sixteenth centuries.

Sight The vision slit in a helmet or visor. Also, the notched projection or other 'sighting' devices on the barrel of a gun, to enable it to be aimed accurately.

Skeggox Anglo-Saxon single-handed axe, used in hand-to-hand combat and also as a missile.

Skull The part of a helmet covering the top, back and the sides of the head above the ears. It can also denote a simple metal cap.

Slow match A slow-burning cord of hemp or flax soaked in salt-petre and then dried. Used to ignite cannon and hand guns.

Socket *see* tilting cuisse

Solleret *see* sabaton

Span The term used for preparing a crossbow to shoot (by pulling back the string to engage with the nut), or preparing a wheel-lock gun to fire (by winding back the wheel a three-quarter turn, with a 'spanner').

Spangenhelm A modern German term describing conical helmets constructed of a number of segments riveted together; descended from Late Roman prototypes.

'Spanish' morion *see* cabasset and morion

Spaudler A light laminated defence protecting the point of the shoulder and top of the arm, especially popular in Germany.

Spear The oldest form of staff weapon, intended primarily for thrusting. The war spear usually had a leaf-shaped or long, thin, triangular head.

Spetum Staff weapon similar to a runka. The head consists of a long pointed blade or tine with two upward-curving secondary blades extending outwards on opposite sides from its base.

Splint Light arm defences used in the fifteenth and sixteenth centuries. 'Gutter-shaped' and intended to protect only the outside of the arm, they were often found on cheap armours specifically designed for infantry use and on certain types of German armour. *See also* almain rivet.

Spurs Y-shaped metal goads strapped to the heel, used to drive the horse on. Dating from early antiquity. Early medieval spurs were of simple prick type; rowel spurs date from the very late thirteenth century.

Standard A mail collar common in the fifteenth century.

Stechhelm A 'frog-mouthed' form of great helm which was worn specifically for *Gestesch*, bolted to the breastplate.

Stechsack A thickly padded bumper for the horse's chest, which was hung round its neck in such a way as to provide protection for the rider's legs; worn specifically for the *Gestesch*.

Stechtartsche A small rect-angular wooden shield for the *Gestesch*, suspended by cords which passed through holes in the left side of the breastplate.

Stechzeug Armour designed for the *Gestesch*.

Steel An alloy of wrought iron and carbon, capable of being hardened by heating and then quenching (rapid cooling) in water. This hardening process could cause embrittlement; gentle reheating (tempering) increased the metal's resilience. These processes were well known in the Middle Ages. *See* wrought iron.

Steel *see* saddle steel

Stinkpot A clay or pottery vessel, usually containing burning sulphur, naptha or quicklime, or various combinations of these, hurled in the face of an oncoming enemy, creating similar effects to tear gas and napalm.

Stock The wooden part of a hand gun or the tiller of a crossbow.

Stop rib Small metal bar riveted to plate armour to stop the point of a weapon sliding into a joint or opening.

Suit of armour *see* harness of armour

Surcoat A flowing garment worn over armour from the twelfth century. It could be sleeved or sleeveless, usually reaching the mid-calf. Later it was shortened and in the fourteenth century developed into the jupon.

Tabard Short, open-sided garment with short sleeves used to display the wearer's coat of arms. Often worn by heralds.

Tace *see* tasset

Tang The homogenous continuation of a sword or dagger blade, often passing through and retaining the rest of the hilt (guard, grip and pommel). By the middle of the medieval period virtually all sword tangs passed through the pommel and were riveted over it to secure and retain the hilt.

Target Small circular shield.

Tasset A defence for the top of the thigh, hung from the fauld by straps to cover the gap between cuisses and breastplate. First appeared in the fifteenth century.

Tiller The stock of a crossbow.

Tilt A barrier of wood covered in cloth to separate the jousters as they ran a course. Introduced in the fifteenth century to stop head-long collisions.

Tilting socket Large plate rein-forcing-cuisses which pro-vided protection for the thighs and knees and hung from either side of the saddle; worn for the rennen. Also called a gard-cuish or gard-cuisse.

Tonlet Also called bases. A deep, hooped skirt of steel worn on armours designed for foot combat from the late fifteenth to the early sixteenth century.

Touch-hole The hole in the breech-section of a muzzle-load-ing gun barrel, through which a jet of flame from the pan ignites the main charge and so fires the gun.

Tournament A mock combat, useful both for practice and enter-tainment, introduced as a 'formal' occasion in the twelfth century.

Tourney Also called in German freiturnier. Although originally implying single combat, within the context of a tournament this term rapidly came to signify a melee, either on foot or on horse-back. *See also* Melee.

Trapper An all-enveloping textile or leather cover for the horse, reaching to the fetlocks and leav-ing only the eyes, ears and nose un-covered. It usually displayed the rider's coat of arms.

Trigger The hand or finger-oper-ated lever that shoots a crossbow, or fires a gun by setting off its ignition mechanism (lock).

Tuck The contemporary English term for an estoc.

Turcopole Light cavalry auxili-ary recruited by the Crusaders in the Holy Land.

Turning-joint An enclosed cir-cular joint above the elbow, en-abling the arm to twist. A flange on the rim of the upper cannon of the vambrace rotates inside an embossed groove along the lower edge of the rerebrace.

Umbo A shield boss, usually in the centre of the shield, covering and protecting the hand as it holds the grip.

Vambrace Armour designed for the lower arm. However, the term can be applied to the whole of the arm defence with the exception of the pauldron.

Vamplate A circular plate of steel set in front of the grip on a lance, to protect the hand.

Vassal An individual owing ser-vice and allegiance to his superior under the feudal system.

Ventail An integral flap of mail attached to the coif in the thir-teenth century; it could be drawn across the mouth to protect the lower face.

Vervelles Staples attached to the base of a basinet for securing the aventail.

Visor Protection for the eyes and face; a plate defence pivoted to the helmet skull.

Volant-piece An English term for the reinforcing brow-piece on a helmet such as the sallet.

Waist lame A horizontal lamina-tion in the breast or backplate at waist level.

War hammer Also called martel and horseman's pick. A short-hafted hammer used mainly in the late fifteenth and sixteenth cen-turies as a percussive weapon. The horseman's pick combined the hammer head with a long, curved pick-shaped fluke.

War hat *see* kettle hat

Watered steel Also known as Damascus steel. Iron and steel forged together to form a homo-genous steel. A visible 'watered' pattern appears if the surface is polished and slightly acid-etched. The term is probably derived from the city of Damascus, which was a famous centre for watered steel blades even as early as the Middle Ages.

Wheel-lock An early sixteenth century mechanical device for igniting gunpowder to fire a gun. Sparks are struck from a piece of iron pyrites held against the ser-rated edge of a revolving wheel.

White armour A modern term for an armour of plain, polished steel without a cloth or any other form of permanently attached covering.

Wrapper An additional defence for the armet or, later, other hel-mets; it was strapped to the front of the helmet and covered the lower half of the chin and visor.

Wrought iron Pure iron which does not contain any carbon to turn it into steel. Wrought iron is very malleable and easily worked, but can only be hardened by 'case-hardening,' not by heat treatment. *See also* steel.

Wyvern A legendary beast with the head of a dragon and body of a serpent. Attached by its head to a long staff, it was a traditional Norse battle standard of the late Dark Ages, continuing to be used on the Continent in the early Middle Ages.

Index

ACKNOWLEDGEMENTS

The publisher would like to thank Martin Bristow the designer, Melanie Earnshaw the picture researcher, Ron Watson for compiling the index, Malcolm McGregor for preparing the artwork, and especial thanks to Jane Laslett the editor. Many thanks to the agencies and individuals below for the illustrations, B=below; L=left; R=right; T=top; BT=bottom:

Aachen Cathedral Treasury/Ann Munchow: p 11T, 54 both, 55. Archiv Gerstenberg: p 10, 45, 49, 58T, 132T, 136. Archivi Alinari: p 62. ATA, Stockholm: p 12. James Austin: p 25, 41. Bern Historical Museum: p 97. Bibiliothèque Nationale, Paris: p 29, 131T, 171B. Bramante Editrice: p 52, 63L. Bodleian Library, Oxford: p 74[MS Bodley 264, folio 51v]. British Library: p 24T, 40, 43, 48T, 50, 51, 58B, 65, 67, 73, 124, 131B, 132B, 133, 158, 160. Courtesy of the Trustees or the British Museum: p 1, 6, 27, 134B, 162TL, 168B. Brussels, Musée Royaux des Beaux Arts de Belgique: p 161. Canterbury Cathedral: p 66, 86T. Chartres Cathedral/Photo Royal Armouries:

p 79T, 81T, 83 bottom two, 87. College of Arms: p 164B. Conway Library, Courtauld Institute of Art: p 56L. The Dean and Chapter of Durham: p 89. Glasgow Museums and Art Galleries, Burrell Collection: p 47, 122. Scott Collection: p 111. Glasgow University Library: p 38[MS Hunter 229]. Gotha, Forschungsbibliothek, East Germany: p 163T. David Harriman: p 182TR. Heidelberg, Universitätsbibliothek: p 155, 157. Herbert Art Gallery and Museum, Coventry: p 114B. Michael Holford: p 13, 15, 21B, 22-23T, 22B, 23, 26, 31, 34 both. Kloster Wienhausen: p 59B. By Kind Permission of the Dean and Chapter of Lincoln: p 82B. Mansell Collection: p 44, 81B. Marburger Universitatsmuseum/Foto Marburg: p 64R. MAS, Barcelona: p 35B, 63R. Memling Museum, Bruges: p 119L. Metropolitan Museum of Art, New York: p 17B, 20, 57, 79B. Munich, Nationalmuseum: p 76L. Museum of London: p 30, 32, 36, 85B, 91, 92, 93T. National Gallery of Art, Washington; Ailsa Mellon Bruce Fund: p 102. Reproduction by

Courtesy of the Trustees, National Gallery, London: p 108B, 122R. National Monuments Record: p 68. Nördlingen, Stadtmuseum: p 110T. Collection of Malcolm Norris: p 56R, 64L, 75L, 80 both, 84, 93B, 112, 116R, 117, 121B. Nürnberg, Stadtbibliothek: p 176 below right. Offentliche Kunstsammlung Basel, Kunstmuseum/Colorphoto Hinz: p 95. Oslo, Kunstindustrimuseet: p 18. Paris, Musée de L'Armee: p 94. Pierpoint Morgan Library: p 39, 59T, 60, 61, 118, 159. Prague Cathedral Treasury/Narodni Museum: p 19B. Royal Armouries, HM Tower of London: p 19T, 37T, 53, 69 both, 82top two, 83T, 88T, 88, 98 both, 99B, 105T, 109, 119R, 121T, 122L, 126, 128R, 129R, 130C, 138T, 139T, 140, 145B, 146TL, 153 both, 162B, 163B, 165 below right, 167, 169, 170 both, 173R, 174TR. Royal Collection, Reproduced by Gracious Permission of Her Majesty the Queen: p 138B. Royal Museum of Scotland: p 71, 128L. Scala/Firenze: p 75top and below right, 87B, 106B, 135. Schloss Churburg/Photo Royal Armouries: p 77. JCD Smith: p 136B. Courtesy

of Sotheby's Inc, New York: p 137. Stiftsbibliothek, St. Gallen, Switzerland: p 2-3. Vienna, Kunsthistorisches Museum: p 8, 9, 21T, 33, 37B, 100, 103, 104. Vienna Museum der Stadt: p 143T, 144B, 148L, 165L, 166T, 168T, 172, 173L, 182CT. Permission of the Trustees of The Wallace Collection, London: p 28, 70, 86B, 90, 99T, 101, 105B, 106 top two, 107 both, 108T, 120, 127, 129 above and below, 130 above and below, 141 both, 142 both, 143B, 144T, 145 top two, 146 both right, 147all four, 148 two right, 149, 151CL and B, 152 both, 154, 165TR, 166B, 171T, 174TL, 175, 176BL, 178 above and below, 180 all three, 181 all four, 182TL and B. Walters Art Gallery, Baltimore: p 134T. Geoffrey Wheeler: p 78, 114T and R, 115, 116L. The Dean and Chapter of Westminster: p 4-5, 110B, 125T. The Dean and Chapter of Winchester: p 46. Winchester City Museums/Photo John Crook: p 139B. Württenburg Landesbildstelle: p 24B, 48T, 156T. York Archaeological Trust: p 11B. Zurich, Schweizerisches/ Landesmuseum: p 76R.